DISCOURSES

ON THE

BOOK OF RUTH.

DISCOURSES

ON THE

BOOK OF RUTH,

AND

OTHER IMPORTANT SUBJECTS:

WHEREIN

THE WONDERS OF PROVIDENCE, THE RICHES OF GRACE, THE PRIVILEGES OF BELIEVERS,

AND

THE CONDITION OF SINNERS,

ARE JUDICIOUSLY AND FAITHFULLY EXEMPLIFIED AND IMPROVED BY

THE LATE REV. JOHN MACGOWAN.

LONDON:

PRINTED FOR G. KEITH, GRACE-CHURCH STREET;
J. JOHNSON, ST. PAUL'S CHURCH-YARD; AND
J. MACGOWAN, PATERNOSTER-ROW.

MDCCLXXXI.

PREFACE.

CHRISTIAN READER,

IT is abfolutely neceffary that thou be firmly perfuaded of the truth and excellency of the Chriftian Religion; *for this is thy life.*—The prefent is an age of infidelity—fcepticifm is arrived at its higheft pitch—men, almoft of every rank, have impudence and hardinefs enough to attack the Sacred Scriptures, and ufe every effort to fap the very foundation of our holy religion: their grand aim is to laugh religion out of the world; which, if they could effect, would be neither to their intereft nor honour. The word of God is, notwithftanding all the fcoffs, prejudice, and enmity of infidels, fupported by the cleareft and fulleft evidence, and the higheft authority. We find, in all ages, that the divinely-infpired Oracles have triumphed over all the power and policy of men and devils,

devils, making its way in oppofition to the wifdom of philofophers, the arts of magicians, the will of princes, and all the temptations and terrors of the world. The kingdom of Chrift, our great Redeemer, has, without force of arms, fpread itfelf through the world, and that by the preaching of a few defpifed perfons, feveral of them being unlearned fifhermen. This demonftrates its original to be divine, and its protector almighty. The real believer derives all his hopes, comfort, and falvation from this facred and never-failing fountain—on the doctrines contained in the facred pages, he is not afhamed to live, nor afraid to die.

Now, although all Scripture is given by infpiration of God, and is profitable for doctrine, &c. and confequently claims our attention and belief; yet, there are fome parts that appear of more importance than others, and that on account of the prophecies which they contain; the hiftoric facts which they relate; the wonderful providence which they difplay; the grace which they reveal, and

the

the experience of the faints which they fet before our eyes; and among thefe, the book of Ruth, which our Author has taken for his fubject, is not the leaft to be admired and efteemed: every one who reads with care and without prejudice, will find a fund of entertainment and inftruction in that little piece of Holy Writ.

I have no inclination to prepoffefs the the mind of the reader with opinions without conviction and examination. Let him pay all due attention to the doctrine contained in thefe Difcourfes, and the manner in which they are handled, and then judge for himfelf.

It may be expected that I fhould give an account of the part I have taken in this publication. I will tell the honeft truth:

The Writer, when in his laft illnefs, intimated to his furviving relict, that he had gone as far as he was able in his defign, in preparing for the prefs his Difcourfes on the

Book

Book of Ruth (for the publication of them was much upon his heart); and therefore he desired, that after his decease, the manuscript might be put into my hands, with a request to revise the copy, and superintend its publication.

With this request I complied, from motives of the most sincere friendship and esteem to the deceased, and a desire to promote the edification of many; especially the church and congregation of which he was pastor near fifteen years.

How far my attempts may have answered the wishes of the Author's particular friends, and the expectation of the public, must be left to their decision—I hope for candour and impartiality—I shall be allowed to say, that in the prosecution of the office assigned me, I met with many difficulties, and that on account of the unfinished state of some parts of the copy. In order to supply that defect, I kept in view the Author's main design, which was a practical improvement of

the

the book of Ruth; and, as Mr. Christopher Ness, an ejected Nonconformist minister of the last century *, was a favourite writer with him, I chose to follow his very entertaining method, in his judicious remarks upon that inspired part of Holy Scripture. This may be seen in Sermon III.

Having got through that difficulty, we arrived at a more agreeable connection, and found the path more smooth and pleasant.

Every one acquainted with the writings of Mr. Macgowan will easily discern his spirit and style in these Sermons. I am certain, that those who sat under his stated ministry will see in a moment the features of the original, and perhaps receive, in the publication of what they heard from the pulpit, a second benefit. Numbers of the dear man's hearers have expressed to me the unspeakable pleasure and satisfaction they received in the delivery of these Discourses.

* See Christopher Ness's History and Mystery of the Old and New Testament.

PREFACE.

It is not possible for an author to please all his readers—he must be a weak man who aims at, or expects it. If the critic is not gratified, sure I am the plain and humble Christian will—for such our Author wrote, and happily succeeded;—many having declared how greatly their souls were refreshed and edified by his writings, as well as by his ministry. For my own part, I am not ashamed to acknowledge; yea, I do it with pleasure, and gratitude to the great Author of every blessing, that Mr. Macgowan was one of the most valuable and improving companions I ever had the honour of an intimacy with. We visited often, and our conversation usually turned on important subjects, which proved very instructive to my own mind. The natural cheerfulness of his temper, the ease and familiarity with which he communicated his ideas, his great integrity, and unaffected piety, rendered him the pleasant companion, the amiable Christian, and the sincere friend: no one more sensibly felt the loss of him than myself.

I frequently

I frequently visited him in his last sickness, when he took occasion, as opportunity offered, of opening to me his whole heart.

At one time he was in great darkness of soul, and lamented exceedingly the withdrawings of the presence of God. Two things, he said, had deeply exercised his thoughts. The one was, how those heavy and complicated afflictions which God had seen fit to lay upon him could work so as to promote his real good. And the other was, that God, his best friend, should keep at a distance from his soul, when he knew how much his mind was distressed for the light of his countenance.—" O !" said he, turning to me, and speaking with great earnestness, " my soul longeth and panteth for God, for " the living God; his love visits would " cheer my soul, and make this heavy af- " fliction sit light upon me. The wonted " presence of Jesus, my Redeemer, I cannot " do without—I trust he will return to me " soon—yea, I know he will in his own " time; for he knows how much I need

" the influence of his grace."—In this conversation, he often mentioned the depravity of his nature, and what a burden he found it—" My heart," said he, " is more and more
" vile—every day I have such humiliating
" views of heart-corruption as weighs me
" down—I wonder whether any of the
" Lord's people see things in the same
" light that I do."—And then turning to me, he said, " And do you find it so, my Brother?" Upon my answering him in the affirmative, he replied, " I am glad of that."

The next time, which was the last of my conversing with him, I found him in a sweet and heavenly frame;—his countenance indicated the serenity of his mind. On my entering the room, he exclaimed—O my dear Brother, how rejoiced am I to see you!—sit down, and hear of the loving-kindness of my God. " You see me as ill
" as I can be in this world, and as well as I
" can be whilst in the body. Methinks I
" have as much of heaven as I can hold."—
Then tears of joy like a river flowed from

his eyes; and his inward pleasurable frame interrupted his speech for a time. He broke silence with saying—" The work will soon "be over—you see what you must soon "experience—But death, to me, has no- "thing terrific in it—I have not an anxious "thought—The will of God and my will "are one—'Tis all right, yet mysterious— "We are to part here; but we shall meet "again.—You cannot conceive the pleasure "I feel in this reflection, viz. that I have "not shunned to declare (according to my "light and ability) the whole counsel of "God—I can die on the doctrines which I "have preached—they are true—I find "them so.—Go on to preach the Gospel of "Christ, and mind not what the world "may say of you."—All the while I sat silent; and rising up to take my leave, fearing he would spend his strength too much, he immediately took me by the hand, and weeping over each other, we wished mutual blessings. Upon parting, he said, " My dear "Brother, farewell—I shall see you no "more."

PREFACE.

Thus I left my much esteemed friend and brother; and the next news I heard of him was, that on the Saturday evening his immortal spirit left the body, to go to the world of light and bliss, and keep an eternal sabbath with God, angels, and saints *.

Mr. Macgowan was well known in the world, and in the churches, both as a minister and an author. His several publications are standing proofs of his great abilities, and singular talents. He discovered a peculiarity of genius in the investigation of divine subjects; and, no doubt, some will object to the method of his treating the book of Ruth,—That he has allegorized too much, and gone into topics that have no foundation in the history, &c. but to such objectors I would say—consult page 3d of the Introduction.

With respect to the Sermons annexed to this work, I have only to observe, that some

* Mr. Macgowan departed this life, Nov. 25, 1780, in the fifty-fifth year of his age.

PREFACE.

of the Author's friends thought it advisable to print them, as there was a probability they would be acceptable, and a prospect of their being useful. I have some reason to believe that the two sermons on Joshua, &c. were designed for publication.

It is my sincere desire and fervent prayer, that this work may answer the labour and design of the excellent and pious Writer; and that those who remain* in the ministry, may be like-minded with him in preaching the gospel, defending the faith, and acting the Christian.

J. REYNOLDS.

Kingsland, *June* 8, 1781.

* The removal of faithful ministers from our world, must be sensibly felt and regretted by every friend to the interest of Christ, and the prosperity of Zion. It hath pleased the wise and sovereign Disposer of all events, to call away by death the Rev. John Conder, D. D. who was employed in a double capacity, that of a divinity tutor and a pastor; which offices he filled up for a great number of years with honour to himself, satisfaction to his flock, and advantage to his pupils. He died on Wednesday, May 30, 1781, aged sixty-seven years.

TO THE

CHURCH OF THE LORD JESUS

MEETING NEAR DEVONSHIRE-SQUARE,

IN BISHOPGATE-STREET,

LONDON.

MY DEAR FRIENDS,

IN a day in which few are found who delight in the purity of that Gospel, which reflects equal glory upon the works and ascribes equal dignity to the persons of Father, Son, and Holy Ghost, it is your unspeakable privilege to be reduced to the lowly obedience of faith, resting secure in the acknowledgment of the mystery of God, and of the Father, and of Christ.

In a day, when instead of adoring the person, trusting in the righteousness of Jesus, and deriving all supply from his inherent fullness, so many men of virtue, natural religion, and of eminent abilities, are straining
every

every nerve to eclipse his personal glories, and bring into contempt his finished salvation; you cannot be thankful enough for that grace which has made you sensible of the plague of your own hearts, with your absolute helplessness, and indispensable need of an interest in Jesus in all that is his, so as to make you flee for refuge to the hope set before you in the gospel. This you would have had neither power nor will to do, if the Holy Ghost had not breathed upon you, as of old upon the dry bones; and quickened you when dead in trespasses and sins.

Therefore by what principles soever others are influenced, you will find yourselves under the necessity of going on in an implicit dependence on the perfect obedience of Jesus, as the only spring of Christian holiness, seeing whatsoever is not of faith is sin.

Thus called out of darkness into marvellous light, and constituted a church of the exalted Jesus; a church whose only rule of worship and discipline is the mind of God revealed in the sacred canon, exclusive of the capricious return of the unsteady, on
one

one hand, and the lordly dictates of popish and prelatic arrogance on the other. This being the case, you must expect but little countenance from gentlemen whose uniform aim is to link the interests of Christ and the world together; rather expect that a great share of tribulation shall be yours; for were you to escape it, the Scriptures would denominate you bastards, and not sons and daughters.

You have indeed, as a church, been called to wade through seas of affliction, and to encounter mountains of difficulty; yet your spark has been kept alive amidst rolling billows; your bow has abode in strength, though galled by the masters of arrows your enemies. You have been helped to cleave to Jesus in his temptation, and as a church have a Scripture warrant to look to him for the appointed kingdom. This He hath promised, and he was never known to forsake them who desired to follow him in the simplicity of his appointed ways notwithstanding he willeth them to wait, and to watch for his blessed coming.

Your

Your trials, my Friends, have been principally from those of your own communion; those who ought to have been helpers of your faith, and promoters of your joy; those who ate bread at your table, have lifted up their heel against you, and, like Achitophel of old, have turned their counsels against your tranquillity. But that unanimity in your judicatures, which God was pleased to give you in your greatest trials, has enabled you to surmount every difficulty. You have encouragement, therefore, still to persevere in following the simple dictates of revelation, for in so doing you shall be established as a church, against which even the gates of hell shall never prevail.

In this militant state, one trial passes away only to make way for another; so that there is no room to expect rest and ease of any long duration. This circumstance loudly calls to the closest attention to instituted means. In times of apparent safety, the mariners may take their rest; but in a storm, all hands must be active, as on activity of individuals the general good depends.

When

DEDICATION.

When you look back to the scenes of trouble through which you have been brought, the dangers which you have escaped, and reflect on your present situation, what reason of thankfulness to the great Keeper, by whom alone you have been preserved. May you, may I, be helped still to go on, making the Holy One of Israel our only refuge in all our trials, and immovable foundation of our hope in the day of evil. Never forgetting that in a little while, those who sow in tears, shall reap in joy; who now groan under the cross, shall wear the crown, be where Jesus is, and behold that glory which he had with the Father before the world began; then shall all your sighs and groans be turned into hallelujahs to God and to the Lamb for ever and ever.

The following Sermons having been preached in your assembly, acceptable to most, and useful to many, when delivered from the pulpit, I dedicate to you as a token of that unfeigned esteem, and fervent regard I have for you as a church of our Redeemer. To you I willingly gave myself, and can truly say, that nothing under heaven could

could yield me more real pleasure than to see my poor attempts to serve you, in the work of the ministry, made successful in the gathering into, and building up the CHURCH of the LORD in DEVONSHIRE-SQUARE.

I have been with you in much weakness, both in body and mind; in much fear and trembling, not so much for you as for myself, lest the Lord should humble me amongst you, by leaving me to myself. I dare not give you the least hope of its being otherwise in future, seeing I feel more, if possible, of the wretched depravity of an heart filled with enmity against the best of Beings, and by nature the seat of every vile affection. I feel a total incapacity of standing one moment of myself, much more so of being of any the least use to my hearers, without a divine blessing. Therefore I earnestly request, yea, I even covet your prayers for me. And indeed in proportion to the desire you have of my being useful among you, you must seek that usefulness from the Author of every good and perfect gift. The more frequent you go to the throne of grace in my behalf, and in behalf of one another,

the

the more flourishing you shall be in your own souls, and the fruits of your prayers shall return into your own bosoms.

My proposed plan was to take a summary view of the whole history of Ruth, as it may be accommodated to gospel purposes and principles. What led me to contemplate the subject, was a desire expressed by a much esteemed friend, now in glory, to have a particular passage of the history, which had been particularly useful to her, opened in the course of the ministry. What induced me to commit them to the press, was the more than ordinary impression which the sacred subject made for years upon my own mind, joined with the wish of many to have the whole in their own possession.

I am very far from considering the work as so much as verging towards perfection, or handled to that advantage which it might have had from another; but this I can say, I myself can go no farther in attempting to render it complete. But as I consider my time and talents your property, were the fruits of my meditations ever so valuable, they

they should with cheerfulness be devoted to your service; and such as they are, I doubt not but they will meet with your kind acceptance.

That the parental tenderness towards young inquirers, which Naomi discovered towards her Moabitish daughter-in-law, be ever manifested in your conduct as a church; and may you, with those holy women, find rest in the portion of Israel; that in your last days, songs of salvation may flow from your lips, and gratitude, for blessings received, warm every affectionate bosom.

I am, my very dear Friends, your affectionate, though unworthy and sinful servant, and brother in the gospel of Jesus,

JOHN MACGOWAN.

INTRODUCTION.

INTENDING, if Providence permits, to take a close view of the several parts of the history of Ruth and Boaz, and as far as may be consistent with the spirit of the text, apply it to gospel purposes; it may not be amiss to make some general remarks by way of introduction.

I. As to the time when the incidents related in the book actually happened, which is fixed with precision in Chap. i. 1. *In the days when the judges ruled;* but under which of the judges the nicest inquirers have never been able to determine. Some think it was in the days of Ehud, and that Ruth was daughter to Eglon; which, if true, would give a greater lustre to the Spirit's work upon her soul in subduing her prejudices, which the untimely death of her father, by the hand of Ehud, might have occasioned; as well as to stoop to glean for her own and her mother's living, notwithstanding the dignity of her family.

Others suppose that this famine took place in Gideon's time, when the Midianites spoiled the land of Israel; and Josephus is for fixing it to the time of Eli's government. But I think that where the Holy Ghoſt is ſilent, it is rather daring to attempt an inquiry. And indeed it appears a matter of no great moment to us, if we can only make a proper improvement of its ſacred contents. Nor does it appear more to our purpoſe, to be informed with certainty by which of the inſpired penmen it was written. Whether Eli, Samuel, Gad, Nathan, or Ezra? It is enough that it is of the ſacred canon, and referred to by the genealogiſts of our moſt holy Redeemer.

II. The leading ſcope and principal parts of the ſtory, are objects more worthy of our preſent attention and ſerious regard. Its leading ſcope undoubtedly is to delineate the intermixture of the ſeed of the Gentiles with that of the Hebrews in the line of Jeſus, ordained the Saviour of thoſe who believe, whether Jew or Gentile, in every age of the world. Mr. Roberts, in his Key to the Bible, obſerves, That Ruth the Moabitiſh widow is inſerted in the liſt of the Redeemer's anceſtors by Matthew, one of his genealogiſts, as well as Rachab, as being the firſt fruits of the Gentiles unto God. By thus taking his fleſh of the ſeed of the Gentiles as well as of the Jews, confiſtently with this natural union he becomes a light to enlighten the Gentiles, as well as to ſhew forth the glory of his people Iſrael; ſo that through him God is glorified in his ſpiritual

Jacob,

INTRODUCTION.

Jacob, even to the ends of the earth; Gentile nations wait for his law, and rejoice in his salvation.

The same judicious writer observes further, That if the book of Ruth was to be taken from the canon of Scripture, the genealogy of Jesus would be incomplete; the whole of the Old Testament, without its assistance, being insufficient to give proper evidence of his Messiahship; so that it is of the utmost consequence to the cause of Christianity, and absolutely necessary to gospel faith.

This remark, made by an author for whom I have the highest esteem, an author who devoted his time and talents to the service of the believing church, was one, amongst other motives, which inclined me to take its contents into closer consideration than I had done before; concluding that, if the Holy Ghost has seen meet to make the book of Ruth necessary to the establishment of Christianity, I should find it fertile of profitable matter, and very capable of a practical improvement.

It is not proposed to inquire into the propriety of their sentiments who embrace this pleasing history under the notion of veiled and figurative gospel, nor to censure such who consider it as no more than a history, having no designed allusion to the gospel of grace. Every man claims a right of thinking and judging for himself, and I shall claim no more than the same privilege.

Thofe who confider the book of Ruth, as no way adumbrative of gofpel myftery, but merely hiftorical, cannot confiftently be offended with an attempt to accommodate even hiftory itfelf to the illuftration of gofpel truth, feeing that "what-"foever was written aforetime, was written for " our inftruction, that we through comfort of the " Scriptures may have hope." On the other hand, thofe who confider Ruth as gofpel veiled, or hidden under the figures of perfonal types, ought not to blame, if I choofe to accommodate it hiftorically, rather than to read it typically, as I am obliged to do fome other parts of Holy Scripture. My intention is, to enjoy my own free liberty, and to give full licenfe to excurfions of thought, without defigning the leaft offence to any man, how widely foever he may differ from me in opinion.

Before I enter particularly into an improvement of the fubject, it may not be amifs to fet before you, in one general view, its principal parts, by way of analyfis, efpecially as it may be fome help to the memory.

The firft thing recorded is Elimelech's departure from the land of Ifrael, on account of the famine, to feek food for himfelf and family in the land of Moab—there his two fons Mahlon and Chilion were married, the one to Ruth and the other to Orpah, both daughters of Moab——there, in this land of ftrangers, Elimelech died, and

and was buried—his death was succeeded by that of both his sons——Naomi hearing that the Lord had visited Israel with plenty, resolved to return to her country and kindred—her tender parting with Orpah, and Ruth's inseparable attachment to her in all her afflictions—their arrival at Bethlehem-Judah, and reception by the kindred of Elimelech—the bitterness of her sorrows on viewing the scenes of past endearments.

Boaz is described in his name—family—in his calling as an husbandman—in the affluence of his temporal circumstances, and piety of his conversation.——Ruth is described, in the humility of her spirit—her industry in her lowly employment as a gleaner—her dutiful regard and implicit obedience to her mother-in-law.—-Naomi's maternal care for her daughter's welfare—her wise directions, by which the desired marriage was brought about.——The tenderness of Boaz to her, and his full justification of her conduct and kindness.

The public settlement of matters, between Boaz and the nearer kinsman, as preliminaries necessary to the intended marriage—Ruth's public espousals to this honourable Israelite—the blessing of the elders upon them both after their marriage—her conception, and deliverance of Obed, David's grandfather—congratulations paid to Naomi, this venerable mother in Israel, on this joyful occasion.

INTRODUCTION.

From this short sketch of the history we may learn,

(1.) That no state is so bad, no circumstances so dark and dismal, as to be considered hopeless. Naomi and Ruth were both in circumstances to the utmost distressing, before the day of prosperity began so much as to dawn upon them. Yet their darkness was but for a night, and the smiling morning brought a train of pleasures to their possession. The waters of Marah were dried up, and the streams of Shiloh flowed abundantly; so that after all their bitterness of spirit, those desolate widows sung songs of salvation. Let us then look up in hope, even when the darkest cloud is drawn over our tabernacle, when we are called to drink most deeply of the wormwood and the gall, seeing it is only preparatory to the cup of salvation; a ruffling storm before you enter into the undisturbed rest of the sanctified. The smoking furnace of trying temptations usually precedes the smiling lamp of gospel consolation.

(2.) We learn hence, That no man serveth God for nought; or, as our blessed Redeemer expresses it, "That no man forsaketh father and mo-
" ther, wife and children, houses and lands, for
" his sake, but who shall receive an hundred fold
" even in this life, as well as eternal bliss in the
" world to come." Ruth left all and clave to her mother-in-law, and by so doing was reduced to

the

the lowest degree of indigence; but she emerged from her distresses, and affluence succeeded her penury. Instead of the enjoyment of her native idols and connections, her name is recorded in the annals of heaven. Fear it not, my dear friends,—never fear that God will let you be losers, by cleaving to his people in the day of their visitation; or by taking up any, were it even the heaviest cross upon his account.—Ruth received an hundred fold even in this world; an hundred fold is promised to all in like circumstances; promised by the TRUTH himself, our ever faithful Redeemer.

(3.) In the case of Orpah, we see that a high degree of natural virtue may be lost for want of divine religion. You hear her lift up her voice and weep at parting with her mother-in-law; but at the same time, you see her return back to her idols and Pagan connections. Her conduct displayed her duty and filial affection in an eminent degree, but not the least inclination to come and put her trust in Jacob's Jehovah. How sad is their state who are governed solely by education principles, and have no higher dependence than mere refined nature? Orpah is not alone in this predicament; there is much reason to fear, it is the case with but too many of our contemporaries. God grant it may not be ours! It is not the holding on a great way with Orpah, but holding out to the end,

end, which evidences the reality of religion; for he only that endures to the end shall be saved. The Orpahs, the stony ground hearers, and half-hearted scribes, shall never sing of salvation within the tents of Jehovah's Israel.

I would now recommend it to you, narrowly to mark the principal characters in the history, as we pass on in its illustration, and endeavour to make them your own, by copying their excellencies, which are truly eminent; and even from Orpah, learn this lesson, that the soul who draweth back is displeasing to Jesus.

BOAZ

BOAZ AND RUTH.

SERMON I.

Ruth, Chap. i. Verses 1, 2.

Now it came pass, in the days when the judges ruled, that there was a famine in the land; and a certain man of Bethlehem-Judah went to sojourn in the country of Moab, he, and his wife, and his two sons. And the name of the man was Elimelech, and the name of his wife Naomi, and the name of his two sons Mahlon and Chilion, Ephrathites of Bethlehem-Judah, and they came into the country of Moab, and continued there.

AS it is not my intention to study method so much, as to draw forth the practical part of the history to view, I shall take the passage, in its several clauses, as it lies before us; which, for ought I know, may be the most ancient as well as the most useful method of preaching, because of its plainness and simplicity. And as I have no

other

other object in view but the glory of God in in our common salvation, I am no way careful what the critical hearer may think of the abilities of the preacher. Yea, in submitting the discourses to public inspection, I am equally indifferent on that head, as I have not the least hope of their being so much as read by any besides the truly serious, the lovers of Jesus, and him crucified; and I would hope that I am now, at this time, equally insensible to popular applause or censure, if the grand end I have in view be but answered in opening the history. The

First clause of which is, *Now it came to pass;* not by chance, or by any combination of fortuitous events, but by the special hand of an all-ruling and Divine Providence, which is the counterpart of the divine decree, or an exposition of the hidden things of infinite Wisdom. *Shall there be evil in a city and the Lord hath not done it?* The times and the seasons, the earth and the clouds, the winds and the rains, are all under his awful controul; so that plenty, or famine, are solely by his appointment. And how should it be otherwise, seeing the life of a sparrow, the dinner of a raven, and even the very hairs on our heads, are under his direction, care, and government? To profit by what you read, or hear, it is necessary that you should mark well what comes to pass, in the course of Divine Providence;

for,

for, says the Psalmist, Psal. cvii. 43. *Whoso is wise will observe these things, even they shall understand the loving kindness of the Lord.* Here, the exercise of true wisdom is made to consist in the marking of those things, and undoubtedly that person who treasures up his own experience under the various dispensations of Providence, has, as it were, a body of divinity within himself, and best knows how to live upon the loving kindness of the Lord, even in seasons of the greatest difficulty, and of the deepest distress.

IId. *In the days when the judges ruled.* It was observed in the introduction, that the Holy Ghost is silent with respect to which of the judges it was who then governed Israel, which consequently precludes any inquiry; but be he whomsoever he might, during his government there was,

IIId. *A famine in the land.* For the fertility of its soil, the land of Canaan was said to flow with milk and honey, notwithstanding which it was subject to famine, as both Abraham, and his grandson Jacob experienced; and at this time the famine was so great in this land of plenty, that it reached even Bethlehem, the house of bread itself. But was there not a cause? Doth the Lord afflict willingly, or grieve the children of men without provocation? No; but he may justly turn a fruitful land into barrenness, for the wickedness of
them

them who dwell therein *. Indeed, through the whole of sacred history, we find that judgment upon Israel was always preceded by their having done evil in the sight of the Holy One; and their deliverance as constantly followed their repentance and making their supplications to him.

What then has Great Britain to fear? Britain, the far greater part of whose inhabitants live as if there were no God, no future judgment, no eternal world, though favoured with higher privileges than are enjoyed by any nation under heaven. Is there not reason to fear, that in the day of visitation, the height of our privileges may make our condemnation the more emphatical, and the judgment of Capernaum be our reward as a people? When the sins of Judah arose to a certain height of aggravation, the God who made the people would shew them no mercy; but laughed at their calamity, and mocked when their fears came upon them. So, in the present case, the presence of even the godly in the land, could not avert the famine, which affected the opulent themselves; for,

IVth. *A certain man, of Bethlehem-Judah, went to sojourn in the country of Moab.* A clear and striking proof that here is no continuing city or place of abode; and shews the necessity of our seeking a city which hath foundations, the builder

* Psal. cvii. 34.

and

and maker of which is God. For if a man is ever so agreeably fituated in the midft of plenty, Divine Providence can foon drive him from his reft, and reduce him to the difagreeable neceffity of depending upon the bounty of even the wicked themfelves, who are, like Moab, for ever fhut out from the fanctuary of Jehovah. This fhould teach us to guard againft fecurity, not to be high-minded, but to fear, and truft in the name of the Lord.

How fovereign are the difpenfations of Holy Providence! whilft bleffed Jacob and his family were in danger of perifhing with hunger, corn abounded in the land of accurfed Egypt. So, meagre famine fpared not even Bethlehem-Judah, whilft the offspring of an inceftuous embrace had not only bread enough for themfelves, but alfo wherewithal to fupply the wants of others in their neceffity. From whence it appears that wicked people may fometimes abound in affluence, while the godly experience the trials of penury, as is indeed apparently the cafe in numberlefs inftances. This evinceth the truth of Solomon's doctrine, Eccl. ix. 1. *No man knoweth either love or hatred by all that is before them:* confequently, they err exceedingly who confider their profperity as an evidence of their intereft in fpecial favour; and equally wrong it is, to draw uncomfortable conclufions from circumftances of diftrefs and penury. Curfed Moab had plenty, whilft the chofen race
were

were pining in famine. Jeremiah says, Chap. xlviii. 11. *Moab hath been at ease from his youth, and hath settled on his lees, and hath not been emptied from vessel to vessel, neither hath he gone into captivity: therefore his taste remaineth in him, and his scent is not changed.*

The case with Moab was simply this, He remained in an unchanged, unregenerated state; his taste for earthly enjoyments, and sensual gratifications, remained entire in him. Earth was the object of his pursuit: earth was his only God. His scent of sinful pleasures, forbidden lusts of the flesh and of the eye continued still the same. He was never led into captivity, to feel the galling chains of his own iniquity, and to know himself, to be a slave to his own lusts, and a very drudge of Satan. He was never convinced that he was held, and by the righteous law, to fulfil its tenor to the utmost perfection, or bear its penalty in the fullest extent of its rigour; the consequence of which was, he settled upon his lees, enjoyed the fatal rest of carnal security, and went on frowardly in the way of his own choice. Nor did the Almighty think it worth his while to pour him from vessel to vessel, as he doth his own people Israel. Woe be to them that are at ease; but blessed is that man who endureth temptation, for when he is tried, he shall receive a crown of life.

This

SERMON I.

This man, though driven by famine from his own land, and from the inheritance of his God, had no intention of making the land of Moab his home, but went merely to sojourn there, till the Lord should visit Israel again with plenty. An Israelite indeed, will find his dwelling in Moab to be as uncomfortable as Lot's was amongst the people of Sodom. What the philosopher said concerning Athens, will apply in the present case, "It is a pleasant place to pass through, but unsafe "to dwell in." Moab might be very well for a temporary sojournment, but would by no means do for a settled habitation.

Let Moab for once symbolize the world, and it will still apply. Here are many blessings to be enjoyed; many excellencies to be viewed; and, so far as we can trace the operations of a God unsullied, every scene is delightful. But where is the saint who would choose the world for his eternal habitation? Where that believer, who would not choose strangling, rather than to be condemned to live for ever in the present state of existence? Yet it is very well to pass through, on our journey to the land of true felicity. The bitterness of time, will make the rest of eternity the more delightful.

Vth. *Him, and his wife, and two sons.* This shews domestic union in the midst of the greatest distress, and that nothing whatever should separate those
whom

whom God hath joined together, either by the ties of nature, or the bonds of sacred marriage. They had lived together, and could not part: rather than part, they resolved to share a like fate at home or abroad. This strongly reproves those husbands and wives who aim at separate interests, or seek different scenes of pleasure; or who indeed can willingly be parted, by any thing short of dissolution: what numbers then must fall under rebuke in this degenerate age? This domestic complacency in Elimelech's family, equally reproves those, worse than brutal parents, who discover a neglect of their offspring, respecting either the present or future life. The very tigress fostereth her young with maternal tenderness; and the helpless hen gathereth her chickens under her wings, and exerts the full extent of her feeble powers in their defence. Yet some parents, sunk beneath the brutes, by idleness, intemperance, and extravagance, make war upon the happiness of their own offspring. But let every such parent know, that he who provideth not for his own family, especially those of his own house, hath denied the faith, and is worse than an infidel.

VIth. *The name of the man was Elimelech,* **My God is King,** a fit name to give consolation in the deepest distress, for he could not even so much as reflect upon it, without being reminded that the Almighty is Governor of the universe, and consequently,

quently, that whatsoever takes place under heaven, is either by express ordination, or by special permission; therefore this famine was to be considered, as an evil of the Lord's sending. A sight of the divine hand in afflictions, sending, proportioning, and over-ruling them, greatly tends to reconcile the mind to the dispensation. It was this which made good old Eli, on receiving the awful message which foretold the final extirpation of his progeny, not from the priesthood only, but from the earth itself, calmly, though doubtless with a griefful heart, to reply, *It is the Lord, let him do whatsoever he pleaseth*. As if he had said, I receive the message as from my God; I know I am guilty with regard to my sons, and fall under his just rebuke. But he is God, and will not do wrong; Jehovah, and cannot err in judgment. Let him therefore do what seemeth good unto him.

It was a custom with the ancients, not unworthy of modern imitation, to give significant names to their children, such names as should be standing memorials of certain mercies received. Hence Rachel named Bilhah's son, born upon her own knees, after a long season of personal barrenness, Dan, which signifies *judging*; because, as she said, God had judged her, and heard her voice *. How much

---

* Godly parents do well, when they give such names to their children as may be memorials of the providence of God towards

much soever her conduct, in giving her handmaid to her husband, may be deemed reprehensible, her fixing a memorial of prayer being heard, was laudable and worthy of imitation.

wards them.—See the history and changes of Joseph's life epitomized, Psal. cv. 17. 20. &c. Now after this turn in his affairs, we are told that he had two sons in the land of Egypt; but what were their names? The text answers, Gen. xli. 51, 52: He called the name of his first-born Manasseh, which signifieth forgetfulness; and he giveth the reason for it; for, saith he, God hath made me forget all my toil, and all my father's house. And the name of the second called he Ephraim, which signifieth fruitful; for said he, God hath caused me to be fruitful in the land of my affliction. He was once very much afflicted, and now he was very fruitful; therefore he called the name of his younger son Ephraim, that he might remember the kindness of God to him, as often as he beheld, or spake to, or of, that son. So Moses called his son Gershom [stranger], for he said, I have been a stranger in a strange land, Exod. ii. 22. We find names also given to things, as well as to persons, by way of remembrance. Thus, 1 Sam. vii. 12. after a great victory obtained against the Philistines, Samuel set up a stone and gave it a name, he called it Eben-ezer, or the stone of help: the reason was, for, said he, Hitherto the Lord hath helped us. The name of the stone was to mind them of the Lord's constant readiness to help them in every strait, and to work salvation for his church to the end of time. So Moses, Exod. xvii. after that great deliverance from the Amalekites, built an altar, and called it Jehovah-nissi, which signifieth, the Lord is my banner, to put them in remembrance how the Lord went forth as a man of war, and mightily confounded their enemies. *See Caryl on Job.*

The

SERMON I.

The first three names given unto man, are so significant as to make a very important sentence. Adam, Earth; Cain, Possession; Abel, Vanity; which may very properly be rendered, "Earthly possessions are vanity." I pretend not to say, whether the imposition of those names was by the spirit of prophecy, or merely, what we call, accidental, further than observing that, the first was given by God himself, and is suitable to all the race of mankind; therefore it is lawful to infer a possibility of the other names being given, some how, under the direction of influence from above.

The import of Elimelech's name, if imprest upon his heart, must necessarily comfort him in his removal from Bethlehem to the country of Moab, when he reflected that, his God was King even in the land of strangers. How happy must that man be whose God is King? he may be driven by famine, by persecution, or otherwise, far from the house of his God; yet he can never be banished to any place, but where God is his King. Every Christian, every regenerated person, may be called Elimelech, and he may justly say, either in a church assembly, on the Exchange, or elsewhere; yea, even on a sick or dying bed; in a dungeon, or at the stake, "MY GOD IS KING." May we not then say, with the Psalmist, *Blessed are the people whose God is the Lord, and whom he hath chosen for his own inheritance.*

VIIth. The name of the woman is next to be considered; Naomi, *My sweet or pleasant one.* What every woman ought to study to be to her own proper husband; therefore there ought to be no forced marriages, let the seeming advantages be ever so great; for how is it possible for a woman to study to render herself sweet and pleasant in the eye of a man for whom she has no particular affection. In such a case, bare civility is as much as a man can expect, and even that must be a force upon her inclination. It is difficult to say who acts the most absurd part, the parent who compels his daughter against her wish and desire, or the man who receives an hand known to be given with reluctance.

Every man ought to esteem his wife as his Naomi, his sweet and pleasant one, seeing that in marriage she has sacrificed her all, conscience excepted, to the will and power of her husband, and now looks up to him as her earthly all. Indeed so near is the relation, that she not only lyeth in, but actually is the wife of his bosom, Deut. xiii. 6. and ought to be as dear to him as the heart that dwells therein. To shew the impossibility of a relation more near, it is expressly said of man and wife, that they are no longer twain but one flesh,

bone

bone of each others bone, and flesh of each others flesh.

The husband may indeed assume a kind of pre-eminence, from the consideration that his wife is but the weaker vessel; but this very pre-eminence of his ought to be turned to her consolation. Is she the weaker vessel? does it not then become his duty to overlook her weaknesses and infirmities? Is she his sweet and pleasant one? will he not then make it one great part of the business of his life to nourish her, and render her comfortable? Happy the man who is Elimelech, and the woman who is Naomi.

The believing church is Christ's Naomi, his sweet and pleasant one, and he is her Elimelech, her God the King. For her he forsook the mansions of plenty and delight—with her he sojourned in a Moabitish world, amongst enemies to the God of Israel—there he died an accursed death to accomplish her salvation—there he was buried to purify the grave for her use—rose again to trample on all her enemies; and is now gone to Bethlehem, the house of bread, to prepare a place for his Naomi on her arrival from the land of Moab.

The love of husbands to their wives, when genuine, is symbolical of the love of Jesus to his church, deep, steady, and uniform, not like the flighty fits of lust after an harlot. Hence Paul exhorts husbands, *Love your wives even as Christ loved his church*; a better example for imitation he could not possibly propose.

Isaac's love to Rebekah as recorded, Gen. xxiv. 67. is worthy of our observation, *And Isaac brought her into his mother Sarah's tent, and took Rebekah, and she became his wife, and he loved her.* First, he put her in possession of his mother's tent, with all its appurtenances; then he owned her and treated her as his wife; lastly, he loved her with an increasing love. All of which is typical of the conduct of Christ towards the Jewish and Gentile churches. Dead Sarah was a solemn figure of the former church, when her children made void the commandment to establish their own traditions; and especially when her law of ceremonies was completely abrogated, and her outward pomp departed; more especially still, when her very place and city were taken away by the victorious Romans.

Young Rebekah, who came from a far country, and was put into possession of all that belonged to Sarah, is a striking figure of the Gentile church, which being called from every nation, people, kindred, tongue, and language, is put into possession of the substance of what the Jewish church enjoyed only in the shadow. And having thus loved his own, who were in the world, he loveth them to the end.

VIIIth.

VIIIth. The names of their two sons were Mahlon and Chilion, both significant, and seemingly prophetic of part of this history.

Mahlon, a song, infirmity. A song, in the early days of espousal love and domestic prosperity; infirmity, prophetic of the sad events which afterwards took place. Chilion, finished, as both father and children were in almost the opening of this history, and which every thing under the sun must eventually be.

Elimelech's conduct and end were represented in the names of his two sons. It was great infirmity in him to leave the promised land, to leave even Bethlehem, the house of bread, for fear of the famine, seeing the word is, *Dwell in the land and verily thou shalt be fed*; but outward appearances being so strong against the promise, the weakness of his faith could not surmount the difficulty. No wonder, for the famine drove even Abraham himself from Canaan to Egypt, for which he had likely to have paid very severely in the loss or pollution of his beloved Sarah. We may truly say, Lord, what is man when left to himself? There is such a thing as fleeing from a lion, and being met by a bear; so Elimelech fled from the famine, and met with certain death in a land of strangers. It is good in every case to have the word, the counsel of God, for the rule of our conduct.

The history of the two brothers seems to be involved in their very names Mahlon and Chilion. From infirmity they both finished their lives in Moab, and with their father made their graves in a strange land. Both were men of infirmity, and both finished their course in Moab. These names are written upon all flesh; numberless infirmities both natural and moral cleave to the best of men. Paul had his thorn in the flesh, Timothy his often infirmities, and the church in general her great tribulations to endure. Moreover, all are hastening to finish their course with Chilion. Good and bad, rich and poor, gracious and profane, are posting towards the house of silence, where there is neither work nor device.

IXth. They were *Ephrathites of Judah*, a name of honourable distinction, Micah v. 2. *Thou Bethlehem Ephratah, though thou be little among the thousands of Judah, yet out of thee shall he come forth unto me, that is to be ruler in Israel; whose goings forth have been from of old, even from everlasting.* So that Jesus, the Son of **God**, was himself an Ephrathite of Judah.

Seeing there was an indelible enmity in the hearts of the Moabites against Israel, it may be asked, How it came to pass that those Ephrathites should not only be permitted to sojourn peacefully among them, for the space of ten years, but also during the whole time to have their wants supplied?

SERMON I.

To which we have this encouraging anfwer. In the time of their diftreffing exile, God fpeaketh for his banifhed people in the very hearts of their enemies: fo that it does not fuppofe the removal of the enmity, but the controul which the Almighty has over the will and inclinations of his peoples' enemies. In Jer. xv. 11. we have this promife: *Verily it fhall be well with thy remnant; verily I will caufe the enemy to entreat thee well in the time of evil, and in the time of affliction.* Enemies ftill, although inftrumental for good to the afflicted faint; and although enemies, under the abfolute controul of the God of Ifrael. An excellent divine * thus paraphrafes the promife, " If I do not effectually intercede for the enemies " of whom thou art afraid, never truft in me " more." The kind treatment which Jeremiah met with from the Chaldean General Nebuzaraddan, was neither lefs nor more than the fulfilment of this gracious promife.

As the banifhed ones muft both fojourn and be fed in Moab during their exile, we learn, that how dark foever the circumftances of the righteous may be, they fhall never be forfaken. He was with Ifrael in Egypt for their redemption, with the three faithful Hebrews in the furnace, with Daniel in the den of lions; and will be with his needy

* Mr. Nefs in his Hiftory and Myftery of the Bible.

people to the end of the world. So that although they may be perfecuted, they fhall not be forfaken; may be caft down, they fhall not be deftroyed *. The Scripture contains not one promife that we fhall be exempted from affliction and temptation, but it abounds with promifes of fupport under, deliverance from, and conqueft over; *for in all thefe things we are more than conquerors through him that loved us.*

* 2 Cor. iv. 9.

SERMON II.

THE CASE OF THE WIDOW AND FATHERLESS CONSIDERED, FROM RUTH, Chap. i. 3, 4, 5, 6, 7.

And Elimelech Naomi's husband died, and she was left and her two sons. And they took them wives of the women of Moab: the name of the one was Orpah, and the name of the other Ruth; and they dwelled there about ten years. And Mahlon and Chilion died also both of them; and the woman was left of her two sons, and her husband. Then she arose with her daughters-in-law, that she might return from the country of Moab; for she had heard in the country of Moab, how that the Lord had visited his people in giving them bread. Wherefore she went forth out of the place where she was, and her two daughters-in-law with her: and they went on the way to return into the land of Judah.

IN opening this passage, three heads of discourse offer to consideration.

Ist. The state of the widow and fatherless.

IId. The marriage of the two sons contrary to the law of God.

IIId. Naomi's return into the land of Judah, which God had again visited with plenty.

Ist. The

1st. The case of the widow and fatherless. The husband died, and the woman was left.

Death in any, even in the mildest form, hath something in it not only awful, but tremendous to nature. Even a Cato, when he found himself, as he thought, under a necessity of dying that he might not see the slavery of his people, could not without painful reflections venture upon an untried state of existence. But when the awful skeleton creeps into the bed of a man, and takes away the desire of his eyes with a stroke of death at once, bereaving him of the comfort afforded by a bosom companion, and entailing upon him more than a double charge, the dispensation becomes truly affecting. Yet none are exempted from circumstances of this nature—none are married longer than death shall them part. The fondest couple must part, though linked in the bonds of holy matrimony. And oh! sad the parting to hearts united! But it must be, the decree is gone forth, *Dust thou art, and to dust thou shalt return*. Remember ye who doat most upon one another, that notwithstanding your present enjoyments and pleasure, you must part also; you hold your pleasures by a tenure to you very uncertain, but at last your union must be finished by a separation; and oh! that you may be united in soul, in heart, and affection in the pure world of spirits.

SERMON II.

Some of God's people have been thus visited under circumstances of peculiar aggravation. Ezekiel must part with the desire of his eyes, and is denied the poor consolation of mourning for his loss. Chap xxiv. 16, 17. *Son of man, behold I will take away the desire of thine eyes with a stroke; yet neither shalt thou mourn nor weep, neither shall thy tears run down: forbear to cry, make no mourning for the dead,* &c. His wife was the desire of his eyes, what every wife ought to be to her husband. Though Ezekiel was the prophet of God, he could not be screened from the stroke of affliction. The injunction laid upon him not to mourn seemed to be an infringement of the laws of common decency, even in a person of private life: but here the prophet of God is, by divine authority, laid under the necessity of violating the rules of civil decorum. Lose a beloved wife, and not be permitted to mourn over her! How hard the case, says nature; but grace replies, it is the command of a covenant God, and shall be obeyed.

Ezekiel's case was undoubtedly trying, but it is still more hard and heavy when death, as in Naomi's case, bereaves a woman of her husband, and devolves upon her a multiplicity of cares in training up a fatherless offspring. The state of widowhood is, in society in general, considered as a very disadvantageous state, which changes *Naomi* into *Marah*, and for the most part attended with many miseries. You may well remember that the woman of Tekoah made use of it as a plea to win David's attention, *I am indeed a widow, and my husband is dead.* The word *Almonah* which we render widow, signifies dumb, the head being gone; and hence it is that the Scriptures so often, and so strongly recommends their cases to the consideration of judges, because the needy are frequently the subjects of oppression. But let the widow indeed remember, that if she herself is Almonah, dumb, she shall see a pleader rise in her behalf who speaks as never man spake, even our great High Priest who speaks well, and whom the Father heareth always. Widows indeed are honourably described, 1 Tim. v. 5. *Now she that is a widow indeed, trusteth in God, and continueth in supplications and prayer night and day.* How different these from those whom the Apostle describes, by saying, they will wax wanton and marry?

Whilst your husbands lived, you looked up to them in a way of dependence; now they are removed from your head, there is none but the Lord on whom you can rely. On him you may safely depend so long as you read that precious passage, Isa. liv. 5. *Thy Maker is thy husband, the Lord of Hosts is his name.* In him you shall find a wise director, a powerful protector, and a bountiful

tiful provider, who will never forsake you in the hour of your necessity. When one reads 1 Kings vii. 14. it gives great encouragement to comply with that injunction, Jer. iv. 11. *Leave thy fatherless children, I will preserve them alive, and let thy widows trust in me:* for the great Tyrian artist who built the temple in Solomon's days was the son of a widow, of which circumstance the Holy Ghost makes particular mention. *And king Solomon sent, and fetched Hiram out of Tyre; he was a widow's son of the tribe of Naphtali, and his father was a man of Tyre, a worker in brass: and he was filled with wisdom and understanding, and cunning to work all works in brass.* This was undoubtedly intended for the encouragement of other widows to bring their fatherless children, and commit them to him who alone can do them essential service.

Of all widows, we read of none whose case was more to be deplored than that of good Naomi. Banished by famine from the house of God, and the inheritance of her fathers, bereaved of her husband in an enemy's country, having two sons to educate in the midst of idolatry; and more especially, when her two sons themselves were taken away, and two young widows were added to her burden. Yet by those things, so grievous for her to bear, Infinite Wisdom was only bringing about the great end originally in view, the salvation of the ends of the earth; and after being thus tried in the furnace of affliction, her faith being found unto praise, she became the honoured nurse of one of the ancestors of Jesus.

A fatherless condition is also a state of misery, and exposed to many disadvantages, and is therefore joined with the widow every where in Scripture, both in point of mystery of the divine paternal care, and encouragement to trust in the goodness of a covenant God. You who are fatherless, may derive much consolation in contemplation of that passage, Exod. xxii. 22. *Ye shall not afflict any widow or fatherless child. If thou afflict them in any wise, and they cry at all to me, I will surely hear their cry.* To afflict the widow and fatherless any way, or in any degree whatever, rouseth the jealousy of a God; nor is it necessary that they should have the eloquence of an Aaron to engage him in their cause; for if they cry at all, though in language ever so broken, and in petitions ever so imperfect, the Lord will hear, yea, he will *surely* hear their cry, and retaliate upon their oppressors.

The fatherless are often neglected by man, but they are the declared objects of heavenly regard, and it is frequently enjoined upon those in power not to oppress them or the widow. You therefore who are forsaken of both father and mother, are particularly called to put all your trust in your
heavenly

heavenly Parent. You may say with David, Psal. xxvii. 10. *When father and mother forsake me, then the Lord will take me up.* He even glories in his near relation to you, and encourages your hope and trust in him as such, Psal. lxviii. 5. *A father of the fatherless, and a judge of the widows, is God in his holy habitation.* Yea, to visit the widow and the fatherless is one part of true and undefiled religion. These considerations tend to soften the aspect of the most gloomy dispensations, and open a door of hope to every Naomi.

IId. The marriage of her two sons to the daughters of Moab, contrary to the laws of the Lord, comes under consideration.

They took them wives. It does not appear that the godly mother had any hand at all in the matter, but rather that they acted uninfluenced by any. Nor was the taking of them wives simply considered at all reprehensible, but rather a favourable event, as thereby the loss of one creature comfort was supplied by the enjoyment of another. They had lost their father, and took unto them wives, for whom both father and mother ought to be forsaken, and who ought to be abode by in every circumstance. It was thus that Isaac was comforted after the death of his mother: he lost Sarah the mother, and found a help meet in Rebekah. May we venture to use this as adumbrative of Christ and his church? The Jewish church

church he possessed for many hundred of years; at last the glory and life departed, and Jehabod was written upon her gates: but he embraced the Gentile church and was comforted, saw the travail of his soul and was satisfied.

Under the most trying dispensations, and the very greatest of losses, the believer may say, "Although I have lost the gift, I have not lost the Giver." The Author of every perfect gift is still my own; my own God and my Saviour: if all my outward comforts were gone, the well from whence I draw consolation can never be dried up. If they were all withdrawn, I have fresh and lively comforts in the living God; the God of all comfort, and Father of all mercies, 2 Cor. i. 3. *Blessed be God the Father of mercies, and the God of all comfort, who comforteth us in all our tribulation.* The Apostle's eye was unto none but God for comfort. He that is in tribulation he can comfort, and declares that in all tribulation he doth comfort. On which observe, that God is the spring of all comfort; true consolation comes from him alone: the creature may yield comfort, but it is like the apples fabled by the poets, beautiful without, but stuffed with ashes and cinders within; but that which is from above is pure and undefiled.

It is he only that bestows all kinds of comforts whether natural or spiritual, for time and for eternity,

eternity, as well as comforts of every degree. It is he begets all our mercies for us, and ever lives to beget new mercies when the old ones are taken away.

But thefe marriages, taken in a moral view, yield reflections of a very different nature. *They took unto them wives of the women of Moab.* Here was a grievous departure from the law of their God, which law excluded ftrangers from the houfe of the Lord for ever. And furely thofe who are excluded from the holy congregation, ought never to be taken to the bofom of an Ifraelite. The law in Exod. xxxiv. forbids the Hebrews to make any covenant at all with the nations; and behold, Naomi's fons enter into the very neareft of all relations with ftrange women!

Yet God may, in his infinite wifdom, fo over-rule the evil actions of men, as to bring about by them the defigns of his grace, never once thought on by the perpetrators themfelves. No greater evil could ever be committed than to murder the Lord of glory, yet by this very evil was the redemption of the world accomplifhed. In like manner, notwithftanding the above marriage was in itfelf unlawful, it was fo over-ruled as to become fubfervient to the falvation of the Gentiles.

However, this gives no licenfe to any man to act contrary to the revealed will of God, which standeth fast for ever, and expressly enjoins all believers to the strictest obedience. The injunction is, 2 Cor. vi. 14. *Be not ye unequally yoked with unbelievers.* The reasons for it follow: *For what fellowship hath righteousness with unrighteousness? and what communion hath light with darkness? What concord hath Christ with Belial? or what part hath he that believeth with an infidel?*

According to the law, a man ought not to plough with an ox and an ass in the same yoke, nor so much as wear a garment of linen and woollen; and whoever departs from the direction given by the Holy Ghost in point of marriage, shall be a sufferer in his own soul. It was Solomon's foible to be attached to strange women, and the consequence was, they drew away his heart from his God. All his wisdom was not equal to their allurements. Let others, therefore, beware of connections so dangerous. Happy had it been for Sampson had he foreseen the danger of any intercourse with Delilah. Then would he have retained his eyes, and his strength; would have continued the terror of the Philistines, and the boast of his own people Israel.

These considerations ought to teach us to guard against all carnal connections, for it is difficult to take fire into the bosom without being burned, or to touch pitch without being defiled. If the strength of Sampson, and the wisdom of Solomon,

could

could not preserve them, we surely can have no reason to hope being more succefsful.

The preceding verse strongly verifies the Psalmist's declaration, Psal. xxxiv. 19. *Many are the afflictions of the righteous, but the Lord delivereth him out of them all.* Here was loss upon loss, trial upon trial. First, the husband died, and was buried in a strange land; secondly, the sons married strange women, the daughters of an accursed race, and enemies unto Israel; and, thirdly, the sons themselves are taken away by death in early life, without being permitted to visit their paternal inheritance: so that the woman was emptied indeed. We are told that God afflicteth not willingly, nor grieveth the children of men for their hurt; and yet, that *whom the Lord loves he chastens, and scourgeth every son whom he receiveth.* One son, and only one he had, who never sinned, but not without suffering; sinless Jesus was the greatest sufferer of the race of mankind, and yet the Holy One of Israel, the only Begotten of the Father, and the immaculate Redeemer of the election of grace, which was indispensably necessary to our salvation.

From what we read of the afflictions of others, we are taught that our own cases are by no means singular, even when our griefs are complicated. What did Israel, the elect of God, undergo in Egypt that house of bondage? what did Naomi endure in the land of Moab? and what is the general character of Jesus himself, but a *man of sorrows, and acquainted with grief?*

IIId. We come now to treat of Naomi's return into the land of Judah; in which we shall accompany her, making the following familiar remarks as we go along.

After being as it were buried in Moab for the space of ten years, this mother in Israel, in the words of the text, begins to emerge from obscurity and resume her proper character.

(1.) *Then she arose.* *Then*, after she had drank the bitter cup, in being stripped of her earthly all: for whilst husband and sons were alive, we hear not so much as of the most distant intention of returning again into the land of Israel. But her God prepared a school of heavenly instructions for her, in the outward corrections, and by the terrible things in righteousness with which he visited her, and thereby taught her that her resting place was not in the country of Moab. Those terrible things which she suffered, made her fit loose from her then present abode, think of the land of Canaan, and long once more to visit Bethlehem, the city of her ancestors, and abode of her husband's kindred.

What more than affliction tends to wean the believing soul from the things of earth and sense? What can tend more to make the heart long to be be at rest in the peaceful mansions above, where sinning and suffering are known no more for ever? David was not the only saint who wished for the wings of a dove, that he might fly away and be at rest. In the present case, the rod had a voice, as it always has whether attended to or not, and the holy woman had an ear to hear, and an heart to understand its language, which was "Arise, de- "part, this is not your rest, for it is polluted;" wherefore she arose accordingly to prepare for her departure.

When afflictions, of what kind soever, reduce you to a state of emptiness and nothingness, take off your dependence upon seen objects, and bring you to the necessity of living upon God as revealed in his word, you may say, that in very faithfulness your God hath afflicted you. Indeed that he could not have been faithful either to your souls, or to himself, without afflicting you in the very manner he has done. How comely is it for the believer to say, *It is the Lord, let him do what seemeth him good.*

(2.) *She arose with her daughters-in-law.* If it is a beautiful thing, as the Psalmist says, *for brethren to dwell in unity,* how lovely must it be to see the mother-in-law, and her daughters-in-law, arising together with an apparent design to forsake the land of Moab, and journey towards Israel, seeing these relative characters are, in general, no way remarkable for their reciprocal affection.

Now there must have been some remarkable cause for the daughters-in-law venerating, and so far cleaving to their mother in the days of their adversity, which could be nothing besides the following: Naomi was a woman who professed godliness, and acted in character; so that her daughters could not but be struck with conviction of her integrity, and the excellency of her religion. How different is this from the conduct of those professors, which in its own nature tends to give the lie to their profession, to excite prejudice in the carnal mind against the religion professed? thus making poor unconverted sinners tenfold more the children of wrath than they were before. Such professors have not only their own transgressions to answer for, but the blood of poor sinners, by their means hardened, will undoubtedly be required at their hand.

It ought never to be forgotten, that the church of the Lord is as a city set upon an hill, the light of which cannot be hid; that the daughters of Moab very narrowly mark the tempers, the life and conversation of an Israelite, and consequently that circumspection is indispensably necessary. Solomon says, Prov. xxx. 29. *That there are four things comely in going;* to which a fifth may very safely be added, A Christian walking in all the commandments

commandments of the Lord blamelefs. How cautious ought people to be who are in providence called to converfe much with the unconverted world, that they may be able to take God to witnefs, that they are clear from the blood of all men. It muft be an awful reflection to a faved foul to think that he has, in any wife, contributed to the ruin of any of his fellow creatures; and muft have yielded a comfortable reflection to Naomi, that God had made her the honoured inftrument of bringing Ruth into the tents of Ifrael.

(3.) *She arofe that fhe might return from the country of Moab.* The Moabites themfelves may reft at eafe in their native land, and worfhip idols of their own formation. So may worldlings of every rank, and every name, continue fatisfied with earthly productions. Not fo with chofen Naomi; for to her, God imbitters every Moabitifh fweet, dries up every well of confolation, and fhuts up every profpect of future happinefs in that land of ftrangers, till her foul became as a child weaned from its mother, and fhe renounces the name Naomi, laying claim to that of Marah. Nor was fhe the only perfon thus taught by terrible things, for we find the Pfalmift, Pfal. cxxxi. 2. thus confeffing, *I have behaved myfelf as a child weaned of its mother; my foul is even as a weaned child.* This alfo is in fome meafure the cafe with every Chriftian, to whom the Almighty is pleafed

to

to imbitter all the enjoyments of the present life, in order to endear unto them the heavenly felicity.

Paul, the holy Apostle of the Gentiles, found to his daily and bitter experience, that wherever he went, bonds and persecutions awaited him; and the effect which this experience produced was an earnest desire of dissolution, as expressed Phil. i. 23. *I desire to be dissolved that I may be with Jesus.* Indeed, it is one evidence of the love of God to his people, that when he sees them inclined to wander from his house and ways, to hedge up their way with afflictions, losses, crosses, and disappointments, that they may say with the church, Hosea ii. 6, 7. *I will return to my first husband, for then was it better with me than now.* And Chap. xiv. 3. *Ashur shall not save us, we will not ride upon horses, neither will we say any more to the work of our hands, ye are our gods; for in thee the fatherless findeth mercy.*

(4.) Emptiness of all Moabitish comforts was attended with an encouraging, inviting voice from Canaan; *for she had heard in the country of Moab, how the Lord had visited his people in giving them bread.* From whence we see that the Lord hath his visiting seasons, as well as times of withdrawment from his people. Sometimes indeed in holy jealousy with paternal chastisement, as Psal. lxxxix. 32. *Then will I visit their transgressions with a rod,*

and

and their iniquities with stripes. And thus he visited Israel with famine, and Naomi with the stripping providences, to which reference has above been made.

He *visits* his people in manifest mercy in giving them bread after famine, and makes them say with the church, Isa. xii. 1. *O Lord, I will praise thee; though thou wast angry with me, thine anger is turned away, and thou comfortest me.* It soon repents the Lord concerning the evil brought upon his servants, and he says when he sees their distresses, as to the destroying angel, 2 Sam. xxiv. 16. *It is enough; stay now thy hand.* It is precisely the same in the case before us; in jealousy for his holy name, he visited his people with a famine; and in tender compassion, he also visited them in giving them bread. This news reached the ear of Naomi, and was good news from a far country, and therefore was to her as cold water to a thirsty soul. O how reviving to the fainting soul is good news from the heavenly country! news of abundant pardon and plenteous redemption to the most abject slaves, the greatest offenders! It is as it were the richest wine of the kingdom of heaven, and makes even babes in grace appear as giants, and excites the worm to emulate Jacob, that wrestler with God, and thresher of the mountains of opposition. But this good news did not reach the ear of this venerable matron

tron till she was bereaved of her husband and sons, and left in a state of desolate widowhood; neither does the news from heaven, in common, arrive till all the springs of creature comfort are dried up; consequently, believers ought not to think it strange, if they see the Almighty to be stripping them daily of their delights.

(5.) *He visited his people in giving them bread.* Notwithstanding it pleased the Lord to visit Israel with a famine on account of their wickedness, his anger was but of short duration; he turned from its fierceness, owns them for his people, and manifests his kindness to them, by visiting them with plenty. We are here taught that the common necessaries and conveniences of life, are as much the gifts of providential bounty, as Christ and salvation are the fruits of everlasting loving kindness. Therefore he is to be sought unto for all things, and to be acknowledged in every enjoyment.

We have likewise a specimen of the divine conduct towards Israel, as different from what it was towards Egypt. The latter had her plenty, and her soil teemed with fruitfulness, before assailed by pinching penury: but although during the seven years of plenty the earth brought forth by handfuls, ghastly famine in its turn stalked through all the land, and soon devoured all that Joseph had carefully laid up in his granaries. Just so it
is

SERMON II.

is with the worldling of every character. They have their good things now, and the evil is reserved for an unthought of hereafter. One possesses his affluence and grandeur, and with contempt treats inferior classes of the people, but the day of downcasting, disgrace, and penury everlasting, is making hasty marches towards his present dwelling; nor shall he be able, in his present circumstances, to evade the just and tremendous judgment. Another sits in a chair of state, and in self-adulation flatters himself that his honour shall be permanent; but death, like a mole, is undermining his station, and preparing him a bed on a perfect equality with the most needy and tattered beggar, where his body shall become a feast to the vilest worms, and, without repentance, his soul the taunt and derision of fiends! Not so with the Lord's people Israel, they are first visited with famine, and afterwards with plenty; the first gives a zest to the last, and the experience of famine makes the plenty more precious and desireable, therefore it is received with the greater thankfulness. The Christian also hath his evil things to bear in his present state of existence, all the best things being reserved till the last. He is now groaning in this tabernacle, being burdened; the reproaches of the wicked fall upon him daily; temptations assail him every hour; losses, crosses, and disappointments pay him frequent unwelcome visits.

To sum up his character in one word, *He is coming up through great tribulation, washing his robes, and making them white in the blood of the Lamb.* But all this is leading to the remaining rest; to the mansions of pure and unspotted pleasure; to the sweet delights of the kingdom of Jesus, where the visions of God shall never be beclouded.

(6.) Having heard this good news from her own country, this holy woman *went forth out of the place where she was, and her two daughters-in-law with her.*

She was in Moab, a place of vanity, therefore an unsuitable dwelling for a mother in Israel, and especially one who was stripped of her all upon earth. *What fellowship can light have with darkness, or what communion hath Christ with Belial?* This whole world is a place of vanity; and vanity is as much to be deprecated as hell itself, seeing the latter is only the end to which the former naturally and infallibly leads its deluded subjects. To die in a state of sin and vanity, is infinitely worse than to die in a ditch, or on a scaffold; for such a death has no manner of influence upon the concerns of the immortal soul: but vanity stamps everlasting infamy upon its slave, were he even to die upon a bed of state, and under a silver canopy. Surely, my hearer, it must be awful to live in a state or place in which you are afraid to die; and yet this is but too frequently the case, even amongst gospel hearers.

hearers. But if you would not wish to die in Moab, or to perish with the world, the word is unto you, *Arise, depart, this is not your rest, for it is polluted.*

(7.) *She went forth, she, and her two daughters-in-law with her.* It is amiable to see mothers-in-law, and daughters-in-law, so to delight in each others company. And O what a pleasing sight to see relations walking hand in hand, in the fear of the Lord from Moab to Canaan, from this world, doomed to destruction, to the upper regions, the seat of rest and felicity! to see husband and wife, parent and child, coming cheerfully up to the house of the Lord together! But it is sad to behold the one set his face towards the house of vanity, when the other goes to worship God in his house of prayer. How many hearts this conduct has broken, and what murder of this kind must be answered for in the day of retribution, Infinite Wisdom only knows; but of this we are certain, that it shall all be brought into judgment before an assembled world. How awful the scene, when all the secret ways of mankind, with their causes and effects, shall be publicly investigated by the impartial Judge of heaven and earth! Well may the wicked and impenitent tremble on anticipating their certain doom. And well may the saints of God rejoice on the prospect of their redemption daily drawing nearer and nearer.

(8.) *They*

SERMON II.

(8.) *They went on their way to return to the land of Judah.* Orpah had not as yet difcovered any inclination to continue in the land of Moab, therefore her mother had no juft reafon to call her fincerity in queftion; as man can be approved or cenfured only by their prefent works, it being wholly within the divine province to judge of the principles which influence the heart. The practical improvement is couched in this obfervation: all who fet out from Moab to Canaan in earneft, do, like unto them, go on in their way; not indeed in the way of perceived fanctity, but rather under a fenfe of heart pollution which lays them and keeps them low in the fight and prefence of their holy Redeemer; and this growing downwards into nothingnefs, is one of the evidences of growing in grace, and in the knowledge of our Lord and Saviour Jefus Chrift, whether a man does or does not enjoy the immediate benefit and comfort of it himfelf.

The righteous hold on their way, becaufe here in this Moabitifh world, they can find no continuing city nor place of abode; nothing to fatisfy the cravings of an immortal mind: and from the very beft authority they have heard, that in their Father's houfe there is bread enough and to fpare; and they juftly conclude, that this being the cafe, it would be madnefs in the extreme for them to tarry in a ftrange land, and perifh by penury.

Indeed,

SERMON II.

Indeed, whilst there are many mansions in his house, and yet room for every comer from every quarter of the globe, why should they be discouraged, or by any means deterred from their laudable pursuit of life eternal? Difficulties you may, you must, you shall meet on your way; for it is through much tribulation that we shall enter the kingdom: but an entrance once administered into the holiest of all, will amply reward your toil and suffering, and cause your present afflictions to appear as waters which have passed away.

To conclude. Remember it is the Spirit of the Lord which discovers the emptiness of Moab, and the insufficiency of all creature enjoyments; which inclineth the heart to forsake father and mother, wife and children, houses and lands, for the sake of Jesus and salvation: it is he who giveth courage and inspireth strength to hold on in the way even to the end, and bring you safe to the heavenly felicity. Let then your eye, and your cry, be ever to Jesus for his Spirit's teaching; for as many as are *led by the Spirit of God, they are the sons of God*, Rom. viii. 14.

SERMON III.

Ruth i. 8,———13.

And Naomi said to her two daughters-in-law, go return each to her mother's house; the Lord deal kindly with you, as ye have dealt with the dead and with me. The Lord grant you, that you may find rest, each of you in the house of her husband. Then she kissed them; and they lift up their voice and wept. And they said unto her, Surely we will return with thee unto thy people. And Naomi said, Turn again, my daughters: why will ye go with me? are there yet any more sons in my womb, that they may be your husbands? Turn again, my daughters, go your way, for I am too old to have an husband: if I should say, I have hope, if I should have an husband also to-night and should also bear sons, would ye tarry, &c.

SPEAKING of the virtuous woman, whose price is above rubies, Solomon says, Prov. xxxi. 26. *She openeth her mouth with wisdom, and in her tongue is the law of kindness:* truly verified in Naomi, from whom we have not heard a syllable till now, and nothing but wisdom and kindness drop from her lips; all is maternal tenderness and piety, joined with the most becoming gravity.

gravity. Far from being like the clack of the foolish woman elsewhere described, and known by the multitude of her words; she acts and speaks as if a type of the church, in caring for the welfare of her daughters-in-law. What a rebuke does this venerable character give to tattlers, backbiters, and busy bodies? and what a fair example is set before every mother in our modern Israel?

1st. *Go, return each to her mother's house.* This breathes the most ardent affection. She loved her daughters, and delighted in their company; but rather than involve them in the difficulties she saw before her, she was ready to deny herself of the only earthly consolation she retained. Much had she lost, her all was at stake, yet her noble, disinterested soul felt more for her daughters-in-law than for herself; notwithstanding she rejected the name of Naomi, and laid claim to that of Marah. *It grieveth me much for your sakes that the hand of the Lord is gone out against me,* ver. 13. What an excellent lesson to parents, teaching you to prefer the good of your children, even to your own personal happiness; and indeed what would not a parent sacrifice to the good of his offspring?

Besides parental tenderness, this experienced mother might have a political end in view in giving this advice. By this she brought them to the test, and proved the sincerity of their affection to her, and to that Jehovah whose religion she professed.

professed. Till this advice was given, the soundness and sincerity of Ruth's religion did not appear; nor did the rottenness of Orpah's profession discover itself: but this brought them to a final determination, and each clave to the company with which they were formed to associate. This will ultimately be the case with all men, and every one shall have his own proper company; the very company which is their choice in the present state of existence.

Poor Orpah, whose religion was superficial, could now go back with credit, and therefore embraced her mother's advice: but steady, amiable Ruth had her heart effectually touched, and no persuasion could possibly divert her from her purpose to cleave to her mother-in-law, in life, in death, and in the very grave itself. O how steady and immoveable is the attachment of the truly godly! where you see much unsteadiness, you have great reason to fear that the root of the matter is absent, for love is a fixed principle, which cannot be quenched even by many waters.

The believing church being the Redeemer's Naomi, his sweet or pleasant one, in his unsearchable wisdom; it is his pleasure sometimes to bring her into the wilderness of afflictions, and tempestuous trials, on purpose openly to try the love of her professed daughters. In such sifting and winnowing seasons, many Orpahs turn their backs on her assemblies, as if no way interested in her internal concerns; notwithstanding at their first entering into her communion, they solemnly professed to cast their lot in with her's for the worse, as well as for the better. But such professors who can walk with the church only in her peace and prosperity, betray their want of affection to the Lord and Master of the church himself; and it is no matter how soon they return back to their own proper company, for they cannot at all profit the Lord's people.

IId. *The Lord deal kindly with you, as ye have dealt with the dead and with me.* This holy woman could not part with her daughters-in-law without praying with and for them; thereby letting us an example truly worthy of the closest imitation; and happy would it be if the same conduct were more generally practised in Christian society; of what union of affection might it be productive! she prayed for both with equal earnestness, not knowing which, if either, the Lord had chosen. Hence it appears, that parents ought to pray with and for their children; for how shall they be convinced, that they have at all a share in your prayers, if they are never offered up in their personal presence?

You may do your offspring more good by prayer and supplication for them, than by all your endeavours to render their fortunes affluent. Naomi had neither silver nor gold to confer, but she had, what was more valuable, an heart which could not cease to pray for them.

Indeed one would suppose that every parent who has an heart to love his children, would also have an heart to pray with and for them; but alas! the case happens very often to be quite the contrary, and many children are brought up, who, from the conduct of their parents, are altogether unacquainted that there is either duty, or privilege in that solemnity. But will not the man of grace imitate the high father of the faithful, who, in the fervour of his spirit, prayed earnestly for the son of even the bond woman, his whole soul going forth in the ardent petition, *O that Ishmael may live before thee!* Where is that parent who will not say, O that my children may live before the Most High; and with Naomi, *the Lord deal kindly with you, and bless you?* Children, bless God for praying parents; it is possible that they many times pray for you, when they hardly have hearts to pray for themselves. And ye parents, go on to pray for your children, let circumstances be ever so unpromising, for the Lord hath never said to the seed of Jacob, *Seek ye my face in vain.*

IIId. *The Lord deal kindly with you, as you have dealt with the dead and with me.* They had shewed conjugal kindness to their husbands whilst alive, buried them honourably when dead, and dutifully

continued

continued with their mother-in-law until this time in mourning: in all these things it appears not that Ruth exceeded Orpah. From whence we gather this striking truth, that how excellent soever moral and social virtue may be in itself, it may possess that soul which is altogether uninfluenced by divine religion; and consequently, that this, abstractly considered, is no suitable foundation for the hope of mankind.

The Lord deal kindly with you, &c. It may be observed that the Holy Ghost, by whom only prayer is inspired, leads his subjects to pray according to the designs of his grace and providence, so that although all blessings are freely given in Jesus, they shall be obtained by us only in the way of asking; for, *for all these things,* saith the Lord, *I will be inquired of by you, O house of Israel.* Hence it follows, that when a spirit of prayer for the nation, church, or family, is in exercise, it is an evident sign that suitable blessings are near approaching. On the other hand, when that is absent, as there is just reason to fear it is in this day, there is reason to apprehend that these blessings are at a remote distance, if at all designed. O Britain! my heart bleeds to contemplate thy situation! may God avert the approaching judgments!

The Lord deal kindly with you, as ye have dealt with the dead and with me. The law of retaliation,

tion, in both good and evil, is of divine institution, and of very ancient authority, Exod. xxi. 24, 25. *Eye for eye, tooth for tooth, hand for hand, foot for foot, burning for burning, wound for wound, stripe for stripe.* This same law is still in force under the gospel dispensation, with this difference, that under the Mosaic dispensation the execution of it was left with the judges, but now the Lawgiver has resumed that province himself. But this alters not the tenor of the law, seeing the same God who commands his people to forgive even to seventy times seven injuries, will, upon their forgiveness, himself retaliate upon their enemies; for himself tells us, Mat. vii. 2. *With the same measure ye mete, it shall be measured to you again.*

Adonibezek, lord of the world, and tyrant of Jerusalem, was fully convinced of the sanction of this law of retaliation, as appears from his own confession, Judges i. 7. *Threescore and ten kings having their thumbs and great toes cut off, gathered their meat under my table; as I have done, so God hath requitted me.* Caleb having defeated his forces, and taken the tyrant himself prisoner, either from his knowledge of his personal history, or by some secret leading from above, ordered his thumbs and great toes to be cut off, which opened his eyes to the villanies he had himself practised on others, and brought him to the above confession,

which

which shews forth the righteousness of the heavenly Governor.

This wretched and unjust tyrant was a lively type of that man of sin described by the Apostle Paul, 2 Thess. ii. 4. *As the son of perdition, who opposeth and exalteth himself above all that is called God, or that is worshipped; so that he as God, sitteth in the temple of God, shewing himself that he is God.* He also assumes the name Adonibezek, lord or father of the world, the princes of which have kissed his toe, and as it were gathered their meat under his table, holding their crowns and kingdoms by no other tenure than his despotic will. In flat contradiction to holy writ, he has practically declared that it is by him kings reign, and princes decree judgment. *One is your Master, even Christ*, says the Scripture; but I am lord of conscience, says the man of sin.

This man of sin is the head of the Roman church, that Antichristian hierarchy, which has ever shut the door of knowledge against the people, and persecuted to death the faithful followers of Jesus; and against which church is already denounced the following awful malediction, Rev. xviii. 6, 7. *Reward her even as she rewarded you, and double unto her double according to her works; in the cup which she hath filled, fill to her double. How much she hath glorified herself, and lived deliciously, so much sorrow and torment give her.*

her. Nor is this to be considered as an empty threatening, for its fulfilment is on its way, and shall be amply accomplished under the third vial, Rev. xvi. 6. where it is represented in point of certainty, as a fact which had already taken place. *They have shed the blood of the saints and prophets, and thou hast given them blood to drink, for they are worthy.* Let the man of sin with all his adherents tremble at the dreadful doom; and let the souls under the altar rejoice, seeing that judgment is hastening, and their God will fully execute the law of retaliation.

IVth. *The Lord grant that you may find rest each of you in the house of her husband.* Benevolence prompted the pious prayer, and shewed that she preferred the welfare of her living daughters, to the memory of her deceased children. She wisely considered them as loosed from the law of their former husbands, and at full liberty to re-enter the conjugal state with whom, and whensoever they pleased. This shews that a life of celibacy was no more known to ancient custom, than it is any part of Scripture requirement. It is evident that she even considered marriage, yea, a second marriage, as honourable, and a state of rest in comparison of widowhood or virginity. Let experience speak, and it will testify the same truth; therefore those who recommend a sequestered life, ought to be deemed enemies to society.

This

This good woman looked to God as the giver of this rest, *The Lord give each of you rest*. Happy, happy it is for that man who can look to the Lord, as the only giver of every good and perfect gift! And assuredly, if men and women were to look to him, instead of fortune, and social connections, there would be many more happy marriages than in general subsist. Blessed is that man who can upon this, and every other occasion, say with David, Psal. xxv. 15. *My eyes are ever towards the Lord.* But as Mr. Ness observes, with but too much justice, in general on these occasions the great bag, instead of the great God, is most regarded. And this we may conclude, that where the first is the object, true conjugal happiness is not to be expected. Begin with God, and he will continue with you even to your dying moments.

Vth. Having prayed with and for them, she kissed them, which shews that a rejection of every form of homage proceeds from superstition, rather than from Scripture usage. Even Abraham, the parent of the chosen race, bowed to the cursed Hittites *; and venerable Boaz, in a pious manner, saluted his harvest people, with *The Lord be with you.*

In Scripture we read of a civil kiss of salutation congratulatory at the meeting of friends, as when Jacob met with his cousin Rachel †. This in the

* Gen. xxiii. 7.   † Gen. xxix. 11.

text is valedictory, at an intended parting. Of a flattering, treacherous kiss, designed to cover the malignity of heart intentions: thus Absalom, acting the traitor to his own father, kissed the people on purpose to win their affections. Thus Joab took Amasa by the beard and kissed him, on purpose to conceal the dagger intended to be plunged into his bowels. And thus Judas comes with his, Hail Master! on purpose to betray the Saviour of the world.

We also read of a superstitious and idolatrous kiss, such as the image of Baal received from his worshippers; not unlike to the former practice of princes stooping to kiss the *toe* of the hoary impostor at Rome. A wanton whorish kiss, Prov. vii. 13. where it is said, *And she caught him, and kissed him*. But above all, there is an holy kiss of precious communion between Christ and his church, or the believing soul.

This is twofold. 1st. From Jesus, when he speaks pardon, peace, and loving-kindness to the poor, lost, and self-condemned sinner, mentioned Song i. 1. *Let him kiss me with the kisses of his lips*, &c. and who, that feels the bitterness of convicted sin, but will join in the ardent petition? 2d. There is a kiss of homage and submission from the believer unto the Saviour, similar to that which is practised by men in civil society. When any person is by the prince entrusted with office, you

hear

hear of him doing homage by kissing the hand of his sovereign and benefactor: how much more reasonably is the pardoned sinner called upon, Psal. ii. 12. *To kiss the Son lest he be angry*, and to take upon him the Redeemer's light yoke and easy burden?

This tenderness and piety of the mother produced in her daughters the softest sensations; they were not like many who can hear the most fervent petitions without the least emotion; who, perhaps, while the parent is groaning for their redemption, can snort away the moments of prayer, moments never, ah! never to return! unless it is like the flying Spartans, to lodge an arrow in the heart of the thoughtless. May the thoughtless and prayerless be enabled to keep this in remembrance.

VIth. *And they said unto her, surely we will return with thee unto thy people.* So said both, and both meant as they spoke. A few remarks here.

(1.) Promises of speech, and purposes of heart, whether to God, to his church, or to individuals, ought to go hand in hand. Speech is the glory of man, and its intent is to express the meaning of the heart. None ought to promise with their mouths what they do not purpose with their hearts; this is to be fraudulent and deceitful, which is destructive to human society; and such act the part of devils, and proftitute the glory of their nature to the worft of purpofes, if a man's word does not exprefs his meaning, and bind him, nothing can: you who have faid to the church, *Surely we will go with thee*, pray that God would give you grace to keep your word, left, like Orpah, you turn back again.

(2.) Promifes and purpofes often proceed from paffion inftead of principle. This we frequently fee exemplified in young converts, who have a paffionate regard to the perfon or manner of a preacher; and who for a while are extravagantly fond, and vehemently carried away. Orpah's was evidently from paffion. Saul, overcome with David's kindnefs, promifed that he would not feek his hurt. Naomi feemed fenfible that this proceeded from paffion, therefore prudently diftrufts them till fhe had put them to a farther trial.

A church will, at leaft ought, to examine into the candidate's principle before admiffion, and that becaufe,

(3.) Purpofes and promifes proceeding merely from paffion foon fall to the ground. A changed heart is neceffary to perfeverance in following God with Naomi. *I go Sir*, and went not was the language of one whom we read of in the gofpel, Mat. xxi. 30. Some perfons' meltings under the miniftry of the word, are but as the fummer brook which Iema's troops drank of, foon dried up, up, Job vi. 15. 20. Good thoughts do only make a thorough-fare upon a wicked heart, they stay not there as those that like not their lodging. Saul may have his religious fits, and Jehu much zeal, but for want of a changed heart both come to nothing.

VIIth. *And Naomi said, Turn again my daughters: why will ye go with me?* &c. Permit me to engage your attention to the following particulars:

(1.) *Why will ye go with me?* She well knew that if their hearts were not formed to it, the customs of Israel would prove irksome. This would have been a stumbling-block to the weak; a scorn to the wicked; an heart breaking to herself. *Why will ye go with me?* says the church. Young candidates should be full of caution, looking well to the grounds of their forsaking their idols: whether a sense of the purity of God and his law; the malignity of sin; Christ's all-sufficiency and fitness be at the bottom. *Why will ye go with the church?* Is it because ye consider it as God's chosen, purchased, and conquered people? Or in Moses's words, *because ye have heard that the Lord is among them?* Numb. xiv. 14. or because the church is Christ's Naomi, his sister, his spouse, his love, his dove, his undefiled? You will enter into a warfare; none have more enemies than the professing Christian; Satan, and all his vassals,

his

his myrmidons, *the luft of the flesh, the luft of the eye, and the pride of life.*

Now, war is to be entered into with caution and confideration, Luke xiv. 31. *What king going to war againft another king, fitteth not down and confulteth, whether he be able with ten thoufand to meet him that cometh againft him with twenty thoufand?* You are called to follow the Lamb, and his gofpel, in good and evil report; to choofe godlinefs though afflicted, and the gofpel though perfecuted.

Naomi's reafoning was full of candour and gentle perfuafion. She ufed not the authority of a mother; but the foftnefs of a friend; for fhe well knew that candour and kindnefs, are better than morofenefs and rigour.

(2.) *Are there yet fons in my womb, that they may be your hufbands?* alluding to the Levitical law, Deut. xxv. 5, 6. in which the brother of the deceafed hufband was bound to take the widow, &c. that the inheritance fhould not be alienated, nor the hufband's name perifh. Naboth loft his life becaufe he would not part with his inheritance, 1 Kings xxi. 3. *And Naboth faid to Ahab, the Lord forbid it me, that I fhould give the inheritance of my fathers unto thee.* This will apply to the gofpel and its ordinances, defcended to us from our anceftors: God forbid that we fhould alienate or fool it away; fhould we not tranfmit it to pofterity, sterity, childrens' children might curse us. Slavery follows a departed gospel. God forbid that our land should cast us out, or that our sins should cast out the gospel, or that Christ's land should be given to Antichrist.

(3.) *I am too old to have an husband.* Second marriages are no where in the word of God condemned as unlawful. Had they not been lawful, Abraham had been reproved for marrying Keturah. Naomi gives no intimation of her having relinquished the world to go into a nunnery, &c. The doctrine of a monastic life is contrary to Scripture usage. Enoch walked with God as prince and high priest of the faithful, in a married state, begetting sons and daughters. If Adam and Eve had been separated in a convent or nunnery, how would the world have been peopled? The Pope contradicts God in this as well as in every thing else. *It is not good for man to be alone,* says God. "It is best for men in orders to be alone," says the Pope. But whether it be right to hearken unto the Pope more than unto God, judge ye.

(4.) *Would ye tarry for them till they be grown? would ye stay for them from having husbands?* None of them thought of having children without husbands. *Nay, my daughters: for it grieveth me much for your sakes.* To a gracious soul, it is very affecting to see others involved in the fruit of its sins. She sinned in leaving Canaan, perhaps she was the principal cause of their removal; but they had not sinned with her, yet they suffer. When the plague went forth upon the people, David spake unto the Lord, and said, *Lo, I have sinned, and I have done wickedly: but these sheep, what have they done? Let thine hand, I pray thee, be against me, and against my father's house*, 2 Sam. xxiv. 17. O that spendthrift husbands would think of this, how their wives and their children are involved in their punishment!

The words are by some read, *It is more bitter to me than to you.* She was a poor, an old, a childless widow. Such are the objects of Christian charity, and to give to such is to lend to the Lord.

(5.) *That the hand of the Lord is gone out against me.* It is well for us if we can see, and are brought to acknowledge the Lord's hand in our afflictions. Divine Providence gives commission to afflictions to seize upon us: Providence orders the measure, the continuance, and the fruit of afflictions. The Stoics ascribed them to inevitable fate; the Epicureans and Atheists to blind fortune; the Philistines to chance. But Christians are of another mind; they hold a different creed, and ascribe the trials and changes of life to a quite different cause. David could see the divine hand through Shimei's wickedness, 2 Sam. xvi. 11. The providence of God regardeth all his works. *The very hairs of your head are numbered.*

SERMON IV.

RUTH i. 14, 15.

And they lifted up their voice, and wept again: and Orpah kissed her mother-in-law; but Ruth clave unto her. And she said, Behold thy sister-in-law is gone back unto her people, and unto her gods; return thou after thy sister-in-law.

THE Son of God being ordained the Saviour of all who believe, of the Gentiles as well as the Jewish race, it was necessary he should derive his human body of the substance of each; that affinity by blood might between them subsist, and consistently he might become their common Saviour; or, in the language of prophecy, *that he might be a light to enlighten the Gentiles, and the glory of his people Israel.* In order to this, the seed of the Gentiles must be mingled with the Jews, in that line from which Messiah was to descend. To accomplish which, a long train of providences are introduced as necessary; as, a great famine must take place in the land of Israel, in which even men of property found it difficult to procure

procure the ſtaff of life. Elimelech and Naomi are driven from their poſſeſſion, to ſojourn in the land of Moab; there muſt their ſons, Mahlon and Chilion, marry each a Moabitiſh woman; die, and be buried in the land of ſtrangers; and old Elimelech himſelf muſt pay his debt to nature, and not return to the land of his God to recultivate his paternal inheritance: by all which, this mother in Iſrael, this deſolate widow, led a life of bitterneſs, and choſe to be called Marah rather than Naomi, becauſe the Lord had dealt very bitterly with her.

' We may ſee from this hiſtory, as well as many others, that by the ſufferings of his ſervants, the unerring Majeſty of heaven and earth is pleaſed to bring his purpoſes to paſs, for his own glory, and their ultimate felicity.

What a mixture of ſweetneſs would the waters of bitterneſs, drank by this good woman, have received, from the knowledge of God's gracious deſigns; by the emptying of *her* to introduce the fulneſs of the Gentiles, and make her the honoured nurſe of the father of Jeſus, the Saviour of ſinners.

The leading ſteps of divine Providence thus briefly hinted at; I ſhall conſider the names, diſpoſitions, and conduct of theſe daughters of Naomi; and in order to which, I ſhall,

Iſt. Speak

1st. Speak concerning Orpah, who was so loving as to kiss her mother-in-law, and yet had not affection enough to cleave to her like her sister Ruth. There is such a thing as being neither cold nor hot, which seems from the issue to have been Orpah's condition; but it is a dreadful situation, if that threatening denounced against the church of Laodicea is to be regarded.

The name Orpah is very significant, intending the hinder part of the neck, and seems prophetic of her conduct, in turning back and forsaking her mother-in-law, instead of accompanying her with Ruth into the land of Israel, where the pure worship of the living God was duly maintained. Orpah signifies stiff-necked, which in one sense was applicable, in another inapplicable. In civil life, and as a member of society, her conduct was amiable: in point of relative duty, she was loving and obedient; but as to her religion, she preferred her Pagan connections to the privileges of the house of Israel. Her country, her kindred, and her gods, were dearer to her than her mother-in-law, and the inheritance of Jehovah. Orpah had been a faithful and kind wife, during the life of her husband, and after his death a loving and dutiful daughter to his mother. But agreeable, natural dispositions, and personal excellencies, being no infallible proof of the love of God, she cannot, with her honoured sister, cast in her lot with her

her afflicted mother, and renounce her natural connections, for the fake of her husband's kindred; neither can she finally forsake her, without sorrow and floods of tears.

Orpah went as far with her mother-in-law as consisted with her hope of carnal enjoyment; but when the door of this hope was shut against her, her resolution failed; her love to Naomi could not prevail with her to leave her native country. Like Orpah with Naomi, some sinners we read of, who followed Christ even a great length, but could not forsake all for the sake of his redemption; such was that Scribe, who, when he heard of the uncomfortable lodgings he was to expect, if he followed the Saviour of mankind, laid aside his resolution of following him whithersoever he went. Such also were those who followed Jesus more for the loaves and fishes, than from regard to the doctrine of that immaculate Preacher. Multitudes may be found who can part with much, but cannot part with all for the sake of that endearing name; who will go as far in religion as interferes not with their temporal emolument, but have not heart to take up their cross daily, and follow him through good and evil report. But the being almost a Christian, never conducted any man to heaven. If any man love father or mother more than Christ, he is condemned as unworthy of celestial felicity; unworthy to be the Redeemer's disciple

disciple here; unworthy of the enjoyment of him hereafter.

As Orpah seems to have gone a great way with Naomi, and after all went back to her kindred and her gods, so we see some put on a profession of religion, and for a season continue with the church. Like stony-ground hearers, they spring up into seeming Christianity on some ruffling of conscience, or some ferment in the passions: but being, alas! destitute of sufficient root, they cannot bear the scandal and mortifying influence of the cross. For want of love to a crucified Lord, they are not able to endure the pains of crucifixion. Having no proper relish for things unseen, they cannot find in their heart to part with carnal delights. As Orpah loved Naomi, and wept at parting, they may love the people of God upon inferior considerations, and it may grieve them to forsake them; but still their country, and their gods, have the ascendency over the promised but unseen pleasures of Israel. Like that young man in the gospel, they may desire eternal life; but they, with him, would have it in the way of doing, rather than in the way of parting with what they have; and although it may cost them a struggle, when they find that eternal life comes in the way of parting with all, and not as they would have it, for doing some good thing, like him, they will prefer their possessions to the divine inheritance, whatever sorrow may attend their giving up their pretensions to heaven. These go out from among us, because they are not of us. These return *with the dog to his vomit, and with the sow that was washed, to her wallowing in the mire.* Jehu drove furiously in the destruction of Baal, till he obtained a kingdom for his zeal, and then returned to the very same idolatry he had been destroying. But know, my hearers, this great, this capital and important truth, that it is only those *who endure to the end who shall be saved;* only those who overcome by the blood of the Lamb, to whom the Redeemer will grant *to sit down with him on his throne, even as he also overcame, and is set down in the throne of his Father.*

The King's daughter is called to incline her ear, and to consider, to forget her own people and her father's house, which call was not obeyed by stiff-necked Orpah. She turned her back upon Naomi and her God, for the sake of her own Pagan kindred, and the house of her father. But where Christ, by the displays of his own amiable, personal excellence, is pleased to allure the heart, all other lovers, all other kindred shall be forgotten; and the enamoured soul shall cry out after her Lord, in such pathetic exclamation as this, *Whom have I in heaven but thee, O Lord! and there is none upon earth I desire besides thee, my God!* All connections, all enjoyments, all pursuits,

suits, must give place to the sweet and endearing influences of drawing grace; and the whole universe will seem a general vacuum, but as God, our chief, our only joy, is pleased to manifest himself therein.

Orpah being gone back to her kindred, we shall,

IId. Attend to pious Ruth, whose conduct differed so widely from that of her sister-in-law. *Orpah kissed her mother-in-law, but Ruth clave to her.* I shall here pursue the same method as in the preceding head, and begin with the name Ruth.

Ruth signifies " made drunken," as this young woman had been by affliction, in the death of Elimelech her father-in-law, and of his son, her husband, as well as her brother-in-law, husband to Orpah. And now, put to this trying alternative, either to forsake her beloved, her godly mother-in-law, and all her hopes in the God of Elimelech, or to forsake all that was near and dear to her in the land of Moab.

The heirs of the kingdom seldom escape tribulation in this mortal life. Instructions are dispensed in the school of our heavenly Prophet, by terrible things in righteousness. Very frequently we see the people of God brought to pursue the honours of his sacred name, by the bitter exercise of stripping providences. Divine Providence was as it were big with signal honours, to be conferred in future on this Moabitish damsel; and in the school of affliction the all-wise Governor was pleased to train her up to a capacity for bearing of them gracefully. He empties those whom he intends to fill, and humbles by affliction those whom he intends to honour. For as on the one hand, *pride goes before destruction, and an haughty spirit before a fall*; so on the other hand, *before honour is humility*, and the way to dignity is through the depth of affliction. Before David is exalted to the throne of Israel, he must not only be banished from the court of Saul, but driven from the house of his father, and hunted in the wilderness as the fowler hunts a partridge upon the mountains. Before the government is established in his hand, he must undergo the fatigues of a civil war; a war with the house of Saul, that turned the land of promise into a horrible Aceldama. Even so, believers, ye must have your bitter, your disagreeable circumstances in the present state, in order to prepare you for the enjoyments of the future world. Ruth the destined bride of honourable Boaz, must drink deep of the cup of affliction before she is advanced to be named in the annals of Israel.

Ruth also signifies watered, as was her soul with the gracious influences of the sovereign Spirit, in order to her future fruitfulness, recorded in the page of sacred history. The grace and goodness of the God of Israel greatly discovered itself in detaching her from her former connections, and rivetting Naomi in her stedfast affection, so as to make her willing to part with all, rather than forsake the woman of adversity. She had the same gloomy prospect before her, which had deterred Orpah from any further pursuit; future consequences were entirely set aside, and whatsoever might befall her, she had fully determined to share in every circumstance in life and in death. Happy Ruth, mistress of such eminent self-denial, to part with all thy Moabitish connections for the sake of a portion in Israel. Go on, blessed damsel, and thou shalt find, *that whosoever forsaketh houses or lands, wife or children, for the sake of our Jesus, shall receive in this life an hundred fold, and in the end everlasting life.* The portion of Israel is not a barren wilderness.

O sinners, ye must be watered in order to become fruitful; born again, that ye may love the Lord with an holy affection; *for if any man be in Christ Jesus, he is a new creature; old things are done away with him, and behold all things are become new.* Divine charity is not a native of this depraved soil, it is an exotic, and its seed is from heaven. That heart, the imaginations of which are only evil continually, cannot of itself produce love to the Lord our Saviour. *Ye must be born again,*

again, says an incomparable Preacher. Lord, I believe, I receive upon undoubted evidence the infallible testimony, and wish no happier lot than to enjoy the precious fruits of regeneration in their most extensive latitude. My God, how happy shall I be to be found the workmanship of thy heavenly Spirit, and an heir of thine eternal kingdom.

Ruth signifies filled, as this holy damsel was with the sacred fruits of the Blessed Spirit; and even with the good things of Canaan, after her God had detached her from her native connections, and emptied her of her former comforts. For, as our God in his ordinary course of operation, fills none before he has sufficiently emptied them, so he empties none of creature trust and self-dependence but those he intends to fill. If he casts down into the dunghill, it is with a view to exalt unto thrones, and to set you among the princes of his people. How low was Jacob laid under the oppressions of Laban, and fears of his brother Esau, before he exalted him to the dignified name of a prince, who had power to prevail with God; or to be the parent of the chosen race? How low was David, who knew what it was to lack a morsel of bread before his accession to the throne? Yet they were filled with riches, with honour and with length of days.

Unbelief

SERMON IV.

Unbelief itself shall never produce an instance of our God having emptied any vessel of its own sufficiency, and then leaving it to be filled with wrath and indignation. It is easily proved, that to empty of self-dependence, by revealing our own insufficiency, is the work of grace; and as easy to shew, that the operations of grace are all perfect and complete; for *we are confident of this very thing, that where God hath begun a good work,* such as to empty the soul of all self-dependence, razing every sandy foundation, and beating down every lying refuge, he will perform it even to the day of Christ, when ye shall be filled with all the fulness of God; overwhelmed in the heights and depths, lengths and breadths, of the unsearchable riches of Christ, and the unspeakable bliss from thence resulting.

Let us note the difference between these two sisters; Orpah kissed her mother-in-law, as an honoured relation; Ruth clave to her with the attachment of a saint. Orpah came along with Naomi to the borders of Moab, and went back sorrowing for having lost her. Ruth would not be entreated to go back with her sister, but resolved to cleave to her mother to the loss of all; to cleave to her even amidst the bitterness which the Almighty had brought upon her. Orpah is soon persuaded to depart; all persuasions served only to strengthen Ruth's resolution of following her whithersoever

whithersoever she went, and cleaving to her till the latest moments, even in death itself. When that Scribe understood that Jesus had not where to lay his head, he soon dropped his purpose of following him as his master; but the blind man who was forbidden to cry after Jesus, because, truly, his crying was troublesome to the disciples, would not be dissuaded from pursuing his suit, and cried out *so much the more* for the opposition he met with. Where the heart is indeed influenced by sovereign grace, and drawn by the eternal Father, opposition will only serve to inflame our love and zeal, as oil cast into the fire serves only to increase its ardour, instead of extinguishing the flame; but if the convictions are merely natural, a small matter of opposition will be sufficient to send us back, that we follow no more with Jesus. Only those who are cleansed by the washing of regeneration, and the renewing of the Holy Ghost, will cleave to Jesus and his believing church, in the dark and clouded day of adversity.

Intreat me not to leave thee, says amiable Ruth; it was painful to her to hear her mother's entreaties. She knew not how to disobey; yet in the present case, she deemed disobedience even a virtue. Her soul clave to her with a warm, an indissoluble attachment; she could do any thing with greater readiness, than part with her beloved
mother-

mother-in-law. What a cenfure is this hiftory upon fuch perfons of that mutual relation, of mothers and daughters-in-law, who are fo far from cleaving to one another, that they are fcarce able to live in the fame town, much lefs under the fame roof with one another. I would recommend this pleafing, facred hiftory to the attentive regard of all who ftand in that endearing relation.

How little of the maxims of the world is here difcovered in the conduct of this pious Moabitefs? How little of that falfe, that hollow hearted friendfhip fo difgracing to mankind? The rich man hath friends enow. But how nobly oppofite to the cuftom of men to cleave to Naomi in her deepeft adverfity? how like is this to the friendfhip of the heavenly friend of finners, who loveth at all times, was born for adverfity, and fticketh clofer than a brother.

Ruth clave to her mother-in-law. To come at the force of the word, ufed by the divine hiftorian to fet forth her warm and clofe attachment, we may a little *note* the fenfe in which it is ufed in fome other places of infpired writ. That great mafter of facred diction, the royal prophet, the princely finger in God's Ifrael, twice ufeth the fame word as here in the text to fignify his own affinity with the duft. Pfal. cxix. 25. *My foul cleaveth to the duft*. Pfal. xliv. 25. *For our foul is bowed down to the duft, our belly cleaveth unto the earth*. Thofe who
are

are acquainted with themselves, cannot be at a loss to know how close their connection is with that dust from whence they were taken, and to which they shall return. In Psal. lxiii. 8. the same word is rendered, *followeth hard. My soul followeth hard after thee:* what he means by following hard you see in Psal. xlii. 1. *As the hart panteth after the water brooks, so panteth my soul after thee, O God.* This shews the intense longing of the Psalmist's soul, for the pleasing enjoyment of his Maker's presence, that he could no more live without it than the hunted hart could comfortably endure without the cooling stream. So pious Ruth *followed hard* to share in her mother's fortunes, whether they should prove favourable or adverse; which naturally supposes that there was a suitableness of temper and interests, and that she had a perfect union with her in her hopes and views.

To follow Christ consistently in his ordinances, such an union in heart and affection with his believing church is necessary. They are but unfruitful vines, unprofitable members of gospel churches, who have interests and views separate from, or opposite unto the common views and interest of Christ in his church; yet we shall find many who most evidently give the concerns of the Redeemer's kingdom, at farthest, but a second place in their care and assiduity. Can it, with any propriety, be said of such, that they are crucified to the world,

world, and the world to them? that they deny themselves, and take up their cross daily? that they love the Lord Jesus Christ with all their heart, with all their souls, and with all their minds? Look to it, my brethren, that your first and principal concern, be the welfare of the church, the honour of Jesus, and his mediatorial kingdom. If you seek first the kingdom of God, and his righteousness, all other things shall be added to you; and you shall never have it to say that you have served God for nothing.

That was a well chosen petition of the royal Hebrew, that he might dwell for ever in the house of the Lord, and inquire in his temple. Psal. xxvii. 4. *One thing have I desired of the Lord, that will I seek after, that I may dwell in the house of the Lord all the days of my life, to behold the beauty of the Lord, and to inquire in his temple.* *One thing,* as if there had been no other thing worthy of his notice, much less that had the possession of his heart. He had a kingdom to govern, all the tribes of Israel to direct; but *one thing,* unconnected with kingly rule, lay warmest on his heart. This *one thing* was, that he might dwell in the house of the Lord all the days of his life, see the beauty of the Lord, and inquire in his temple. He had all the brilliance of a regal court to attract his attention, and allure his desire; but

regal magnificence, and courtly parade, were by no means the objects of David's supreme regard. He had the beauty of kingly majesty every day in his palace to sooth his wishes; but the *ultimatum* of his desires was, to behold the beauty of the Lord; not barely to have a glimpse of it in a transient manner, but to behold it with steady eye; to behold the beauty of the Lord, so that the eye shall be satisfied with seeing. Might I have this *one thing*, I think that heaven and earth might reserve all their other beauties to themselves. This *one thing he desired of the Lord*. He well knew it was not in man in general, nor in himself in particular, to command the precious, the much desired blessing: that it was not to be found in the horrid din of noisy war, nor in the tinseled grandeur of kingly levees, he sought it of the Lord. His heart was resolutely set upon obtaining it, therefore he would seek after it: *and that will I seek after*. The near and interesting concerns of my numerous family, the softest endearments, and nearest attachments of consanguinity, shall never divert me from seeking after this, as my chief, my superlative good. Not all the weighty, the important and arduous concerns of government, nor the deep machinations of war, shall prevent me from seeking thy face, my God and Father, from beholding thy face, O blessed
Immanuel.

Immanuel. In the church, only in the believing church, are the brighteſt glories of our gracious God, the pure and illuſtrious beauties of ſovereign grace, conſpicuous and manifeſt. There, O believer, thou mayeſt inquire, and there ſhalt thou behold his ineffable beauty beaming forth through the manhood of Jeſus.

SERMON V.

Ruth i. 16, 17, 18,——22.

And Ruth said, Intreat me not to leave thee, or to return from following after thee: for whither thou goest, I will go; and where thou lodgest, I will lodge: thy people shall be my people, and thy God my God: where thou diest, will I die, and there will I be buried: the Lord do so to me, and more also, if ought but death part thee and me. When she saw that she was stedfastly minded to go with her, then she left speaking unto her, &c.

SEE in the person and disposition of Ruth the Moabitess, the believer's firm attachment to the gospel church. Hear her endearing and resolved words, *Where thou goest, I will go,* through smiling fields, or gloomy fens; through verdant meadows, or howling deserts; whether in prosperous or adverse circumstances, I am resolved to cast in my lot with thine. If thy way should lie through the land of Beulah, and the voice of the feathered songsters animate thee for thy journey; if thou mayest happily emerge out of the

ocean

ocean of afflictions, which long has overwhelmed thee, and the candle of the Lord be rekindled on thy tabernacle; I shall account myself blessed to behold thine enlargement. But although thy way should be more dismal than the shadow of death itself, and the future part of thy life be more afflicting than that part elapsed, I can have no pleasure, no other joy, besides what ariseth from assiduously ministring to thy distress, and sharing in, if I cannot alleviate, thy sorrow.

Where thou goest, I will go, will be the language of every truly converted soul to the gospel church. The society of the wicked is held abominable, as the synagogue of Satan, and the maxims of the world as an unclean disease. Even when there is not a full persuasion of interest in Israel's portion, and sharing with the church in her future felicity, you will find a settled, unalterable resolution of seeking her advantage, and sharing in her adversities whilst here, whatever may happen in that world which is to come. This is a noble evidence of Christian affection, and a signal display of the conquest of grace upon the heart, and I may boldly assert, that he who is willing to cast in his lot with the people of God here, shall not be excluded from their enjoyments hereafter.

No man ever did forsake all in this world for he sake of Christ, his gospel and church, but he found the Lord to be as good as his word, and received eternal life according to the full tenor of the promise.

Where thou lodgeſt, I will lodge. Here was no proviſo made for its ſafety and delicacy. Ruth might have made this reſolution conditionally. *Where thou lodgeſt, I will lodge,* provided thy lodging is ſafe, eaſy, and commodious. Like that Scribe who, it is probable, would have followed Chriſt, provided he had been aſſured of agreeable accommodations in the way; but finding great reaſon to apprehend a deficiency in this reſpect, in point of worldly prudence, laid aſide his deſign. It has not in any age been common for the greateſt of ſaints, to have the ſofteſt beds, and moſt comfortable lodgings; and yet, in every age, God has had his followers and witneſſes, and the church her unfeigned lovers.

That reſplendent cloud of witneſſes, of whom the world was not worthy, wandered about in ſheep ſkins, and in goat ſkins; were deſtitute of houſe and home; lodged in dens and in caves of the earth, notwithſtanding they were the choſen heirs of the kingdom of glory. Nor was the Lord from heaven, the only Begotten of the Father himſelf, better provided in his ſojourning below; for although the foxes had holes, and the birds of the air had neſts, the Son of man had not where to lay his head. Notwithſtanding which penury, his faithful diſciples forſook him not,

but

SERMON V.

but were contented with such lodgings as their Lord had for himself, deeming it sufficient that the servants should fare as their Lord and Master.

Thy people shall be my people. The forsaking of her own kindred, kingdom, and household gods, is followed by an adherence to the kindred of Mahlon and Elimelech. *Thy people shall be my people.* Hereby, says the inspired divine, *do we know that we are passed from death to life, because we love the brethren.* Without such a love to the brethren, as will cause us to cleave to them in every situation, we give no adequate evidence of our having passed from a state of nature, into the kingdom of the loving Jesus. Wherever this love to the brethren does discover itself, it evidently shews the soul to be born from above. The reason why you love the brethren is, because they love and follow the blessed Jesus; because in their spirit and temper you see the image, or likeness of the amiable spirit, by which his whole conduct was influenced. Thus it is, that the love of Christ, and only the love of Christ, constraineth you to pay a distinguished regard to those who worship the immaculate Redeemer. Wherever the heart is right with God, as enlivened by the quickening influences of the Holy Spirit, it will discover itself by this unfeigned love to the brethren. The saints of God will be esteemed the excellent ones upon the earth, in whom is all your delight, the only people with whom you choose to associate.

Thy God shall be my God. This is indeed the foundation of Ruth's attachment to Naomi, and from this it appears she had seen, that in the spirit and conduct of her mother, which endeared the God of Israel to her affection and supreme regard. That she had seen in her what she had never met with among her own kindred and people, therefore this becomes her cool and determinate resolution, *Thy God shall be my God.* What a noble and encouraging incentive is this to stimulate us to an observance of the spirit and laws of Christianity, that thereby we may win dark and benighted Heathens, our unconverted fellow sinners, to the love of Jesus, and worship of the Father through him! What an honourable, what an illustrious figure does this mother in Israel make in the annals of heaven; as by her pious and endearing conduct, having allured Ruth the Moabitess to the love of the true and living God!

This exalted instance of genuine piety, is inserted in records subject to no future erazement, and to Naomi's honour, shall be made venerable mention of when fleeting time shall have run his destined race, and all shall be immense, unspeakable, inconceivable eternity. O my soul, may this be the highest point of thine ambition in this life,

life, to be enabled, by grace to draw the attention of young and thoughtless Moabites to the love and worship of thy holy, thine adorable Redeemer, the perfection of beauty, and center of heavenly excellency! Mayest thou sojourn here below no longer than this shall be thy ardent wish and daily study!

What shall we think of those called Christians who never visit Pagan shores, but with a view to plunder the inhabitants? what must the old Indian inhabitants of Mexico and Peru think of the religion of the Spaniards? what must the inhabitants of Indostan think of the Christianity of the English? must not the conduct of the Company's servants in the East Indies, fix in the breasts of the unhappy natives an indelible disgust against the name of Christ, as the patron of ruffians? I fear it, and I think upon solid and scriptural grounds, that the time is coming when a just God will revenge the tyranny of that infamous Company, and plead the cause of the unhappy Pagans with the whole British nation: and who shall be able to stand when an avenging God shall stir up himself as a man of war against us?

Thy God shall be my God, will be the language in which every true convert shall address the believing church. *O Lord, other lords have had dominion over us, but henceforth we will serve thee, the living and true God. Ashur shall not save us, we will not ride upon horses, neither will we say any more to the works of our own hands, ye are our gods; for in thee the fatherless findeth mercy.* Because the presence of the incarnate God is in a peculiar manner with the believing church, her assemblies will ever attract the Christian's attention.

Where thou diest, I will die, and there will I be buried. In life and in death, she fully cast in her lot with her mother-in-law. She would not so much as have her body carried back to her native country for interment. With thee will I be buried, and repose my dust in thy hallowed tomb. That affinity and union which hold out for the full term of life, must be strong; but stronger still that which holds good in life and death. Such only is the Christian union. In life, in death, at judgment, and to eternity it is indissoluble. Those who come to Jesus for life and salvation, consider their bodies as well as their souls as bought with a price, and therefore commit them to him even in death, and in hope lay them down to slumber in the grave, till awakened by that awful voice, compared to which the loudest thunder is but as the softest whisper, and the ruffling hurricane as the breathings of zephyr.

Ruth being inclined and enabled to forsake all, met with a suitable and encouraging reward for her pious attachment to the seed of the promise. She was married to an honourable Israelite, of
whom

whom we shall have occasion to take further notice in some future discourse. "That no man shall "serve God for nought," is a good maxim, notwithstanding laid down by the parent of error, and was exactly fulfilled in the case of this illustrious Moabitess. She was honoured with becoming the ancestor of the man after God's own heart, and through him, the mother of a race of monarchs; not only so, but she became the mother of the glorious Immanuel, that only and blessed Potentate, the King of kings, and Lord of lords, who is possessed of all power in earth and in heaven. This bounty of divine Providence towards our Moabitish heroine, beautifully confirms the truth of our Lord's words, where he says, *Whosoever shall forsake father or mother, wife or children, houses or lands for his sake, shall in this life receive an hundred fold, as well as life eternal in the world to come.*

You, therefore, to whom the world is crucified by the cross of Christ, and who resolve to follow your Redeemer conscientiously, even if it should cost you your *earthly* ALL, you see the good set before you in the promise—*Even in this life ye shall have an hundred fold;* not always in kind indeed, but you shall be sure of it in value. Riches, honour, ease, and pleasure, such as this world boasteth the power to give, are no parts of the good included in the promise. But you shall receive

ceive righteousness, peace and joy in the Holy Ghost, and thus have the kingdom of God set up within you. Such a righteousness as shall render you all holy and complete, lovely, and beautiful even in the eye of infinite Holiness; righteousness, that for its splendor, shall be as a mirror, to reflect the illustrious excellence of every divine perfection: peace, which only God can bestow, which can be obtained only in Christ; peace, which none but the children of sorrow, and sons of warfare are capable of receiving. This is the *peace of God which passeth all understanding*, bequeathed to thee by thy departing Redeemer, and such as the unregenerated heart never experienced. This is the portion of *your* souls, O ye who fly for refuge to the hope set before you in the gospel, *joy in the Holy Ghost!* Little of heavenly joy is experienced, before you are brought down to the very margin of destruction. It is impossible to know the joys of pardoned sin, before the sentence of the law has been denounced in the conscience, and we are brought as guilty criminals to Jesus for a free pardon; none besides the condemned being capable of receiving pardon. But when sin is set before you in all its aggravations, and threatens your ruin by its formidable terrors; when the law has denounced the condemnation due to it, and instead of the execution of the sentence, you receive redemp-

tion

tion through the blood of Chrift, the forgivenefs of fins; how fweet is the joy! how tranfporting the pleafure from thence refulting! fuch righteoufnefs, peace, and holy joy, are connected with a forfaking of all for the fake of Chrift, and his great falvation.

Is it then your holy refolution to part with all, to feek firft the kingdom of God, and his righteoufnefs? may grace ftrengthen your refolution! you will find your account in the wifdom of your choice, and have caufe to blefs God for the gift of this wifdom. You renounce your unlawful gains, and ungodly pleafures, and lo, there is before you an inheritance incorruptible, undefiled, and that fadeth not away; a kingdom that fhall never have an end, and a crown that is not liable to be tarnifhed. Doft thou forfake thy carnal companions, in whofe fociety thy heart can no longer take delight? behold the faints of the Lord, the excellent ones of the earth, are appointed the companions of thy warfare, whilft here, under the guardianfhip and protection of holy angels in the days of thy pilgrimage, and the fharers of thy joy when thy warfare is accomplifhed. Haft thou loft the good will of thy relatives? has father and mother forfaken thee, becaufe thou wilt worfhip the Lord God of thy fathers, after the manner which the world account herefy? be not concerned at it; for when father and mother forfake thee,

thee, *the Lord will take thee up.* Thou hast made a goodly exchange. Thou losest indeed thy natural parents, but the everlasting Father himself becomes thy ALL. The Father of Jesus, and thy Father, are now identically the same. Blessed, O Lord! are the people whose God thou art, and whom thou hast chosen for thine own inheritance. I cannot set before my hearers the extent and glory of the privileges provided for those, who by grace forsake their native *all,* for the sake of Jesus, and his great salvation; but the reapers are commanded to drop handfuls on purpose for them, and bring forth all the treasures of the gospel for their relief. How happy! how truly blessed is your lot, if ye be indeed the followers of Jesus!

Would you follow the Lord Jesus whithersoever he goeth, but for that unworthiness and sin that cleaveth to you? learn then a profitable lesson from amiable Ruth. You have many objections against yourself, and so might she have had, if grace had not prevented; objections in all respects equal to your own. She was a descendant of Moab, the son of incest, and therefore instead of blessing, might have expected cursing for her father's sake. She had been brought up an idolatress, and an enemy to the Lord God of Israel; had always been a follower of the customs disapproved by the law of the Hebrews, and a

stranger

stranger to the constitution of the kingdom of Messiah; but notwithstanding all her objections, she was determined to worship the God of heaven, and trust in the portion of Israel: therefore she expresseth her resolution, *Thy people shall be my people, and thy God shall be my God; where thou diest, I will die, and there will I be buried.*

It is an happy thing to be brought to resolve to cleave to the people of God in this life, whatever become of you in the future world; to resolve to die, and be buried with the people of God, whether you have the assurance of rising with them on the morning of the great day or not: to walk in the ways of Immanuel *now*, if you should even be spurned from his presence hereafter. Never were there any brought to this resolution, but who found it to terminate according to their highest wishes, and who were admitted into that felicity for which they dared not to encourage even the faintest hope, in the drooping days of their gloomy despondency.

Are you covinced that Jesus, our Redeemer, is the true God and eternal life? are you satisfied in your own mind that his ways are the right ways of life and salvation? would you desire to be worshippers of him; to worship him in his own appointed way? worship him then in his own way, and leave the issue entirely to him; he will certainly deal as favourably with you, as he did with Ruth

the

the Moabitess; for he is no respecter of persons. We may very safely challenge Satan and *unbelief* with their united counsel, to produce a single instance of any poor penitent, humbled, desirous soul, following Jesus, cleaving at all events to his people, and at last becoming a cast-away. An instance cannot be produced; no! perish who may at the Libertine's gate, intreating for the crumbs which drop from the voluptous table, none ever perished at the gates of Immanuel; for he, only he, is the friend of sinners; and of none among the human race besides sinners.

So they two went on till they came to Bethlehem.

Here is an instance of God's faithfulness in restoring comfort to his mourners.——Elimelech and his sons were taken away, Ruth is given as a fast friend.——When Abraham lost Sarah, Rebekah is brought into her tent. Types of the Jewish and Gentile church.——When all men forsook Paul, the Lord stood by him, 2 Tim. iv. 16.——When the people spake of stoning David, he encouraged himself in the Lord his God.

It is the Lord's time to bring new comforts when there is a death upon our helps, and damp upon our hopes.

SERMON V.

So they two went on.

Their principles were one, the life and love of God in the foul.——Their object was one, to come and truſt in the ſhadow of divine wings.——Their intereſt was common, the ſalvation of their ſouls, and communion by the way.——Theſe made their friendſhip invariable; heartened them to hold on their way.

Until they came to Bethlehem, the houſe of bread.

How many accompany each other to Beth-aven.——But this is betraying inſtead of befriending one another.——Had Jonadab curbed Amnon's paſſion, inſtead of deviſing means to gratify it, he had done like a friend.——Many Jonadabs infeſt kings courts, but the curſe of God will follow them.

Our travellers are an emblem of the righteous, who hold on in their way, *&c.*

And all the city was moved about them.

Seeing the great change in Naomi's circumſtances.——God worketh great changes in perſons, families, cities, and countries.——What a change on the proud Aſſyrian monarch.——He looketh upon every one that is proud, and bringeth him low, Job xl. 12.——On families, as Job's and Saul's.——On cities, as Jeruſalem, Lam. ii. 15. *Is this the city that men call the perfection of beauty, the joy of the whole earth?*——On countries, as the Aſſyrian, the Grecian, the Roman empire.

empire.——Such changes will affect beholders: Is this Babylon, Athens, Rome, or London?

And she said unto them, Call me not Naomi, but call me Marah.

The condition of creatures is soon changed.——Those who look on themselves to be delightful ones, he maketh Marahs; both Pharisees and his own foolish children.——Those who look upon themselves as Marah in God's sight, he constitutes Naomis.——He calls no man Benjamine, son of the right-hand, who has not first been Benoni in heart.——Before honour is humility.

I went out full, but the Lord hath brought me home again empty.

Her going out was of herself, but her coming home was of God.——People usually get full before they go out from God's way and habitation.——How full soever when they go out, God brings them home empty. See the Prodigal.

Note. To seek for gain or pleasure out of God's way, is the ready way of coming to loss.——To go out of God's way, is to go out of his protection.

To go from the land of promise to the land of curse, is the way of certain danger. Let those who slight church fellowship think of this.——Many are tempted to go out of God's way for gain, but they meet with gall and wormwood instead of honey.——Jehoshaphat had like to have lost

lost his life for going with Ahab, 2 Chron. xviii. 31.—He quite lost his ships, 2 Chron. xviii. 37. ——Good Josiah lost his life by going rashly out of God's way, 2 Chron. xxxv.

The Lord hath testified against me, and the Almighty hath afflicted me.

It is a great alleviation of pain to eye God in our affliction, though even brought by ourselves. —God has come in as a witness against me for choosing Moab rather than Canaan. Thus she kissed the rod.——We may see how the believer differs from himself at different seasons.———In an humble frame, David could see God had bid Shimei curse him.—In another, he could not see how God had bid Nabal be churlish.——Eyeing of God in our troubles, is a sovereign help to true patience.

Remark. Their arrival was in the beginning of barley harvest:

David's extremity was God's opportunity, 1 Sam. xxiii. 20.———There is a fulness and fitness of time for every event.———The redemption of Israel from Egypt.—The coming of Shiloh, when the scepter was departing from Judah.—Old Testament vision sealed.—The converting of the soul by grace.—Deliverance from affliction—finishing our appointed period and work.—You will all get to the house of bread in the beginning of harvest —a full and plentiful harvest eternally before you.

SERMON VI.

Ruth ii. 1,———14.
Naomi had a kinsman of her husband's, &c.

THIS widow was not forsaken of her husband's rich kindred, as is usual in such cases.—When otherwise, it is of the Lord.———God never wants instruments to succour and comfort those who trust in the shadow of his wings.———If Elimelech dies, Boaz is raised up.———David says, Psal. xxxvii. 25. *I have been young, and now am old, yet have I never seen the righteous forsaken, &c.*———There was a time when no Jew durst assist Jeremiah, Chap. xxxviii. and the princes were his mortal enemies.———God had then an Ethiopian Ebed-melech, *the king's servant*, to serve him in his prophet.—An Ethiopian outwardly, but Jew inwardly.—His kindness was well rewarded, xxxix. 16, 17. *I will deliver thee, saith the Lord, and thou shalt not be given into the hand of the men of whom thou art afraid. Because thou hast put thy trust in me faith the Lord.*—Whoever does so shall receive a prophet's reward.

A mighty man of wealth. It is rare that religion and riches meet. *Not many rich men,* &c.—

SERMON VI.

yet there are some. Abraham was very rich, yet he was the righteous man of the east, Isa. xli. 2. David and Solomon.——Riches neither further nor hinder salvation but as loved and trusted in.—Boaz was both rich and religious.—He was a type of Christ, who is also a mighty man of wealth in a twofold sense.——In a natural way, *the earth is the Lord's with the fulness thereof.* In a spiritual way, *It hath pleased the Father*, &c. Col. i. 19.—*In him are hid all the treasures of wisdom and knowledge*, Col. ii. 3.—Durable riches and righteousness are his.—The riches of grace, of love, of mercy and glory.

It is the whole work of gospel ministers to publish his unsearchable riches.—Eternity itself will never count them.

He was a kinsman of her husband's, of the family of Elimelech, therefore the Goel.——Jesus is our near kinsman and Goel. Nearest and dearest—Elimelech—my God the King—Jesus is of the family of our God the King. Only begotten, &c. —Elimelech—the counsel of God.——Jesus is our kinsman appointed in the council of God.—Our kinsman who sits in the divine council—the wonderful Counsellor.

And his name was Boaz. In strength; or strength and fortitude.

Boaz was strong in the Lord, and in the power of his might.—He made the joy of the

Lord

Lord his strength.—-Applicable to Jesus—the strength, arm, and power of Jehovah.——His strength is shewn by his works.—He exhausted divine wrath—spoiled principalities and powers—redeemed his people with a strong hand and stretched out arm.—protects his servants, reapers, and gleaners, and gives them all till they are sufficed and leave.

And Ruth the Moabitess said unto Naomi, &c.

This is the first movement of the grand machine which brought such grand things about.—From gleaning she arose to be the ancestress to Jesus.—Great things often arise from very small beginnings.—A restless night by Ahasuerus, produced that great revolution in favour of the Jews, Esth. vi.—So of our Henry VIII.——What a small beginning had the American Empire?—What dreadful work is likely to arise from the destruction of a little tea?

High buildings are raised upon the lowest foundations.

Let me go now into the field to glean.

She was for improving the present moment.—She would do nothing without her mother's consent and approbation.——Some think they may dwell under Naomi's roof, yet act as they please. *A church is no prison;* the words of a mother ought to be as law to children. Prov. i. 8. *Forsake not the law of thy mother.*—Lev. xix. 3. puts the

the mother before the father, *Ye shall fear every man his mother and his father.*—Because wicked children despise her authority. Yet every child is a Jabez, a child of his mother's sorrow—in conception and travail.——Female feelings are keener than those of men.——Ruth murmured not, but submitted to her circumstances.—Though a young convert, she had learned to be in want. —What a lesson Paul learned, Phil. iv. 11, 12. *I have learned in whatsoever state I am to be content; I know both how to be abased, and how to abound; every where and in all things, I am instructed, both to be full and to be hungry, both to abound and to suffer need.*

It is heaven upon earth to see better things in the will of God than in our own will.—To be willing to be without what God sees not meet to bestow.

Into the field to glean.

Some cannot dig, being accustomed to idle habits, are too proud to glean, are ashamed to beg.—Therefore they cheat, defraud, and steal; the extortioner is as bad as the thief.——Ruth was not above using every honest endeavour to maintain herself, and assist her mother.—An excellent pattern for church members.—Strongly reproves the idle, the dishonest.—An honest heart will rather starve than steal; die, than do wickedly.

After

After him in whose sight I shall find grace.

She would not glean, though lawful, Lev. xix. 9. without the owner's consent.——An heart influenced by grace, will ask—Is it lawful? is it decent and lovely? is it expedient?

Those who having found favour with God, look to him for supplies; shall find favour with man also in the time of necessity. Jer. xv. 11. *Verily I will cause the enemy to entreat thee well in the time of evil, and in the time of affliction.*—— When a man's ways please the Lord, he maketh even his enemies to be at peace with him, Prov. xvi. 7.

And she said unto her, Go my daughter.

It is difficult which to admire most, Ruth's submission, or Naomi's meekness and endearing language.——She had a meek and quiet spirit, 1 Pet. iii. 3.—God hath promised the earth to the meek, who are the least fit to take care of it, because most likely to be sworn out of it, as Naboth was.—To what end then is the promise made? God will take care of the meek. The less that Moses was moved at Miriam's murmuring, the more doth God plead his cause. Numb. xii. 1. *to the close.*—— Let this encourage you to bring all your difficulties to the Lord, saying with Micah, vii. 9. '*I will bear*, &c.

And

SERMON VI.

And her hap was to light on a part of the field belonging to Boaz, who was of the kindred of Elimelech.

With regard to Ruth this was hap, or chance; she knew not his field from another.—With God it was providence.—Those things which with us are accidental, are all the determinations of holy providence.—Her's was to go out to glean; but God directed her to this field.—It was in the eye of man mere chance that brought Jacob and Rachel together, Gen. xxix. 9.—Likewise Pharaoh's daughter going to bathe, both as to time and place.—Moses meeting with Zipporah, Exod. ii. 17.—The Syrian shot at a venture, but God directed the arrow.——The various incidents by which our present connections were formed, religious and civil.—Sometimes crossing our inclinations to bring about his own purposes. *O Lord, I know that the way of man is not in himself, it is not in man that walketh to direct his steps*, Jer. x. 23.

And she came and gleaned: a mean but honest employment.——Mean, not suited to her former circumstances.—Honest, answerable to the integrity of her heart.——Mean employments honestly stooped to in the time of need, are frequently preludes to preferment. *God resisteth the proud,* &c. Jam. iv. 6.

To have the mind brought down to our circumstances, is the forerunner of exaltation, 1 Pet. v. 6. *Humble yourselves under the mighty hand of God,*

God, that he may exalt you in due time.——The lowly are like Jesus,—The proud like Satan.—The one honoureth God, the other invades his prerogative.—God dealeth differently with them. The Lord looketh upon the contrite;—He beholdeth the proud afar off. Pſal. cxxxviii. 6. *Though the Lord be high, yet hath he respect to the lowly, but the proud he knoweth afar off*.——In Ruth we have diligence and its reward, diligence naturally tends to advancement, Prov. xxii. 29.

And behold, Boaz came from Bethlehem.——A note of attention to this special providence.——Ruth is led to the field,—Boaz is sent to meet her, to bring about the great design of providence.—The footsteps of providence contemplated drop much fatness. Pſal. lxv. 11, 12. *Thou crownest the year with thy goodness, and thy paths drop fatness; they drop upon the pastures of the wilderness, and the little hills rejoice on every side.*——Providence is the execution of the divine decree, like it, always infallible and well timed.—Eſau could not come in with his veniſon, till Jacob went out with the bleſſing.—How opportunely it brought Pharaoh's daughter to infant Moſes!——Pharaoh's dream was Joſeph's deliverance.

Boaz came to look after his country affairs; though a mighty man of wealth, he looked after his country affairs.—His eyes were every way;—On the ſervants, reapers and gleaners, yea, eating

with

with and lodging among his labourers, Chap. iii. 2, 4.

He said, The Lord be with you.—Of all salutations this is the best.—It was the practice of the church of old, Psal. cxxix. 9. *The blessing of the Lord be upon you: we bless you in the name of the Lord.*—Holy religion rather requires than prohibits civil salutation, Matth. x. 12. *When ye come into a house, salute it.*—How grace humbles the heart! makes mighty men of wealth not above their fellows.—How beautiful the pious strain!

Boaz. *The Lord be with you.*

Servants. *The Lord bless thee.*

Then Boaz said unto his servant that was set over the reapers, Whose damsel is this?

This servant Josephus calls his bailiff, or steward.——*Whose damsel is this?* Her dress, or complexion, but especially her diligence, caused her to be noticed—*A man diligent in his business,* &c.—Strict inquiry should be made respecting those damsels suffered to glean in the field of gospel ordinances—Whose are they, God's, or Satan's?—It is when men sleep respecting this the enemy sows tares.——More especially should inquiry be made after those designed to be made reapers.—The ruin of religion arises from a depending more on human learning than the Spirit's teaching.

And the servant said, &c. Without hesitation, being faithful, he could give a good account of those
whom

whom he suffered to glean in his master's field.—Those who are the church's stewards ought to be capable of giving a good account of those they suffer to partake of her bounty.

Three things are requisite to be found in them.

1. That they have indeed cast in their lot with Naomi.

2. That they have laboured from the morning until now; not idle in either sense.

3. That they have been meek and modest, *I pray you let me glean*, ver. 7.

This is the Moabitish damsel, that came back with Naomi out of the country of Moab.

Little did he think this damsel was his intended mistress any more than Boaz did.—Her cleaving to Naomi made her name known, and procured her favour in Israel, and with the master of the field.—So with church members.—All are Moabites by birth who glean in the gospel field.

And she said, I pray you let me glean after the reapers amongst the sheaves.

Advancement of a lasting nature usually begins in humility. It was so with Joseph, with David, and with their antitype Christ.—She little thought that this rich field was to become her own.——What mean thoughts have young converts of themselves, when they come first to glean in the gospel field?—They cannot think they have a right to the handfuls, much less to the sheaves, less still that the field is their own; and least of all, that the unsearchable riches of the owner are theirs.

She hath continued from the morning till now.

This diligence recommended her to Boaz's attention.—*Seest thou a man,* &c. Prov. xxii. 29.—*The hand of the diligent maketh rich.*—What the Lord gives we gather.———It is not a beginning well, but continuing in diligent application to the use of means that is crowned with success.

Then said Boaz unto Ruth, Hearest thou not my daughter? &c.

Hearest thou not my daughter? How grace humbles even mighty men of wealth, to utter the law of kindness even to the poor and needy.—*My daughter?*—a kind interrogation to rouse her to what he was going to say.———We have need to be roused when Jesus speaks, our ears being heavy, and our hearts inattentive.—Hearing is often without taking heed, goes in at one ear and out at the other.—To take heed how, what, and who you hear, is good advice.—Ye young are particularly called to attend to the grave advice of age and experience.

His directions begin.—*Go not into another field to glean.*

Here was good will shewn to a necessitous person, not in word only, but in deed and in truth.—There is nothing meaner than lip charity, yet

some

some go not even so far.—It is not easy to make a fire or a garment with mere words.—Boaz acted godlike.—God is more kind to his gleaners than Boaz to Ruth.—He turns all his promises into performances.——There are who rob God in his cause and ministers; but they are cursed with a curse, Mal. iii. 8, 9. *Will a man rob God? yet ye have robbed me; but ye say, wherein have we robbed thee? In tythes and offerings—Ye are cursed with a curse.*

Go not to glean in any other field.

God's gleaners have or should have their peculiar gospel fields in which constantly to glean. John x. 5, 8. Christ's sheep hear not the voice of strangers.—They have their senses exercised to discern both good and evil, Heb. v. 14.—They have a spirit of discerning by which they distinguish between the voice of Christ and of Antichrist.—Hence they hate every false way of either doctrine or discipline, Psal. cxix. 104. *Through thy precepts I get understanding; therefore I hate every false way.*——They ought not to glean in another field that is even orthodox, to the neglect of gleaning in their own proper field.—Duties are reciprocal; where the pastor is obliged to preach, the people are obliged to hear, where circumstances of time and place will admit.—There will God come and bless you, Exod xx. 24.—In wandering, a snare is more likely to be met with than a blessing,

SERMON VI.

a blessing, Prov. xxvii. 8. *As a bird that wandereth from her nest, so is a man that wandereth from his place.*

Only three things can dispense with our duty here, except in the case of servants.—Old age, illness, and distance of place.

Some reasons to enforce this duty.

1. In her assemblies is a body politic. One foot cannot be in London, and the other in Westminster. Separation of members naturally tends to dissolution.—2. A faithful attendance was promised at admission, when members gave up themselves to the church.—3. The example of primitive Christians calls for it. *They met with one accord in one place*, Acts ii. 1.——4. Officers cannot watch over those who are given to wander, yet to their watchings all are called to submit, 1 Thess. v. 12. Heb. xiii. 17.——5. Forsaking the assembling of ourselves together is the forerunner of wilful sinning, Heb. x. 25, 26.——6. If one member has a right to wander from his place, all have; if all have, the pastor must have, being a member; then there is an end to all communion.

But abide fast by my maidens; for society and for safety.——For society; of them she would learn the language of Israel, and the worship of the God of the Hebrews.——With them she would be safe—for the presence of this mighty man of wealth is particularly promised to his assembled people.

SERMON VI.

people.—God will be kind to thofe gleaners who induftrioufly keep to their own company, like Peter and John, Acts iv. 23.

Hence members fee their duty and privilege joined.—And officers fhould be ftirred up to watchfulnefs.

Let thine eyes be on the field that they do reap.

Let thine eyes be on the gofpel field, it is long, wide and rich.—Here reapers do reap, gleaners do glean, and Bartholomews do draw water.

Go thou after them, So long as they reap in the field of Boaz, for the fuftenance of his houfehold.—But fhould they go into another field, go not after them.—Even Paul wifhed not to be followed farther than he followed Chrift, 1 Cor. iv. 16. *Wherefore I befeech you be ye followers of me.*—How far? *Be ye followers of me, even as I alfo am of Chrift,* 1 Cor. xi. 1.

Have I not charged the young men that they fhould not touch thee.——Either wantonly to defile her, or cruelly to rob her of the fruits of her gleaning.—Some will, at the clofe of a day, rob a poor gleaner of all fhe had picked up through the whole, wantonly ruining her comforts.—But God thus chargeth, *Touch not mine anointed, and do my prophets no harm,* Pfal. cv. 15.——On the contrary, God chargeth to comfort his people, Ifa. xl. 1, 2. *Comfort ye, comfort ye my people, faith your God; fpeak ye comfortably to Jerufalem,*

and

and cry unto her, that her warfare is accomplished, that her iniquity is pardoned.

Have I not charged the young men? &c. An excellent example for masters of families, to charge their household, that no wickedness should dwell with them, Psal. ci. throughout.—Nebuchadnezzar's law, Dan. iii. 29. was good.

When thou art athirst, go unto the vessels and drink of that which the young men have drawn.—With hard labour in that hot country.—But mercy is never stingy, nor churlishness to be found with charity.——Faint type of the liberality of our Jesus, who gives the water of life to his people, John iv. 10. *If thou knewest the gift of God, and who it is that saith unto thee, give me to drink, thou wouldst have asked of him, and he would have given thee living water.*—This revives the drooping soul, as a well of living water springing up unto eternal life.—He gives it freely, Rev. xxii. 17.—To every one that thirsts, Isa. lv. 1.—To every comer, even the unworthy, Ezek. xvi. 6.—The waters which Christ give quencheth our thirst for worldly vanities, John iv. 14 Such as thirst for these never drank heartily of that.—Not water only, but blood, the blood of God, Acts xx.—This blood is drink indeed, John vi. 55.

God hath his Beer-Elims, or wells of the mighty ones. Prophesies, declarations, promises. All wells of salvation.—He hath his Bartholomews or water drawers,

drawers, who draw forth the words of eternal life.—These young men draw for the gleaners, those thirsty souls who bear the heat of the day.—It costs them much sweat of both brow and brain.—Yet they do it with singing, because the work is pleasant. Numb. xxi. 17. *Spring up, O well, sing ye unto it.*—They draw it with joy, because they drink of the water themselves, Isa. xii. 3.

A Puritan observes, that the day consecrated to Bartholomew, was the very day on which the Bartholomews were bound by an act of uniformity;—and black day of the Parisian massacre.

Then she fell on her face and bowed herself to the ground.—Overcome with his condescension and benevolence.

O how low bows the soul when God speaks words of peace!—The lowly shall be exalted, 1 Pet. v. 6—Humble Lazarus to Abraham's bosom.—When Job abhorred himself, and repented in dust and ashes, God turned again his captivity, Job xlii. 6, 10.—David was little in his own eyes when made king over Judah.

Why have I found grace in thine eyes that thou shouldst take knowledge of me, seeing I am a stranger?

Nothing but necessity on her part.—He could not profit by her gleaning.—This was all her own.—Our goodness extendeth not to God, Psal. xvi. 2. *My goodness extendeth not to thee, but to the saints in the earth, and to the excellent, in whom is all my delight.*—What faith the sinner when divine love is manifested?—Why have I found grace in thine eyes?—Lord, what is man?—What am I or my father's house?—I am but a stranger—to God, to godliness—to thy ways and people—possest of an estranged and a straying heart.

And Boaz said to her, it hath been fully shewed me all that thou hast done to thy mother-in-law, &c.

Her faith in God, and love to Naomi, were noted by all; as when a poor sinner sets his face Zion-ward, how the godly take notice of him.—Her obedience to her mother-in-law, parting with all, joining herself to a strange people, could not be hid.——True religion cannot be concealed, hence the church is a city set upon an hill, Matt. v. 14.—True religion is connected with due praise which follows it, even as the shadow the body, Heb. xi. 2. *By faith the elders obtained a good report.*—The religion of the Thessalonians sounded through the world, 1 Thess. i. 8. *Ye were ensamples to all that believe in Macedonia and Achaia, for from you sounded out the word of the Lord, not only in Macedonia and Achaia, but also in every place your faith God-ward is spread abroad.*——It is an evidence of grace to prize its work upon others. *Hereby we know that we are passed,* &c. 1 John iii. 14.—Ruth valued that she saw in Naomi—Boaz that he saw in Ruth.

SERMON VI.

The Lord recompence thy work, &c.

He could not recompence her pious work of faith and love himself, therefore appeals to God in her behalf.——Every work of love is sure to meet with its proper reward; a disciple's reward, a prophet's reward, Mat. x. 41.—43.

Such as shew the kindness of God to distressed saints particularly, shall receive the same kindness in their own distress, Mat. vii. 2. *With what measure*, &c.—David was greatly distrest, and Jonathan shewed him kindness, 1 Sam. xix. xx. chap.—David shewed the kindness of God to his seed, 2 Sam. ix. 3.—So Ruth to Naomi, Boaz to Ruth.

Under whose wings thou art come to trust.

A metaphor taken from the hen and chickens.—Or the ark which covered a cursing law.—The mercy seat covered the ark—The cherubim covered the mercy seat.—This typified Christ in whom the law has its end.

Ruth left all to come and trust, &c.

Certain refuge here, every perfection, purpose, &c. being a safeguard. *Ye are dead*, &c.

SERMON VII.

RUTH ii. 14.

And Boaz said unto her at meal-time, come thou hither, and eat of the bread, and deep thy morsel in the vinegar. And she sat beside the reapers: and he reached her parched corn, and she did eat and was sufficed, and left.

IN some preceding discourses, we have followed Naomi and Ruth in their journey towards the land of Canaan. In this we find them amongst the Lord's inheritance, seeking for rest after the long series of affliction which had passed over them. When they came to Bethlehem, the native city of Elimelech, from whence they departed in the beginning of the famine, the whole city was moved with tender affection to this venerable matron and her pious daughter, and to welcome her return to the land of her fathers. Their kind congratulations, far from yielding her the intended consolation, only served to rip open her wounds, and make her sorrows to bleed afresh, by bringing past endearments to her remembrance, and presenting the images of her lost husband and sons to her disturbed imagination. Wherefore she thus answers their welcome with apparent anguish: *Call me not Naomi; call me Marah: for the Lord hath dealt very bitterly with me. I went out full, and the Lord hath brought me home again empty: why call ye me Naomi, seeing the Lord hath testified against me, and the Almighty hath afflicted me?* From which pathetic exclamation we may note.

Those whom the Most High intends in a peculiar manner to honour amongst his people, frequently have the bitterest cup of afflictions put into their hands prior to their exaltation. So it was with Abraham, as well as with his daughter Naomi. First he is called upon to cast out Ishmael his son, for whose life he had so earnestly entreated the Almighty in this ardent petition, *O that Ishmael might live before thee!* Even the father of the faithful entreated in vain, when his desires corresponded not with the will of his God, whose pleasure it was " *that in Isaac should Abraham's seed be called.* Ishmael cast out and rejected, a cup more bitter still is prepared for him. His Isaac, upon whom the hopes of his family depended; his Isaac, with whom was the promise of life, and from whose loins the seed of the woman, the Saviour of mankind was to descend; even Isaac,
who

who was by a miracle brought into the world, was demanded; demanded a burnt offering; and, strange to speak it! demanded by that God who says, *Thou shalt not kill:* that God who had promised, *That in Isaac should all the families of the earth be blessed:* yea, demanded to fall by the hands of his own father, at his command whose characteristic is MERCIFUL. Thus was his holy soul tried to the uttermost. But had he not been thus tried as by fire, he had never borne the honourable name of *Father of the faithful,* by which he is known in the church through all generations. In like manner, if this mother in Israel had not drank so deep of the cup of sorrow, she had not been so honourably mentioned as she is, in every nation blessed with the light of revealed truth.

She is now emerging out of her former distress, and the day of consolation begins to arise upon her, and continues to advance, though indeed by slow degrees, till it arrives at its meridian splendour. To the tracing of which advances, I hope a discussion of our text may in some degree contribute. In attempting of this, I shall not at all enter into the controversy, whether this book is to be considered as typical and mysterious, or merely historical. My hearers are at liberty to judge for themselves. It is sufficient for me to know assuredly, *that whatever was written afore-*

time was written for our instruction, that we through comfort of the Scriptures might have hope; and to find the history of Ruth capable of being *accommodated* to gospel purposes. Apprehending therefore from these premises that we have a right to improve all, or any part of the Old Testament history to the illustration of the blessed gospel, without exposing ourselves to the charge of enthusiasm, I shall proceed to prosecute the subject in the following manner.

Ist. Speak concerning Boaz the husbandman and master of the field, who invites to come hither at meal-time.

IId. Of the damsel invited to come hither, &c. *Ruth the Moabitess.*

IIId. Consider the invitation itself, *Come thou hither at meal-time, eat of the bread, and dip thy morsel in the vinegar.*

IVth. Enlarge upon the conduct of Ruth on this occasion, *She sat beside the reapers, she did eat, and was sufficed, and left.*

In which conduct she is an eminent example of holy industry, an example worthy of the imitation of every professor of Christianity.

According to this plan, I am

Ist. To speak of Boaz the husbandman and master of the field, who invites to come hither at meal-time; concerning whom we may note,

(1.) His

(1.) His name, Boaz. (2.) His profession, an husbandman. (3.) His circumstances, a mighty man of wealth. (4) His disposition; generous, hospitable, and benevolent. (5.) His pedigree, a kinsman of the family of Elimelech. On each of these, I would offer a few remarks.

(1.) His name, Boaz. The father of Obed, and David's great-grand-father, Boaz who makes a principal figure in this history, and whose name signifies, *In strength*, which is more applicable to Jesus the Husband of the church. Jesus is the arm and power of the Lord, who is revealed in the heart of every believer as the sole ground of his hope, and spring of true enjoyment. He is strength to the weak, and power to those who are ready to faint. He only is the dwelling place and fortress of his people, where the fearful hide themselves in the day of indignation; where they are everlastingly secure from every future evil. He only is that munition of rocks, and rock of defence, in which the righteous dwell on high, eat their promised bread, and drink the vital streams.

His works sufficiently evince the greatness of his power, and prove him to be the mighty God, as well as the loving, the compassionate friend of sinners. He left no work unperformed which was requisite to fulfil the purposes of infinite love, and illustrate the transcendent excellence of the divine perfections. Did the Eternal Father before all worlds choose a people for himself; a people appointed to salvation for the praise and glory of his grace? and did this people, this elect church, fall in the common ruin of the lapsed race? had guilt, interposing between God and them, made their access to his presence impracticable? Behold Jesus appears as the sealed and sent of God; appears as the sinner's friend, and legal substitute. The mighty God appears a son in our nature; the Everlasting Father is born into our world; the Prince of peace makes war upon the powers of darkness, and the holy child Jesus sustains the wrath of avenging Omnipotence.

Great is this mystery of godliness! God manifested in the flesh to take away the sins of his offending creatures. O believer, thy strong, thy loving Redeemer stood in the breach between thy God and thee, to reconcile thee to him; to bring thee to the divine embrace, willingly yielded up himself as thy propitiatory sacrifice. O my soul, mayest thou never forget the wormwood and gall which thy Redeemer drank as thy representative. Infinite wrath was thy due desert; infinite holiness was by thee affronted. The curse, by thee procured, fell all upon him that loved thee unto death. Thou escapest indeed from the dire arrest of incensed justice; but not one of thine innumerable sins, no part of thine aggravated guilt, has been overlooked and passed by with impunity;

nity; in Jesus, thy common person, thine iniquity was punished to its utmost demerit. Ask thine own heart, O believer, what wrath thy sinfulness has deserved? see if any thing short of the deepest hell, and the most extreme torture of the dreadful pit be adequate to thy rebellions? yet see innumerable myriads, whose sin was as atrocious as thine, as highly aggravated in every circumstance as thy black transgressions, saved; completely saved to the uttermost, saved with an everlasting salvation; saved only through his obedience unto death.

Not one member of that vast assembly; not an individual in all that numberless throng, but what deserved the wrath of God to the uttermost. That wrath and indignation due to all, and every individual of them, fell at once upon the holy soul of thine immaculate Jesus. How ponderous the weight! how tremendous the burning curse! what power less than divine could rise superior to infinite guilt as did thy triumphant Jesus? It is done! guilt is no more! sin is for ever annihilated, respecting its dismal consequences to thee, O believer. Come then, ye saints of the Most High, ye sinners redeemed from hell and destruction, come see the works of your conqueror, and say, *Is not this the true God and eternal life?*

Thus it was that your Boaz was made sin for you, that you might become the righteousness of
God

God in him; and thus it was by the power of his hand he finished transgression, made an end of sin; and, for you, brought in an everlasting righteousness, a righteousness in which ye shall shine in the brilliant assembly of paradise.

After such a splendid and memorable instance of our Redeemer's strength, there is little occasion to take up much of your time in speaking of his triumphs over death and the powers of darkness. Yet as such an heavenly truth should not be wholly omitted, I would just observe, that he entered the house of the strong man armed, spoiled him of his armour, and rescued the prey out of his potent hand. He bruised the head of Satan; he wounded the dragon that is in the sea; he spoiled principalities and powers, and openly displayed the trophies of his victory; for he ascended up on high, led captivity captive, re-entered the mansions of light, and received gifts for rebellious sinners.

Nor is the conquest of our adorable Jesus over the hearts and affections of his people to be wholly neglected; for this is one part of our salvation, which greatly tends to shew forth the excellency of his power. Beneath the attractive influence of his heavenly goodness, the most obdurate heart softens into tender relentings; the loftiest looks of the vain-glorious and self-conceited, sink down into profound humility and self-abhorrence; and

the

the iron sinews in the necks of the most stout and rebellious, are bended into submissive obedience. In the day of his power the most backward are made willing to be saved by grace alone, as it reigns in Jesus through righteousness to eternal life.

(2.) As the name of Boaz is not inapplicable unto Jesus, we shall now consider his calling, *An husbandman.* This great man so eminent in Judah, and from whom their future kings descended, was it seems not above cultivating his inheritance himself, and superintending the affairs of husbandry. A noble instance of ancient simplicity, worthy to be imitated even by the moderns, as such an imitation would be an effectual curb upon that licentiousness which stains the annals of the present times.

The calling of Boaz is not inapplicable to the adorable Jesus, who also is an husbandman himself. He hath his field in which he delights; his vineyard where he drinks of the spiced wines, and of the juice of the pomegranate; over which he watches day and night, and waters it every moment to render it fruitful. He has his garden of spices, of myrrh, and lilies, in which he delights to walk and ruminate on the loves of his spouse. He hath the times and seasons which he daily observes for the purpose of his husbandry, and which he improves to the great advantage of his

church

church and people. He hath his sowing and planting times, in which he gives additional numbers to his believing church, and comforts to individuals. The time was that places which are now like a barren wilderness, were like a garden, well watered, and a field which God had blessed: places that are now like the garden of God for fruitfulness, were heretofore like the sandy desert, uncultivated, without any plants therein grafted by the hand of Zion's Husbandman. In particular churches, he hath his times of ingathering and building up; in which times the work shall prosper be in whose hands it will, and feeble worms shall surmount the highest mountains of opposition. With individuals it is the same at certain seasons; every circumstance produceth agreeable and comfortable effects; every sermon, every opportunity is owned to the souls advantage and growth in grace.

But he hath also his weeding and cleansing times. When persecutions and public troubles come upon the church, they usually prove as a fan in the hand of the Son of God, by which he cleanseth his floor, and thoroughly purgeth his wheat. The tares are now rooted out and cast over the wall of the vineyard; hypocrites are returned back to their own master again. This is a scorching season that puts professors to the trial, and withers the stony ground hearers at the root; a wind a wind that drives the chaffy hypocrite before it, and purgeth the threshing floor of our heavenly Boaz. Besides this he hath his weeding, trying, and cleansing time, which he observeth in his conduct towards individuals, in which he proves them, and makes them know what is in their heart for their humiliation, and mortifying of them to sin and to the world. As a rank soil is the best nursery for tares, so plenty of earthly enjoyments are apt to foster vitious lusts; he sees meet to cut off the fuel, lest the fire should devour us. The greatest of men and best of saints have not escaped such humbling visitations. Job, the most patient man upon earth, was visited with accumulated sorrows, insomuch that one messenger of bad tidings came, as it were, treading upon the heels of his fellow, till the worse that could happen was reported to him. David, the most pious of Jewish monarchs, the devoutest of militant saints, knew what it was to roar aloud by reason of his affliction, and to tremble at the hand that was upon him; yea, his heart and flesh were ready to faint, because of the depths through which he was called to pass.

That fervent, affectionate prophet, who bedewed the mount of God with sympathetic tears, found himself in such circumstances, that he cursed the day of his birth, and the messenger who reported his mother's delivery. Paul had his

frequent

frequent buffettings, and Timothy his often infirmities, for *whom the Lord loveth he chasteneth, and scourgeth every son whom he receiveth.* Ruth went through these cleansing and weeding operations, before she began to take root and grow in the inheritance of the Lord. Attachment to carnal pleasure, love to her native country, veneration for the laws of the Gentiles, family and education prejudices were in measure rooted out before the Lord began to water her with the comforts of his house. So that ye need not think it strange, my brethren, concerning the fiery trial, as if some strange thing had happened unto you, for it is the lot of all the children of the kingdom to have tribulation in this world.

But he hath his watering and growing seasons in the Christian life, in which he sheds abroad the sweetness of his love, and causes all his paths to drop fatness to the souls of his people. Indeed all those trying and afflictive seasons serve to prepare for the consolation, and holy growth now under consideration, even as the severest winter frost is the best and most suitable introduction to the smiling spring. When he hath rifted the rocky heart by the voice of his rod, he utters the still voice of his consolation, and shews the glory of his grace. In proportion to which discoveries, our innate corruptions will be brought forth to view, and we shall grow downward in self-abasement

abasement and abhorrence, as well as upward in admiration of that fulness and excellency of grace revealed in the person and gospel of Jesus. Churches also have their genial seasons, in which their Almighty Lord is pleased to water the souls of his people with heavenly influence under the word and ordinances; adds to their number, and builds them up in comfort and holy communion. Then the Lord is as the dew to Israel, his people grow as the lily, and spread forth their roots as Lebanon, and the believing church becomes fruitful as Eden, the garden of God.

He, as the heavenly husbandman, hath also his ripening time, in which his fields are white for the harvest. Now the hoary head is a crown of glory, and the imbecillity of stooping age is a proper emblem of the humility of the grown Christian. That description of old age given by the wise man, Eccl. xii. 3, 4, 5. seems picturesque of the ripening saint; *The keepers of the house shall tremble*, because of the known dangers to which they are exposed from innumerable enemies without, and from that grand traitor, a wicked deceitful heart within; an heart that may not be trusted, not for a moment trusted, because it is of the enemy's party, notwithstanding an inhabitant in our own bosoms. *The strong men shall bow themselves*, under a sense of that body of death that is upon them. Every lofty look shall be brought low, under a sense of their own nothingness and insignificancy, ignorance and folly. *The grinders shall cease because they are few*; so that they shall find themselves incapable of receiving that nourishment, which the word of God actually imparts; that they are as much dependant on sovereign grace, for the least degree of refreshment, as for salvation itself; and as needy of Christ, as if they had never any prior communications from him. *All the daughters of music shall be brought low.* The daughters of music shall still be there, but their songs shall be upon the solemn bass. In the more early days of Christianity, before man was sufficiently discovered to himself, the daughters of music might sing in elevated strains, and might even despise the humble notes of the bass, which is universally allowed to be the foundation of harmony; but alas! their instruments were frequently out of tune, and hung upon the willows, so that the voice of joy was not to be heard; for as they understood not the bass, their music subsided when they could not sing in more elevated lays. But when the soul is grown in the divine life, under the husbandry of Jesus, the daughters of music learn to descend to the use of the bass, and mingle judgment with all their songs of mercy. And many advantages do they find attending this transition, amongst which are the following. They find that although

there

there is lefs noife in the fongs of the bafs, there is greater folemnity, and more profound harmony than in their former premature triumphs. That although its folemn found does not fo exceedingly ravifh the fenfes; it is more fteady, uniform, and confiftent; lefs liable to be out of tune, and more becoming a ftate of warfare.

They shall be afraid of that which is high. Young David could encounter any danger, overcome every difficulty however great; yea, he could break through a troop, or leap over a wall, becaufe through God his mountain ftood ftrong: but the aged Pfalmift was taught not to exercife himfelf in great matters, nor in things too high for him. The young Chriftian, as well as the mere fpeculatift, can venture upon every high thing, and fet himfelf to explain the hidden, the invifible things of God. But further experience teacheth us that fecret things belong to the Lord our God, and that only thofe that are revealed belong to us. So that from a fenfe of ignorance, and aptitude to err, there will be a fear of being too free with things that are not fo clearly revealed, left we fhould inadvertently eclipfe that glory which we fhould wifh to recommend to human efteem. Such a fenfe of perfonal weaknefs fhall attend them, fuch a fenfe of utter incapacity for good, that the very *grashopper shall be a burden*. Thus the higheft attainment of the Chriftian here below,

below, is to be reduced to nothing, that Christ may become all in all. This is the mark at which we ought to aim; this is the standard to which grace shall bring all its subjects, ere they are taken to their long, their exalted home. When the corn bends its weighty head towards the earth, it indicates the reaping time at hand, and the gathering of it into the husbandman's granary. The heart of man bowed down in low abasement, indicates a speedy dissolution, and heavenly exaltation and happiness fast approaching.

(3.) The affluent circumstances of this Hebrew are as worthy of note as either his name or calling, and as applicable to our adorable Redeemer. He is said to be *a mighty man of wealth;* not only *a man of wealth*, but a *mighty man of wealth*, to point out his abundance of riches. Jesus the Virgin's son, Jesus the sinner's friend, is also a mighty man of wealth, notwithstanding when sojourning amongst men he had not where to lay his head; had not accommodations equal to the monsters of the desert, or to the winged inhabitants of the aerial regions. In a natural way he is a mighty man of wealth, for *the earth with all its fulness is his possession:* therefore saith he, Psal. l. 10, 11, 12. *Every beast of the forest is mine, and the cattle upon a thousand hills. I know all the fowls of the mountains; and the wild beasts of the field are mine. If I were hungry, I would not tell thee;*

thee ; for the world is mine and the fulness thereof. Hence it is, that the whole family of heaven and earth subsist upon his bounty and munificence; for these all look unto him, and he giveth them their meat in due season, and satisfieth their mouths with good. The bread which feeds you, and the raiment which keeps you warm, yea, the very air which you breathe, and every other gift in nature, are all the fruits of your Redeemer's bounty. How vast! how mighty must that wealth be, out of which universal nature is fed, adorned, and clothed?

He is a mighty man of spiritual wealth also. With him are durable riches, and undecaying springs of comfort, for it hath pleased the Father that in him all fulness should dwell. The fulness of grace, of life, salvation, and glory. Of grace in covenant transactions; the promise of life for the elect was made to their federal Head, in whom there is all grace, to be exhibited in their behalf, in a way of redemption, adoption, and justification; all grace to be communicated to them in time for their sanctification, and preparation for glory, and all the manifestations of his glorious presence when time shall be swallowed up in eternity. *In him*, saith the great Apostle of the Gentiles, *are hid all the treasures of wisdom and of knowledge ;* the riches of grace, of love, of mercy, and of glory. It is the whole work of gospel ministers to publish the unsearchable riches of Christ. But the greatest, the most intelligent amongst them seeing but in part, and prophesying but in part, it follows, that after all the glorious testimonies that have been borne of him from the pulpit, and at the stake, that little, comparatively, of his excellency hath been known to the militant church. It is the whole business of every believer to be searching into the riches of his grace; and after all their strict inquiries, after all their attainments in experimental religion, when they come to the latest hour, they are obliged to confess, that so ineffable is his worth, so exceedingly inestimable are his riches, that they know nothing at all of them in comparison of their reality; they being exceeding abundant above what we can think of; possessing heights infinitely transcending our highest reach; depths to a finite arm altogether unfathomable; lengths commensurate only with a divine duration; and breadths unspeakably more extensive than the immeasurable universe. Such are the riches of thy Redeemer, O my soul, that saints and angels may exert their utmost powers to reckon the sum of them, and numberless ages prosecute the delightful exercise, they shall still, ravishing thought! they shall still have before them an eternity of the same pleasing employment; grow every hour riper in knowledge of the riches of Jesus, and still at an

infinite

infinite distance from comprehending them. Encouraging consideration, O my needy, my fearful soul! thou canst not possibly ask so much as thy loving friend can bestow, for he is a mighty man of boundless wealth.

(4.) The disposition of Boaz, evinced by his conduct, is worthy of our attention, being humane, benevolent, and bounteous; the very reverse of what is apparently the governing principles with mankind in general, of whom it is truly said, *All seek their own.* A character descriptive of none more than the people of this generation, of what rank or degree soever. *All seek their own,* is a general rule admitting but of few exceptions. Yet although few, there are, there always have been some exceptions to it, in instances similar to the character before us; and wherever found, it is truly noble and godlike. God is great in his goodness, and good amidst all his essential greatness, and a faint adumbration of this divine character we have in Boaz, who was a mighty man of wealth; humane and bountiful, as he was mighty in riches. It was the custom of his countrymen, in after times, to despise the inhabitants of the Gentile world, as a people whom God had cursed, and who had no inheritance in Jacob; but good Boaz took knowledge of Ruth notwithstanding she was a friendless stranger, and an helpless alien from the commonwealth of Israel. He very well knew her descent from Moab, the son of incest; but he despised her not for the intemperance and uncleanness of her otherwise great ancestor.

He not only inquired after her, and spake kindly to her, but he made her welcome to the free use of his field and table, without laying any the least restraint upon her conduct; directs her what course to pursue for safety, in abiding fast by his maidens; gives his young men charge concerning her, forbidding them at all to molest her: and even commands the reapers to drop handfuls on purpose for her; and at last sent her home to her mother with as much provision as she could carry; which at once discovered the benevolence of his heart, and the bounty of his hand. Unlike to Boaz are those who say to the needy and friendless, *Be ye warmed and clothed*, but have not hearts benevolent enough to contribute in the least degree towards either. We wish you well, say some; we should be glad to see you out of these difficulties; we wish some who have it in their power, would make a point of assisting you; there are who could readily do it without exposing themselves to any inconvenience; but alas! as for us, our affairs are so circumstanced that it is out of our power to be of any service to you. Thus the farthest that the religion and benevolence of some people can carry them, in the works of charity, and labour of love, is to form such a denial as shall least expose themselves, or be offensive to the distressed suppliant. But Boaz, whose holy heart glowed with genuine benevolence, gives before she asketh, and equal to her present necessities. Let professors see and learn from his example, what the Lord our God requires of us in the works of mercy, as well as of justice and integrity. For it is not enough that a Christian is strictly honest, if he is not also merciful, tender, compassionate, and bountiful in proportion to what divine providence hath put into his possession.

This conduct of Boaz beautifully adumbrates the benevolent conduct of the blessed and adorable Jesus towards his needy church. For he also takes knowledge of his people who are all strangers by nature, *aliens* from the commonwealth of Israel, and strangers to the covenant of promise; children of wrath even as others. He makes you welcome to his gospel field; leaves you at large to range through all his institutions, and bids you be free with the grace of every promise; he requires on your part no other quality than your necessity. If you are athirst, he bids you welcome to the waters; if hungry, to eat of the bread; if naked, to make free with his wardrobe; if sick, to apply to him for a cure; if guilty, for a pardon; if black and polluted, to wash in his blood and

be

be clean. You say that you are black and not like unto the maidens of your Lord; he says that you are comely; all fair, without spot or blemish. You condemn yourself as worthy of the deepest hell, a sinner of the deepest dye; but he hath adjudged you to the highest heaven, to be for ever with himself.

During the whole of reaping season, he hath charged his reapers to drop handfuls on purpose for you, for all that glean after them without exception; that is, he hath given it in charge to his ministers that they should deal forth plenteous consolation from the word of revelation, and not reproach the poor and needy for making free with the declarations of grace, seeing it is not to foster sin, but to feed the cravings of an hungry soul. *Comfort ye, comfort ye my people, speak ye comfortably to Jerusalem*, is the language of our God; and shews that gospel ministers are expected to speak in a language very different from that of Pharoah's taskmasters, who charged the oppressed Israelites with idleness, and demanded the full tale of brick from the complainants. Therefore we are charged to CRY unto her, *that her warfare is accomplished;* to demand no conditions on her part, but to comfort her with the ministry of a free, a finished salvation. There is a singular beauty in that charge given to the Prophet, Isa. xxxv. 3, 4. *Strengthen ye the weak hands, confirm*

ye

SERMON VII.

ye the feeble knees; say to them of a fearful heart, be strong, fear not: behold your God will come vengeance, God, a recompence, he will come and save you. The supplementary reading serving only to eclipse the glory of the text, I quote the original text without it, and would remark upon it, that it is admirably calculated to promote the consolation of saints, who find themselves to be poor and needy, and are therefore glad to glean in the field of grace and mercy.

Strengthen ye the weak hands, who cannot work out their own salvation, by performing the conditions of the legal covenant; who cannot perform duty, resist sin, nor exercise grace at pleasure; but find that when they would do good, evil is present with them; that they are carnal, sold under sin, and that therefore the good which they would do, is frequently left undone; and the evil which they hate is given into. For those people who can resist sin, perform duty, and exercise grace, can with no propriety be said to have weak hands, and therefore are no objects of our ministrations.

Confirm ye the feeble knees, who cannot stand up under a sense of their sinfulness, whose hearts are overwhelmed with the weight of their iniquities, which have gone over their heads as a burden too heavy for them to bear, and whose spirit faints by reason of the handwriting of apprehended

condemnation

condemnation that is gone forth againſt them. Thoſe feeble knees which cannot of themſelves ſtand ſteady in the day of affliction, when the hand of a ſtripping God is ſtretched out, and the Almighty writes bitter things againſt them. Thoſe who can reaſon themſelves into a philoſophic fortitude againſt every event, can in no ſenſe be ſaid to be people of feeble knees, and therefore no part of our buſineſs is with them. Neither are thoſe who never were oppreſſed with a ſenſe of ſin, any way entitled to a part in the comforts which grace has prepared for thoſe who tremble at the word of the Lord.

Say to them that are of a fearful heart, be ſtrong, fear not. To them that are of a fearful heart, fearful of ſinning againſt an infinitely holy God, and bringing guilt and condemnation upon their own ſouls, of being left to bring diſhonour upon the people and good ways of God; fearful that their ſpots are not the ſpots of God's children, and therefore that Jeſus hath no connection with ſinners of ſuch a ſtamp as them; fearful that all their croſſes are vindictive curſes; their afflictions the effect of divine indignation, and juſt judgments on account of their ſinfulneſs: *ſay to them, be ſtrong;* the foundation of Chriſtian ſtrength lies in conſcious weakneſs. O Jacob, know thyſelf to be but a worm, and thou ſhalt threſh mountains, and beat them to powder. Know that thou

SERMON VII.

thou canſt do nothing, and thou ſhalt do all things through Chriſt ſtrengthening of thee.

Your God will come, vengeance. Your God notwithſtanding all your fearfulneſs, and unbelieving miſgivings of heart. Your God in covenant relation, everlaſtingly the ſame. *Your God will come* although he hides his face from thee, and thou are troubled: although he tarries far beyond your expectation, and ſeems to weary out your hopes, inſomuch that you ſuppoſe yourſelf to be forgotten by him. He will come; his word is paſſed, and he will not revoke it; his promiſe is gone forth, and what ſhall hinder the egreſſion of the grace promiſed? *He will come vengeance* upon thine enemies, into whoſe hands he ſeems to have given you up. You ſhall be ſafe, for when he ſhall be revealed in vengeance upon his enemies, he ſhall come as your God in new covenant relation. *God, a recompence:* God himſelf ſhall be to you a recompence; not of yours indeed, but of the Redeemer's obedience, your adorable ſubſtitute. *He will come and ſave you.* When he ſhall come, come a recompence, come in vengeance, the ſalvation of his weak and fearful people ſhall be his object. What an amazing plenty of conſolation does our divine huſbandman ſcatter in his goſpel field for the uſe of hungry aliens?—Yea, ſometimes he is pleaſed to load with ſoul food as much as you can carry. To give ſuch an overcoming

coming sense of his pardoning love, as to make you sick of love, and cry out, Lord stay thy hand, thy servant is but an earthen vessel.

(5.) Of Boaz it is said, he was a kinsman of the family of Elimelech; and therefore according to the Jewish law, it was his province to redeem the alienated inheritance for Naomi and her daughter after the nearer kinsman had refused, or was become incapable of acting in character. Accordingly when the nearer kinsman actually refused, lest he should thereby mar his own inheritance, Boaz stepped forth openly before the elders of his people as Goel, or the near kinsman, and redeemed the alienated right of the inheritance of Naomi's sons, Mahlon and Chilion; and in purchasing of it, became possessed of Ruth the Moabitess as the reward of his acting the part of a kinsman.

Jesus also is our Goel, or near kinsman, upon whom the right of redemption devolved, when the law, our first husband, became incapable of acting the kinsman's part. When by the sad misconduct of our Eden parent the inheritance was alienated, and we by our own act and deed had confirmed the alienation; our inheritance thus estranged, and the first in kindred incapable to redeem, our Goel, our near kinsman appears in the gate, to redeem to himself both the inheritance and its natural and legal heirs.

Boaz

Boaz was not only a near kinsman, but a kinsman of the family of Elimelech: so Jesus is not only our kinsman, but a kinsman of our own family, of the seed of Abraham, and David after the flesh, although in his divine nature God over all, blessed for ever more.

Elimelech signifies, according to some, *My God the King*, which sense is truly applicable to Jesus, who is our kinsman, of the family of our God the King; being the only Begotten of the Father, full of grace and truth. The only Begotten of the Father is our elder brother, bone of our bone, and flesh of our flesh, therefore our kinsman, of the family of God our King. The word may be likewise rendered *the counsel of God*, and in this sense is equally applicable to the case before us. Jesus is the highest object of the divine counsel, in which he was sealed and appointed. He is our kinsman who sits in the council of God, and therefore is our wonderful Counsellor. How vast and unspeakable that love by which man is taken up into God, and God condescends to dwell in man? Behold what manner of love is this! how boldly may we come before God, seeing we have a near kinsman sitting in his council: this is the Lord's doing, and it is marvellous in our eyes.

SERMON

SERMON VIII.

Ruth ii. 14.

And Boaz said unto her at meal-time, come thou hither, and eat of the bread, and dip thy morsel in the vinegar. And she sat beside the reapers, and he reached her parched corn, and she did eat, and was sufficed, and left.

HAVING in the former discourse spoken concerning Boaz the husbandman, who so generously entreated this fair and worthy stranger to partake of the bounties of his hospitable table, and found that whatever reflects honour on this distinguished character, is found in a superlative degree in the amiable Jesus. We shall now endeavour to shew what likeness Ruth the Moabitess may bear to the bride, the wife of the Lamb; that Shulamite, in whose mysterious person you behold the company of two contending armies. In describing this favourite damsel, we shall note —Her name—her kindred and former connections —her late remarkable conduct—and her present deportment.

Ist. He

1st. Her name, Ruth, hath been spoken to already as applicable to herself, I shall therefore consider it now as suitable unto every truly converted sinner, every real believer in the blessed Immanuel; for they also may be called watered, according to the signification of her name. It is remarkable how Old Testament names are adapted to personal characters, as if divine Wisdom, foreseeing the conduct and after circumstances of the party, led to the fixation of the given name. It has been shewed what analogy there is between the name of Ruth, and the providential occurrences which attended her lot: we shall now consider the name as applicable to the child of grace.

(1.) Ruth, *made drunken* *, as most young converts are with sorrow and affliction. When Paul was convinced of the evil of his way, and found himself to be a real persecutor of Jesus of Nazareth, and in him of the cause of God, of truth, and of holiness, we read that he was three days and three nights without either eating or drinking, so intense was his sorrow and anguish. In ordinary cases it is even so. When the sin of the soul is brought to open light, and actual transgressions lay hold of the conscience; when the whole of

* *Drunken*, the allusion here is to that of Isa. xxix. 9. *They are drunken, but not with wine; they stagger, but not with strong drink.*

the nature and conversation is viewed in the light of the changeless law, that abstract of infinite holiness, and the whole appears vile and abominable; when the awful consequences of a life of rebellion, and utter estrangement from God are discovered, none can tell but those who have felt it, what anguish lays hold on the heart, what tortures the horror of guilt brings upon the alarmed conscience. Sorrow invades the whole soul, and bears down every thinking faculty before it: sorrow for loss sustained; the loss of innocence; the loss of capacity for good; the loss of God and the divine favour; the loss of heaven, and all happiness both here and hereafter: sorrow for danger incurred; danger that makes the heart tremble to reflect upon it; danger of being deprived of the pleasure of every enjoyment in this life, and instead of earthly felicity, to walk under the curse of a broken law; danger of dying an accursed death, and of being everlastingly miserable: miserable with regard to the company dreaded, devils and damned spirits; miserable respecting the place of abode, the lake, the sulphureous lake, which burneth for evermore; and miserable in the keen sensations of growing anguish, when time shall be no more, and when all is unspeakable, immeasurable eternity. This is experience that will make the stoutest heart to give way, and the loftiest look to descend into the dust;

dust; that will make the most daring to cry out, *Men and brethren, what must we do?* and the obdurate heart breathe, *God be merciful to me a sinner.* Such a state of soul made David roar from the bitterness of his spirit, and water his couch with repentant tears, whilst he cried after mercy in a sovereign way, according to the loving kindness of his gracious Maker.

(2.) Ruth, *watered and filled:* very applicable to believers, who are watered with the heavenly influence of grace, and filled with the fruits of the Holy Ghost. By nature we are dry as the scorched mountains of Gilboa, and barren as the Lybian sands. So wild, so uncultivated, and so unfruitful is degenerate man, that by nature, touching every good work, all are reprobates; yea, even enemies in our hearts by wicked works against God: to whom the language of the natural man is, " Depart from me, O Lord, I de-
" sire not the knowledge of thy law, I will not
" have thee to reign over me; for I have loved
" idols and after them I will go. I will delight in
" the fatness of my own olive, and rejoice in the
" blood of my own vine. Is not this great Babel
" that I have built for the house of my kingdom,
" and for the glory of my majesty?" But the time, the set time to favour being come, heavenly influence descends from above and waters the soul; the Comforter comes down as a spirit of conviction, ploughs

up the fallow ground of the heart, and prepares the soul for bringing forth fruits meet for repentance; fills with the spirit of faith, of love, and holiness. It is recorded of Stephen, that he was a man *full of faith* and of the Holy Ghost. What is true of the greatest of saints, is also in his measure true of every believer.

Full of faith, and could not be shaken, or tempted to swerve from the profession of his faith; stedfast and immoveable, respecting that one thing needful, being determined to know nothing in this world, save Jesus Christ, and him crucified. Such is the case of every believer, in his better frames, respecting faith of the operation of God. Likewise, at times, he is so filled with love, that he knows not how to express his grateful sentiments. His cry is, " O Lord, how do I love thy " law! It is my delight all the day long. What " shall I do to praise, to honour and glorify my " lovely, my adorable Saviour: his mouth is most " sweet, yea, he is altogether lovely; he is white " and ruddy, the chief among ten thousand.' Filled with such a sense of his loving kindness, as to be overcome with the transporting pleasures of his presence, that with the spouse you cry out, *Stay me with flaggons, comfort me with apples, for I am sick of love.*

IId. Her kindred, and former connections come next under our notice.

A Moabitess,

SERMON VIII.

A Moabitess, a stranger, the daughter of strangers, whose patriarch was the son of incest, begotten by Lot in a fit of drunkenness on his own daughter, therefore there was nothing respectable in her ancestry. She was by nature of the wild, uncultivated race of idol worshippers, accustomed to bow down to the vanities of the Gentiles, and therefore a child of wrath even as others; afar off from God, and even darkness itself. But these connections were now dissolved; she was plucked off from her native stem, and grafted into the vine of Israel; she was brought nigh by the drawing power of immortal love; out of darkness into the marvellous light of the kingdom of God.

She was not a virgin, but the widow of Mahlon, the son of Elimelech, who died in the land of Moab, before she had any intention of quitting her native country. The spouse of Jesus also was married to a previous husband, the legal covenant, which must be dead to the sinner, and the sinner dead to it, before he can heartily approve of salvation by, and marriage with the Son of God. Mahlon, her former husband, signifies *a song*, which is answerable to the law in its original constitution, and to man in his primitive purity and holy obedience. When man at first dropped from the Creator's hand, he was like unto all the rest of the divine workmanship, perfect and good, capable of the moſt conſummate conformity to the moral law, and in every tittle of obeying his Maker's pleaſure. Whilſt he continued in his primitive rectitude, and ſpotleſs obedience, he could rejoice in the works of his own hands, and ſing of acceſs to the ſacred preſence, in virtue of his own performances. He obeyed, and he reaped the fruit of his doings, which fruit was joy and confidence in God. If they have great peace who but love the law, what holy joy, what ſacred pleaſure muſt have been the reſult of perfect obedience to its demands! Whilſt the law remained inviolate, it was the ſong of ſinleſs man; notwithſtanding, in his lapſed condition, it is to him the miniſter of condemnation. Who can reflect on that mutual intercouſe between God and Adam before the fall, without admiring the felicity of human innocence, and making the ſad compariſon between our own ſtate, and that of our great anceſtor? The Lord God walked with Adam, and freely deigned to converſe with him; yea, Jehovah vouchſafed to conſult with man concerning the names of his creatures. But, O man! where art thou now? from whence haſt thou fallen, O my inſtable parent? Alas! Adam, doſt thou flee from thy Maker's preſence, not long ago in thy ſight ſo delightful, ſo amiable? ſtill doſt thou flee? wilt thou never return Adam? aſk not the cauſe; for ſin is born into the human world:

moral

moral evil is become perfect, and has ruined primitive integrity. Unhappy parent! what awful ruin haft thou brought upon thy natural defcendents. *My God!* how great is thy forbearance, that ftill prolongs the exiftence of felf-ruined and rebellious mankind? It would have been equitable and juft with thee to have cut them down whilft fhuddering in the lonely thicket, and denounced irremediable ruin upon the whole delinquent race. But thou art God, whofe purpofes are unalterable, and whofe loving kindnefs is not fubject to any change whatever: thy counfel ftands for ever faft, and thou wilt do all that is in thine own heart.

Mahlon fignifies, fecondarily, *infirmity*; which is alfo anfwerable to man under a broken law, which law is become weak through the flefh to fave any that come unto it. Sin having entered and obtained dominion over man, it difabled him to perform any part of true obedience. This imbecillity of man rendered the law incapable to fave; as in its original conftitution it never could approve of any thing inferior to confummate perfection. It is weak, indeed, in point of the finner's falvation; but all its weaknefs comes through the infirmity of our flefh, who by nature have loft the power both to will and to do of his heavenly, his good pleafure. Do you queftion the truth of this defcription of fallen man? afk then your own hearts what part of the divine pleasure you can perfectly perform? what branch of practical godliness you can take delight in, before grace is pleased to form your hearts anew? The more you try to search your own hearts, and bring forth to view the springs of action in yourselves, the more shall you be convinced of the affecting truth, that *in man there dwells no good thing*, but that his whole *heart is deceitful above all things, and desperately wicked;* and that *all the imaginations of the thoughts of man's heart are only evil continually*, ever since that awful period on which it might be said, *that all flesh had corrupted his way*, and *we all as sheep went astray, turning every one to his own way*. Bring then the tempers and dispositions of your hearts forth to the trial; forth to be tried by the infallible records of infinite holiness, for by that you must ultimately stand or fall. If weighed in that impartial balance, O my soul! who shall not be found wanting?

By this impartial balance your every action, whether secret or open, must be weighed; it is virtuous, as it agrees with that only unerring standard of virtue and religion; or vicious, as it deviates from its sacred dictates. It was a sense of this that drew forth that remarkable confession from the mouths of the apostolic church, *In many things we offend all*, Jam. iii. 2. We saints, believers, quickened by the grace of God; we evangelists,

vangelists, preachers of the gospel, and apostles of Jesus; we offend, all offend, offend in many things; not only in time past, but we *now* offend, even in our regenerated state. Now, if the apostolic saints, favoured with privileges so exalted, were constrained to make such an humbling confession, would it not be the most daring presumption for sinners, who never felt the power of renewing grace, to flatter themselves that their obedience to the law is perfect? would it not be the most diabolical delusion thus to flatter ourselves, even after conversion, seeing an infallible pen has testified, *that if any man say he hath no sin, he deceiveth himself, and the truth is not in him.*

All mankind being thus concluded under sin, and incapable of that which is truly and spiritually good, it follows that the law is weak through the flesh, utterly weak to save any individual of the human race; so that by the works of the law shall no flesh living be justified or saved. The reason of this proposition is obvious in the highest degree. The law having required perfect, universal, and eternal obedience, in the creation state of man, was it now to abate in its demands proportionably to man's incapacity to obey, it would be mutable, *and therefore not a transcript of the mind of the Deity.* Every deviation from the law being truly and properly sin, it follows that the law

would

would be inconsistent with itself, if it could pass by any, the least sin, without ample atonement being made for its honour: having declared that he who keepeth the whole law, and offendeth but in one point, is deemed guilty of the whole. It would be unworthy of God to say, and not to do; but he hath spoken the word, and who shall disannul it? he is of one mind, and therefore liable to no mutation.

Mahlon, her former husband, was dead before she came to glean in the field of Boaz. It is likely that during his lifetime she was under no necessity of stooping so low as to glean after another man's reapers. But now Mahlon was dead, she was fain to live upon the bounty of another, however unworthy she might deem herself of being numbered among his maidens. It is just so with the perishing sinner, he must be dead to the law, and the law dead to him, before he can live with pleasure on the bounty of Jesus. Whilst the first, the natural husband lives; whilst there are the smallest remains of hope by the law, it is impossible that the soul can cordially submit to the righteousness of Christ, and embrace salvation upon gospel terms, without money and without price. The inspired Apostle of the Gentiles, beautifully states the doctrine under consideration, Rom. vii. 1, 2, 3. *Know ye not brethren, (for I speak to them that know the law) how that the law hath*

hath dominion over a man as long as he liveth? for the woman which hath an husband, is bound by the law to her husband, as long as he liveth ; but if the husband be dead, she is free from the law of her husband. So then if, while her husband liveth, she be married to another man, she shall be called an adulteress ; but if her husband be dead, she is free from that law, so that she is no adulteress, though she be married to another man. Wherefore, my brethren, ye also are become dead to the law by the body of Christ, that ye should be married to another, even to him who is raised from the dead, that ye should bring forth fruit unto God.

Here the law is represented as the natural husband, to whom mankind in general are married; and from whom there must be a total divorce, before we can embrace and live upon Christ, as is clear from the case of the husband and wife specified in the text. The woman cannot be married to another man, till after the death of her husband.

By nature, all our dependence is upon, all our hopes center in the law; nor do our expectations cease till beaten out from every subterfuge, and that is dead wherein by nature we are held. Whilst we place our hope in any sense in the law, it has full dominion over us, as the husband hath over the wife, and requireth perfect, personal, and perpetual obedience : but its authority over us

ceaseth

ceaseth the moment that by grace our hope finds no further foundation in the legal covenant.

When all hopes by the law of works are cut off; when the sandy foundation is washed away by the rising floods, and the fabric reared at such vast expence becomes a general ruin; when every refuge of lies is torn to pieces by the storm awaked in the conscience, the poor dismayed sinner begins to look abroad for some suitable ground of dependence; no longer now being able to find in himself any good thing towards the Lord God of Israel. Thus dead to the law, by the body of Christ, ye are brought to consent to the suit of the Son of God; having nothing wherewith to pay, ye are at last content to be frankly and freely forgiven, and rejoice to be justified as altogether unworthy and ungodly. Then can ye, or at least ye may say, with our holy Apostle, *I through the law am dead to the law, that I may live unto God.* This is the first and greatest end of your death to the law, and marriage to him that was raised up from the dead, that ye might bring forth fruit unto God. This death to the law, on your part, implies the death of the law to you ward, respecting its authority in form of a covenant; Christ having become the end of it for righteousness to all that believe.

There is an amazing force and beauty in the expression of his becoming the end of the law for his

his people. The law has dominion over the sinner to the very moment of his closing with Christ as an all-sufficient Saviour, and from that very moment forward, ceaseth to be his lawful *lord*. The avenger of blood might pursue the manslayer to the very gates of the city of refuge, but he might not touch him after he got within the gates. We may suppose the avenger in hot pursuit of the slayer to the very gates of the city, and seeing him safely enter within the gate, thus expostulate with himself, " So far as I was warranted " by divine appointment, I pursued him; had I " been able to come up with him within my own " dominion, I had sacrificed him to my fury. " But I can go no farther. The city gate is the " end of my authority, therefore I drop my pursuit, " as my vengeance cannot reach him within " the city walls." Will it be too bold to suppose the language under consideration to be something akin to the following: " Whilst he was under " my dominion, I cursed him with indignation; " whilst he sought salvation by obedience to me, " I scourged him with many stripes; but now " he has taken sanctuary where I cannot reach " him, under a covert through which my fury " cannot penetrate. He is safe in him upon " whom I have no farther demands; in him who " has honoured me to the uttermost, and must be
" safe

"safe under such an honourable protection, where
"I leave him for ever blessed."

O Sirs, look narrowly to the spirit of your obedience, and ground of your expectations. Beware of dividing your dependence between Moses and Christ: the dominion of the latter begins precisely where that of the former ceaseth. Ye may sooner intermingle noonday sunshine, and the gloom of midnight, than divide yourselves between the law and gospel in point of dependence. The law must be dead to you, and you to the law, before you can live upon the righteousness and atonement of Jesus; before ye can perform one action acceptable to an infinitely holy God. If you have the least dependence upon your obedience to the law, ye are bound to fulfil it perfectly; look therefore to be damned for the least deviation from the purity of its tenor. On the other hand, if you have no ground of hope but the perfect obedience of Christ; no spring of consolation but his bleeding wounds, ye have nothing to fear at the hand of a relentless law; it may storm, and threaten you with what it would do were you under its dominion, like the disappointed avenger before the gates of the city of refuge, but ye are safe. The inhabitants of the rock may sing of their safety within the gates of salvation.

IIId.

IIId. Having confidered her name, her kindred, defcent, and former hufband, we fhall now attend to her late and prefent conduct, as fomething akin to that of the truly gracious foul whom God has drawn to the love of Jefus.

(1.) She clave faft to her mother-in-law, with full purpofe to abide by her, in all circumftances whatever, refolving that nothing but death fhould divide them.

Entreat me not to leave thee, for where thou goeft I will go, thy people fhall be my people, thy God my God; where thou dieft I will die, and there will I be buried: fimilar to the refolution of the believer under divine anointings, to cleave to the militant church even to death, as has been exemplified in the firft difcourfe of this hiftory. I fhall therefore at this time attend,

(2.) To her prefent deportment, which eminently difcovered a grateful and humble frame of mind, becoming one who is brought to a fenfe of the bafenefs of her original, and alienation from the commonwealth of Ifrael. She fell on her face, and bowed herfelf to the ground; expreffeth her wonder at being taken notice of by this generous ftranger, and freely confeffeth herfelf unlike to his handmaidens of his own kindred and people. His venerable prefence ftruck her with awe, that fhe could not but do him reverence: his generofity filled her with wonder, that a friendlefs, de-

folate

solate stranger should be thought worthy to share in his munificence; and the sight of his retinue filled her with humility and self-abasement. So it is with the believer, who has the same experiences respecting his heavenly and adorable kinsman.

1. His adorable presence strikes them with awe and reverence, that they, like Ruth, fall to the ground with their faces to the earth, and wonder that they should find grace in his sight.

2. His generosity and his retinue lay them low in their own eyes, with their hands upon their mouths, and their mouths in the dust before him, confessing to be less than the least of all, and unlike to the meanest character in his train.

1. His adorable presence strikes them with awe and reverence, that, like Ruth, they fall to the ground, and bow themselves with their faces to the earth, wondering that they should find grace and favour in his sight. Nothing has such a tendency to lay the soul low, in the very dust before God, as the displays of his grace, love, and transcendently excellent and venerable presence. O how low does this bring the lofty looks of aspiring and ambitious man! at this the highest mountain sinks down into a valley, and the tall cedar of Lebanon into the meanest and most contemptible shrub.

Job

Job retained his integrity, and thought himself justified in so doing, whilst conversing only with his friends and equals; but when God himself in the person of the Logos appeared, though in a cloud, and spake from the midst of the whirlwind, Job is all humility and attention. Hear his becoming reply to the divine interrogatories, Chap. xl. 4. compared with Chap. xlii. 3, 5, 6. *Behold I am vile, what shall I answer thee? I will lay mine hand upon my mouth. I have uttered that I understood not, things too wonderful for me, which I knew not. I have heard of thee by the hearing of the ear; but now mine eye seeth thee. Wherefore I abhor myself, and repent in dust and ashes.* The presence of Infinite Holiness brings all the secret defilement of his heart to open view, so that his integrity departs as a nonentity, and nothing but vileness appears in his eye; therefore he lays his hand on his mouth, he abhors himself, lays his mouth in the earth, and repents in dust and ashes before him in whose presence there is no room for created excellence to appear. O Sirs! the nearer you are brought to Jesus, the lower you will lie in your own esteem, and the deeper will be your sense of your own pollutions.

It was at a time when God had, in a particular manner, made himself known to David his servant, that in the sacred presence he thus worshippeth in humble strains of holy gratitude, *Who am I, O Lord*

O Lord God? and what is my house, that thou hast brought me hitherto? and this was yet a small thing in thy sight, O Lord God; but thou hast spoken also of thy servant's house for a great while to come; and is this the manner of man, O Lord God? and what can David say more unto thee? for thou Lord God knowest thy servant, 2 Sam. vii. 18, 19, 20.

From which passage two things are apparent. First, that a sense of mercy is the spring of humble gratitude. David was overwhelmed with a sense of the divine goodness, and was struck with its sovereignty, and independence upon human merit; *for what am I? or what is my house?* saith he. Secondly, David does not abound in words, in the expression of his grateful affection; he wanted words to express his inward sensations; and found himself obliged to leave it with God, to read the thankfulness of his heart, in its inexpressible workings: *And what can David say more, O Lord God? for thou knowest thy servant.* From whence we are taught this comfortable and instructive truth, that the more our hearts are overcome with thankfulness to the God of love for the blessings of our salvation, we may be the less abundant in words, by which we can express the grateful sensations of the soul.

Another instance we have of the humbling nature of the divine manifestations of the Redeemer's presence in the case of Isaiah, in the sixth chapter of of his prophesy. This holy, this eloquent, and evangelic prophet, was laid under the deepest sense of his nothingness and defilement, not by any immediate affliction that was upon him, but by the revelation of the Lord of Hosts, Isa. vi. 2, 3, 4. *In the year that King Uzziah died, I saw also the Lord sitting upon a throne, high and lifted up, and his train filled the temple. Above it stood the seraphims: each one had six wings; with twain he covered his face, and with twain he covered his feet, and with twain he did fly. And one cried unto another, and said, Holy, holy, holy, is the Lord of Hosts! the whole earth is full of his glory! And the posts of the door moved at the voice of him that cried, and the whole earth was filled with smoke.* This courtly prophet had been accustomed to the magnificence of earthly monarchs, and could have beheld the swell of human grandeur without emotion; but when he beholds the glory of Zion's gracious Monarch, he is overwhelmed with its unsufferable blaze. He cries out, ver. 5. *Woe is me, for I am undone, because I am a man of unclean lips, and I dwell in the midst of a people of unclean lips.* But why so alarmed thou venerable prophet? thou wast such before when fear was at a distance from thee; neither thine own lips, nor the lips of the people with whom thou dwellest, are more unclean than they were before: therefore why so alarmed? why so shocked at thine own pollution? *O! mine eyes have seen the King, the Lord of Hosts!* If so, thou hast had an insupportable discovery of thine own utter wretchedness and pollution, and I wonder not at the agitation of thy spirit.

These may serve as a specimen of the humbling nature of divine discoveries. I shall therefore now,

(2.) A little note the humble confession of Ruth, as being unlike unto the handmaidens of Boaz. Ver. 13. *Then she said, let me find favour in thy sight, my lord, for that thou hast comforted me, and for that thou hast spoken friendly unto thine handmaid, though I be not like unto one of thine own handmaidens.* Ver. 10. *Why have I found grace in thine eyes, that thou shouldst take knowledge of me, seeing I am a stranger.* The train of our adorable Immanuel is so august, so glorious by his communicated grace, that the poor believer cannot easily be brought to consider himself amongst the happy number. All the holy angels, all the glorified saints, day and night attend upon his pleasure; ten thousand times ten thousand stand before him, and thousands of thousands fly at his command. The patriarchs and prophets, the apostles and evangelists, the noble army of martyrs, and all the spirits of just men made perfect, swell his brilliant train, and how can I who am so black and swarthy, so wretched and sinful, be numbered

amongst

amongst company so honourable? whence is it to me that my Lord should regard me with favour, and permit me to approach thy sacred presence, and encourage me to feed on the bounties of thy grace? It must indeed be astonishing, when the sinner expecting nothing but destruction, equivalent to the demerit of his sins, finds himself pardoned fully, justified freely, and admitted into the gospel church to partake of all the privileges of his children. What thankfulness must he not feel in his heart? what heavenly joy must transport his soul? and how will he feel his desire incited to seek after the honour and glory of the Redeemer, his Lord and Master, in the use of all appointed means. O God, I will love thee! I will praise thee! for although thou wast angry with me, thine anger is turned away, and thou comfortest me.

SERMON IX.

Ruth ii. 14.

And Boaz said unto her, at meal-time, come thou hither, and eat of the bread, and dip thy morsel in the vinegar. And she sat beside the reapers: and he reached her parched corn, and she did eat and was sufficed, and left.

THE names of the parties having been opened and applied to gospel purposes, in the preceding discourses, we shall now attend to the invitation itself. *At meal-time, come thou hither, and eat of the bread, and dip thy morsel in the vinegar,* which we find to be very capable of a spiritual, evangelic improvement, such as, if divinely blessed, may be an incentive both to our comfort and holiness. With this view, I shall consider it as containing the three following branches.

Ist. *At meal-time, come thou hither.*
IId. *Eat of the bread.*
IIId. *Dip thy morsel in the vinegar.*

SERMON IX.

1st. *At meal-time, come thou hither.* The servants of Boaz had their meal-times, their times of refreshment and rest, in which they retired from their several departments in labour to the place appointed, and fed upon their master's provision. At meal-time their honourable lord disdained not to join them, and fed upon the same food which was provided for his reapers; a beautiful instance of ancient simplicity, the very reverse of modern ambition, voluptuousness and dissipation. Labouring men have need of rest and refreshment, and unto the labourer they yield an agreeable sweetness. Even the bed of down is hard and uneasy to the children of sloth and indolence, and to the voluptuary the most tasteful viands yield no pleasing relish: but to the labouring man who comes at meal-time, prepared for eating by labour-procured hunger, every bitter thing is sweet, and the coarsest bed is soft and agreeable. The voluptuary spends his time to procure the brutal pleasures of eating and drinking, but his pursuits are baffled by idleness and plenty; whilst the rustic swain, upon his humble allowance, feeds with the keenest gust of which sense is capable. When the man of pleasure can by no means procure the due visitations of sleep, even upon his bed of down, the country ploughman enjoys all its charms upon humble chaff, or the coarsest feathers. He comes with an healthy hunger to his plain repast, and wearied by the labours of the day, to his smiling consort and homely pillow, and is gratified by all the pleasures of vigorous sensation.

The church, the believing church, as the family of our divine husbandman, the servants of our holy and adorable Master, have their meal-time, on which they feed in company on such provision as infinite bounty has made for them. The divine Master has appointed one day in seven as his own day, and which is a season of feeding. The Lord's day is so nominated, not because it is a day of receiving ought at the hands of his people, but because it is a day on which he calls them together to display unto them the bounties of his goodness. The remark which I sometimes make cannot be too often repeated: the Christian religion does not consist in a bringing to God, but in a receiving all from his sovereign mercy in Christ Jesus: and the religion of Antichrist, whatever form or name it assumes, consists essentially in a bringing to God, instead of receiving all from him in a way of free favour.

Boaz associated with his servants at meal-time, as is apparent from the words of our text, *He reached her parched corn, and she did eat.* Jesus is also with his family in a peculiar manner on his own day, sitting at his table, and causing our spikenard to send forth the smell thereof, or feeding the souls of his saints in the banquetting house

of

of love. You who now hear me can recollect many instances of your being sweetly regaled with the delicacies of paradise in the house of God. Ye have found many a banquetting table in the house of prayer; the cup of trembling has been graciously taken away, and the nectarine cup of gospel consolation has been administered in its stead. Perhaps, like a weary reaper, ye have come hither at meal-time, heavy laden with a sense of guilt and pollution, groaning under a sense of your mental languor, scarcely daring to hope for any soul repast; yet ere you are aware, your souls were raised by the precious allurements of your Redeemer's voice, saying unto you, *Arise my love, my fair one, and come away;* and in an instant ye were become like the chariots of a willing people: ye were made on that day to sing of his salvation, *O God, we praise thee! for although thou wast angry with us, thine anger is turned away, and thou comfortest us.* Then were ye like giants refreshed with new wine; your hearts were glad as with espousal endearments, and your only boast was of God your Saviour.

Every ordinance of God is a meal-time to the needy believer, and its use stands in connection with covenant promise. These are the vehicles of his provisions, which he has promised to bless to the satisfaction of the poor and needy; with which, as with good things, he filleth the longing soul of the hungering believer. Every servant of God has a right to come hither to the ordinances at meal-time: the duty is general, and is enjoined upon all that would eat of the bread: *Ho! every one that thirsteth, come to the waters!* Ho! every hungry sinner, come hither at meal-time! take and eat without money and without price. You cannot expect to eat unless you attend at meal-time; at meal-time therefore come hither, eat of the bread, and dip thy morsel in the vinegar.

Many you shall find with visage meagre, and with the drauling voice of languor, complaining of their leanness: O my leanness, my leanness; who if duly attended to, will be found to neglect coming hither at meal-time; or, if they do come hither at meal-time at all, they come with such listless steps, and such sickly appetites, that their coming answers little to the purpose of soul nutrition; therefore their leanness and barrenness still continue. That heart which is overcharged with worldly concerns, is no way likely to profit much by the sacred institutions of the gospel. How shall the corn of heaven grow amongst thorns and briars of worldly cares.

The coming together of the servants at meal-time leads me to observe, that all gospel ordinances ought to be administered on the Lord's day in the assemblies of his worshipping people.
The

The master of the field has an undoubted right to direct his own reapers: he that provides the sustenance of his servants, surely may appoint the times and manner of their refreshment. There is one ordinance of the blessed gospel that appears to me of great importance, and is notwithstanding treated with great indignity: I hope I shall be excused, if I should even express my abhorrence of privately smuggling people through the ordinance of baptism into the Christian church; yet both by baptists and pedobaptists, this is sometimes allowed. Without entering at all into the controversy between ourselves, and our esteemed brethren of a contrary persuasion, I shall take the liberty of observing, that with both parties the ordinance of baptism is treated as inferior to other gospel institutions, and frequently is administered on a working day, in a private manner; whereas it being confessedly of divine appointment, and an ordinance of Jesus Christ, it ought to be administered on his own day in the assemblies of his church; at least where this can be done with any tolerable convenience, it certainly must have the preference, as by far the most eligible, and most likely to answer the ends for which it was instituted.

But to return to the thread of my discourse, it may be observed, that if the reapers are laborious, they will have an healthful appetite; and if hungry, they will be glad to come hither at meal-time.

time. They will be so far from being careless in the use of means, that they will find it difficult to hold out to meal-time. You will not find them entering the place of worship when service is almost over, but waiting in time to hear what the Lord our God will say unto them; waiting with as diligent attention as they watch for the morning. Their waiting will be far from formal and customary, and, with the Psalmist, their very souls will wait; wait for God and the visits of his grace, encouraged by the word on which their hope is placed: glad to embrace every opportunity of soul refreshment, such as mutual converse about the things of God, social, family, or private prayer: glad when athirst to go to the vessels and drink that which the young men, the Prophets and Apostles have drawn. More especially, in seasons of great afflictions, when the sun of temptation beats vehemently upon them, will they seek unto the word with that good man, who declares that he had certainly perished in his afflictions, if the law of the Lord had not been his peculiar delight. So then at meal-time, if hungry, come hither: all that thirst, come ye to the waters; all that hunger, come to the banquet of free lovingkindness. Ye are the guests which wisdom hath invited; for you her table is prepared, and her wine is mingled; behold all things are ready,

and

and ye shall be welcome to come hither at mealtimes. This leads me to the

IId. Particular under this head, which is, *Eat of the bread. Come thou hither at meal-time, and eat of the bread.* Coming hither at meal-time will answer but little purpose, if we eat not of the bread prepared. Indeed, if we are an hungered, we shall need but little invitation to eat, if a covered table is presented to us; on the contrary, it would be no small degree of mortification for us in such a case, to see others plenteously to feed upon nutritive and inviting delicacies, whilst we ourselves were shut out from partaking with them.

Eat of the bread, here is a generous and free invitation, to use the means of sustenance with cheerfulness and freedom; it is freely provided, freely given, and thou art perfectly welcome. The bread of life was early provided, even from everlasting: it is the provision of unmerited, of infinite goodness; and, as it was freely provided, it is as freely given; for nothing could excite the Most High to give his Son as the bread and spring of spiritual and eternal life, but his own ineffable lovingkindness: he only is the bread of God; he only is the Christian's life; and he is fully and freely given to all who see their need of such a Saviour: to him is every sensible sinner welcome; and from his salvation shall none be turned empty away. Personal unworthiness is here no reasonable

able impediment, otherwife none had ever partook of the bread of heaven, feeing all are unworthy, becaufe all have finned and come fhort of the glory of God; befides we have the unalterable promife of him who cannot lye, *That of all who come to him, he will in no wife caft out.* How groundlefs then the unbelieving fears of many fenfible fouls, left they fhould be turned away from the banquetting houfe of Jefus, under the tremendous weight of the deferved anathema. But know this of a truth, it is the rich, and only the rich, whom he fends empty away, for he feedeth the hungry with the good things of his gracious kingdom.

Eat therefore of the bread; afk not if it was defigned for fuch as thee: it is certain that bread is prepared for the hungry; if hungry, it was prepared for thee. Ruth, with all her relative and perfonal difadvantages, ate of the bread, and was fufficed, and left. Nothing is more common than for the awakened finner, alarmed with a fenfe of his own danger, earneftly to long for an intereft in gofpel falvation, and to live upon Jefus the bread of heaven. But, ah! the mifgivings of an unbelieving heart lure him afide from his true happinefs, and add to the burden of his weary mind, by vainly prying into the infcrutable decrees of eternal Wifdom. Here you fhall find fuch unneceffary queftionings as thefe. Am I among the number of his people for whom he died? I heartily approve of his great salvation; but have I any interest in it? he is just such a Saviour as I stand in need of, but is he designed a Saviour for such a sinner as me? Such questionings are not only in themselves altogether unnecessary, but are contrary to the genius of the gospel, and dishonouring to God and his Son Jesus. Jesus derives his name of Saviour from the relation in which he stands to sinners; and sovereign mercy in the Deity always hath human misery for its only object; therefore if thou wast not a wretched sinner, thou couldst not have hope in the merciful Saviour. As the case stands, there is a perfect suitableness between Christ and thee: thy misery is exactly suitable to his mercy, and gives it an opportunity to exert itself in its most unlimited scope; and this boundless mercy is in all respects adequate to thy most extensive wretchedness.

All that is requisite then to the freest use of Christ, and all his salvation, is to know thy need of such a one as a Saviour. If thou art a condemned sinner, he is thy all-sufficient Saviour: if thou hast nothing of thine own on which thou canst rely, he is thy portion for ever, and the Lord thy righteousness and strength. Is he therefore held out unto thee as the bread of God and of life? *eat of the bread,* without inquiring for whom it was prepared; it is enough that thou art in a famishing condition to encourage thee to eat of the bread. Whatsoever is set before thee, in the ministry of the word, eat, asking no questions for conscience sake. Jesus, with all his grace and salvation is set before thee, and by sovereign grant thou, though the vilest of sinners, hast an indubitable right to embrace both the one and the other, to make free with Christ and all his unsearchable riches; to trust in him as almighty to deliver and save to the very uttermost, the most abominable sinner that trusts in his mercy. Talk not then, deluded soul, of thine unworthiness, for there are none in heaven more worthy in themselves, than thou art with all thy vileness. Say not, I am a stranger of an uncircumcised nation, descended from a race of evil doers; I am of a swarthy complexion, and not fit to appear among the family of God: but if hungry, eat of the bread.

Eat of the bread, be sure it is bread on which you feed: beware of feeding upon chaff or ashes. That heart is deluded and turned aside which feeds upon ashes; and they are swine who can be satisfied with husks. It was not in his father's house, but in a land of strangers, that the poor prodigal would have been glad to fill his belly with husks that swine did eat. God provides bread, the staff of life, for his household; whilst the servants of sin and Satan are put off with swines' provision.

Look

Look carefully to what you eat; see that it be bread, of the kidney of the wheat: every thing that springs from self or the world is but chaff or corruption; but the promises and declarations of grace are wholesome bread by which ye shall live for ever.

Eat of the *bread, plain* bread, and not dishes elegantly dressed and richly sauced; bread the staff of life, apt to nourish, without gendering humours disagreeable or dangerous, or in any wise injurious to the constitution: bread upon which there is no liklihood of your surfeiting, as you possibly might upon more tasteful viands. Of all the surfeits ye hear of, of all the diseases which abound, none proceed from the eating of the bread, and dipping of the morsel in the vinegar. Surfeiting and disease have their spring in practices very different from these. The full soul will indeed be apt to consider plain bread as a very coarse entertainment; but my concern is not at present with him, seeing the honey itself is nauseous and loathsome to such: it is to the hungry that my message is sent; to you to whom every bitter thing is sweet; and unto the hungry, the plainest healthful bread will be welcome provision.

Our gospel is equally plain and nutritive: so plain, that it is foolishness to the wise philosophic Greek; so nutritive that whosoever feeds upon its provision shall live for ever. In my view of things, it could not be half so majestic, if it was not altogether so plain: its plainness and simplicity suit with none but the hungry and needy; and its majesty gives full scope to the most extensive powers of the human understanding. The gospel of our salvation is so constructed that it can receive no embellishment from human wisdom and science: its spirit is a spirit of independency, and can incorporate with nothing earthly: its noble and beauteous structure is equally adapted to give relief unto every necessitous person, and to humble, abase, and mortify the self-sufficient. Of course it tends in itself to thwart every view of the natural mind, and is in itself that cross which is equally an offence to the unregenerate, and the believer's glory and rejoicing. Here is nothing to nourish pride or tickle our self-conceit. The gospel strips the creature of all its excellency, and lays the whole race of mankind low on a perfect level, in one common ruin before God, and leaves no room for so much as whispering * one boast of either willing or doing.

* *Whispering one boast*—It is indeed unusual for boasters to speak in whispers: but there is such a thing as a self-righteous person speaking privately his own commendation, that which he has not courage enough openly to declare to the multitude, and to this is the allusion here.

But

SERMON IX.

But plain and mortifying as the gospel is, there is no other scheme of life revealed. Ye must either eat or die: no other alternative is known in the volume of revelation but, *He that believeth shall be saved, and he that believeth not shall be damned.* If you eat, ye shall live for ever; if ye eat not of the bread, the whole creation cannot save you from endless despair, and consummate ruin for ever and ever. May God give you an healthful appetite, and teach you to feed upon the bread of his kingdom, the food of his favoured children, that ye may escape the horrors which await the foes of the immaculate Redeemer. You who eat of the bread, and drink of that which the young men have drawn, are blessed indeed, for ye shall never die; your food is the spring of eternal life, and ye shall live for ever with him from whom ye derive your life and all its nourishment. But a

IIId. Third thing is contained in the words, which I know to be very familiar to many of you. *Dip thy morsel in the vinegar.* Our holy Boaz hath indeed provided ample provision for the sustenance of his people, but every morsel must be dipped in the vinegar: such is the purpose of infinite Wisdom, and every saint shall find its fulfilment. To explain a thing so well known as vinegar, might well be deemed superfluous; but as its medical uses are less understood, it may not be amiss a little to amplify them, in order the better to accommodate our object to gospel uses.

It is of excellent use in all kinds of inflammatory and putrid distempers, in all ardent bilious, pestilential and malignant fevers, acting as a certain and very powerful sudorific, which is certainly the most likely way of conquering those diseases, by driving the venom from the heart to the surface of the body *. It is used also as an excellent antidote against all contagious distempers whatever, either by washing the body of the healthy therein, sprinkling the chamber of of the sick, or pouring it in the room upon a burning brick †: taken inwardly it greatly promotes concoction, braces up the relaxed fibres of the stomach, and of course helps the appetite. In weakness and relaxation of the nerves, palpitation of the heart, and all hysterical and hypochondriacal complaints; it is of great use either taken inwardly, or applied to the mouth and nostrils. So that from its great force in medicine, it is not impossible that its plenteous use among the ancients might, in the hand of the Almighty, be one means of promoting their longevity and healthful frame of body.

But to return to my principal design, I may observe, that the people of God are indeed fed

* Vid. New Dispensatory, page 68.
† Sydenham Pract. of Phys.

with bread of the kidney of the principal wheat, and no expence is thought too great for their provision; but then such is their constitution and habit, that during their minor state, it is necessary that every morsel should be dipped in the vinegar: this regimen is apparently necessary, for the preservation of soul healthfulness and prosperity. The paschal lamb was never, at any time, to be eaten without bitter herbs: nor is the bread of mercy to be eaten but as dipt in the vinegar of judgment, so that the one gives an agreeable, qualifying relish to the other.

Of the vinegar in which thy morsel must be dipt, O believer, there are two kinds, equally salutary, equally necessary.

(1.) The vinegar of personal afflictions and sorrows.

(2.) The vinegar of the sufferings and sorrows of thy holy Redeemer.

Each of which hath its physical uses in perfectly restoring the soul to its pristine purity, and to fit her for enjoyments infinitely superior to those of which she was capable in the days of her primitive innocence.

(1.) There is the vinegar of personal afflictions, in which every morsel of comfort or soul provision must be dipped, because, whilst here, the plague of the heart still remaining, we are subject to disorders the most malignant. No situation of the air, however contagious, could generate disease in the human body, if there were not a fitness in its construction or habit to receive the infection; even so temptations however violent, however subtile, could not infect the soul with the malignancy of sin, if there were not an aptitude in our hearts * to fall in with the designs of the powers of darkness. Whilst therefore there is in our mental habit an inclination to the disease of sin, we shall have need, by way of prevention, to dip

---

* *Aptitude in our hearts,* &c. This may be thought to militate against the purity of the creation state of Adam, and of the fallen angels: but when it is considered that there may be in intellectual beings, a principle capable of malignant impressions, without any the least bias to evil before that impression is made, the difficulty vanisheth. That such a principle did dwell in our first progenitor, the event has fully demonstrated; but to suppose that he was created, possest of any inclination to moral evil, would be no less than blasphemy, and indeed an impeachment of the purity of the Creator himself. The tinder of itself would remain for ever without burning, but whenever it is touched by the smallest spark of fire, in virtue of that contact, is changed into the nature of fire itself; whereas the same spark, let fall upon earth or water, would languish and die away of itself. The first and second Adam are essentially different in the natural formation of their minds, as is apparent from the effects.—When Satan came to the first Adam, he found in him a principle capable of being influenced by temptation; which principle but for temptation might never have been discovered; but when he came to the second Adam, he found nothing in him of which he could avail himself. But the author is here speaking of man in his fallen condition.

our morsel in the vinegar; more especially, as the infection is already caught, and disease works in every member, as it did in Paul; this is the way in which our heavenly Physician effecteth our cure.

Who, that knows himself, does not see that the plague of sin in his heart has infected every faculty of his soul, and defiled every organ of the body, making it the instrument of unrighteousness unto sin. What hypocrisy, pride, and self-will dwell in the heart? how have the eyes and ears been open to vanity, and how frequently the lips have moved deceit? what hand has not perpetrated evil? and whose feet have not trod the paths of foolishness? even in a converted state, how sad are the Christian's feelings! How does he sometimes feel inordinate affection and unlawful desire, glowing within him as a burning fever, to the drying up of his vital spirits? and is it not necessary, in such cases, that the fewel of his lusts should be cut off, and medicated vinegars be ministered for assuaging the burning desire? Happy had it been for Sampson if his fair and alluring Delilah had been cut off before she had betrayed him; then had he preserved the sight of his two eyes, the loss of which he lamented even in his death: then had he retained the youthful vigour of his brawny limbs unimpaired, and continued a terror to Israel's enemies.

The very objects, the loss of which we mourn with the greatest bitterness, might perhaps, if continued ours, have proved as so many Delilahs unto our souls. In such a case then, the ministration of the vinegar along with our bread, must have been the result of the wisest counsel. It was more healthful to the soul of Sampson, and more instructive to the tribes of Israel, that he should grind in the prison house, than that he should loll effeminately on the lap of a strumpet. It was more to the honour of God; more consistent with the divine conduct in general, to punish Sampson by his own devices, and correct him by his own wickedness, than to leave him at large to walk at pleasure in the way of Sihor, and with impunity to drink the poisoned streams of a strange river *.

Behold how comfort and sorrow have been blended together, even from the beginning in the lot of God's people. You are by no means the first whose morsel has been dipt in the vinegar of personal tribulation and sorrow: no strange thing has befallen any of you in this respect; no, they are common to men: Abraham, on the gift of Isaac, must cast out his son Ishmael, which was very trying to a parent of his sensibility. Isaac and Rebekah were weary because of the rebellions of Esau, and because of his attachment to the daughters of Heth. All the blessings of a

* Jer. ii. 18, 19.

well

well ordered covenant did not make David forget his diforderly houfe. Solomon's wifdom was counterpoifed by the vanity which he faw infcribed on every fublunary object. Paul's love to Jefus, and fuccefs in the miniftry, could not prevent his groaning in his tabernacle, and crying out under the body of death; prevented not the fmart of the thorn in the flefh, the meffenger of Satan. The cafe is general, all, as well as you, dip their morfels in the vinegar.

That it ought to be fo, is further apparent from our pronenefs to thirft after the things of this world, fometimes with as much ardour as the unhappy patient in a burning fever thirfts for the cooling draught. The pleafures, the honours, and profits of this world, are very alluring, adapted to work upon our viciated tafte, and but too frequently carry away the heart from God and ferious religion. It is profitable for us that God fhould take fuch meafures with us, as to reftrain our licentious inclinations, and make us happy, as it were, contrary to our inordinate defire. What parent, if he fhould fee one of his children going to fwallow a cup of poifon, would not with eagernefs fnatch it from his hand? and does God do more by his people, than prevent them bringing ruin and deftruction upon themfelves and their purer comforts, by wrefting from their hands that which would be fatal to them in the end.

If

If a parent shall see a beloved child labouring under weakness, loss of appetite, and the prevalence of disease, will he not by all means endeavour to exterminate the disorder, though he should find himself necessitated to make use of medicines, even the most unpalatable?

By the use of the vinegar of afflictions in the Christian life, great advantages are obtained in point both of knowledge and affection. Let experience speak, and it will tell you how much you learn of creature emptiness; how insatisfactory to the immortal soul; how insignificant in comparison of that good of which you are in the the pursuit. Disappointments, losses, and crosses in trade, are blessed means by which your Father prevents your taking up your rest in this world: bodily afflictions and darkness of soul give you such discoveries of your own absolute weakness and nothingness, as cannot without them be obtained. How are the hidden principles of iniquity dragged from their deep recesses in the heart, and brought forth to open view? how exceedingly sinful do our hearts by these means appear? how abject our attainments? how consummate our helplessness?

By these things the Christ of God becomes precious to you, and you cannot live a day, an hour without him. As you sink in your own esteem, Christ advances, he rises upon you in worth and
excellence:

excellence: how adorable does his person become? how valuable his righteousness, because of your total privation of righteousness of your own? how inestimable his pardoning blood, because of your most aggravated guiltiness? By these means you learn to live upon Christ who is your life, and the life of every believer.

Dip then thy morsel in the vinegar of afflictions, for it is healthful and salutary; what is indeed necessary for thine enjoyment of any tolerable degree of spirituality; it must be done whether agreeable to thy will, or disagreeable; and it is best that it should be thine own act and deed; and better still, if it is done with cheerfulness. Jeremiah ate the dipped morsel, but it was by constraint, *It is a grief, and I must bear it.* Micah did it voluntarily, *I will bear the indignation of the Lord, because I have sinned against him, until he plead my cause, and execute judgment for me.* But Paul gloried to do it cheerfully, *Much rather therefore will I glory in my infirmities, that the power of Christ may rest upon me.* It is easy to see which of these makes the most graceful appearance; he that wrangled with his heavenly parent, and bore his will merely by constraint, or him that willingly endured, even gloried to endure the whole of his pleasure. Impatience only tends to add to the burden; and rebellion of will, to procure a greater number of stripes. Dip thy morsel

morsel willingly in the vinegar, seeing it is for thy health, O believer, and at the same time the command of thine unerring Parent: dip thy morsel in the vinegar, for it must be done; if not voluntarily, thou shalt do it by constraint.

Blessed is that man who endureth temptations in a Christian temper of mind, without daring to quarrel with God, and saying to him, *What dost thou?* That was an holy resignation in good old Eli, to say, *It is the Lord, let him do what seemeth him good.* This was dipping the morsel willingly in the vinegar.

(2.) There is the vinegar of Christ's sufferings in death also, in which our morsel must be dipt in order to our growth and healthfulness. In this present state of weakness and adversity we are subject to fainting, and as an antidote to it, we have need to dip our morsel in the vinegar of Christ's excruciating pains and dying agonies, that our morsel may be a restorative to us: this David evidently did, when he tells us, that *he had fainted, unless he had believed to see the goodness of the Lord in the land of the living.*

Dip thy morsel in the vinegar; it will eat by much the more pleasant, and nourish thy faith, hope, and love exceedingly.

Dost thou eat the bread of comfort and pardoning love? Dip thy morsel in the vinegar of the expiatory sufferings of Jesus, as the only channel

nel of pardoning lovingkindness, and the only means by which it is procured. No bread more pleasant than this to the soul; yet still it will be both more pleasant and nutritive, for its being dipped in this vinegar. How pleasant, how delightful is the voice of pardon, when I behold my bleeding Lord wrestling to obtain it! My healing is never so divinely ravishing, as when I feel the cruel stripes of the macerated Jesus. My bread can never eat with such a gust, as when I contemplate the penury of the Son of the Highest. How divinely fitting is the justifying robe when dipt in the ardent obedience of the sinner's substitute? Art thou accepted by infinite Holiness, O believer, and admitted to the table of the children of heaven? ask how it comes to pass that a rebel such as thou art is admitted to privileges so sacred and valuable? Then shalt thou be referred to the agonizing groans, and heart-breaking sighs of thine immaculate Redeemer. The heavenly glories themselves shall receive additional lustre from their procuring cause: let the songs of paradise revive upon thy memory, the mournful accents of thy plaintive surety. Let every comfort, that breathes heavenly delight on the heart of sinners, revive the dying Sabbacthani of Jesus of Nazareth.

Is thy soul at liberty? think on the procuring cause of thine enlargement: see the penalty of thy

thy transgressions; the dreadful curse of a broken covenant, lying in its utmost weight, on the only Begotten of the eternal Father. These things if attended to, thy morsel thus dipt in the vinegar, will make thy life more lively, and thy comforts more comfortable. Are the promises thy support, the daily food of thine immortal spirit? they all come to thee dipt in the wormwood and gall which thy Redeemer's soul shall for ever have in remembrance. A promise to the believer is nothing at all, unless it thus comes; for promises, as a reward of obedience can yield no pleasant reflection to one who cannot obey perfectly in thought, word, and deed. But divine revelation shows the whole system of promises as yea, and amen, in the person of the adorable Immanuel. Let every comfort, every privilege, and every means of grace, refer you back to Calvary, the bloody mount of the Lord, where salvation is seen in its utmost extent and glory. How sovereign is grace; how free is salvation and divine favour? My soul, be it the subject of thine eternal contemplation; dwell upon it with incessant and ravishing delight.

God is not a barren wilderness to his people in respect even to temporal things; all have natural comforts in greater abundance than had the Son of God himself in the days of his humiliation. We having forfeited our title to every comfort, natural and divine, and he appearing as our substitute and common person, he had not a legal title to so much as earthly benefits, and therefore when upon earth he had nothing that he could call his own *. This was poverty indeed! the poverty due to law-breakers whom he represented: but poor as his circumstances were, through him law-breakers obtain many natural as well as spiritual enjoyments. Let then thy ever comfortable morsel be dipped in thy Redeemer's sorrow, and comfort itself shall be yet more comfortable.

Dip thy morsel in the vinegar, in all the kindnesses thou receivest at the hands of man; dip them in the unkindnesses which were cast upon him. Remember that in him there was nothing desirable apprehended, he was esteemed as one smitten of God and afflicted; was deemed an enemy to God, and to the common rights of mankind; was tempted, and to his face calumniated; was vilified, set at nought, spit upon and buffetted. When man caresses you, remember how your dear Redeemer was despised and rejected by men of

---

* This circumstance is a beautiful explanation of that of the Apostle, 2 Cor. viii. 9. *For ye know the grace of our Lord Jesus Christ, that though he was rich, yet for our sakes he became poor, that ye through his poverty might be rich.* As the blessed Immanuel, all things are his, the earth with all its fulness, the cattle upon a thousand hills; but as the sinner's substitute, he stood in the place of his people, and was treated in all respects according to their demerit.

the

the moſt reputable ſtations and talents. If thus dipped in thy Redeemer's ſorrow, the careſſes of men will never be injurious to thy ſoul's proſperity; whereas without ſuch a qualifying acid, the favour of men might ſwell thee with pride, and draw thy affections away from thy God.

In all thy ſeaſons of pleaſure and joy, when pleaſure ſparkles in the eye, and joy dances in thy boſom, forget not that Jeſus, thy holy One, Jeſus, thine excellent Redeemer, was a man of ſorrows and acquainted with grief; from his cradle to his croſs he was daily converſant with conſummate grief. Indeed, how ſhould it be otherwiſe, when ſuch a load of guilt was laid upon him; a load ſuch as would have ſunk millions of worlds into utter deſtruction. When I hear my bleſſed Redeemer, pathetically complaining that his ſoul, his holy ſoul, is exceedingly ſorrowful, even unto death; that that immaculate Spirit, which never exiſted but in perſonal union with Almighty Deity*, was juſt ready to ſink under the enormous weight of human guilt, it greatly tends to qualify my mirth, and reduce it to rules becoming the Chriſtian. That Jeſus wept, the

---

* *With Almighty Deity.* Although the human nature of the bleſſed Jeſus, exiſts in perſonal union only with the divine word, there is, there muſt be a certain union between the ſaid nature, and the Father, and Holy Spirit, in virtue of the unity of the divine Eſſence.

ſacred

SERMON IX.

sacred Evangelist testifies; but that he laughed is no where said. Indeed he rejoiced in spirit, but with such a joy as was untinctured with, even the appearance of the bursts of mad and foolish laughter. Dip every morsel of the bread of joy therefore in the vinegar of thy Redeemer's sorrow, so shall it be neither unbecoming, unseasonable, nor excessive.

When thou sittest down at thy well-furnished table, and partakest liberally of the bounties of providence; remember that thy Lord had no table of his own at which he could feed his followers, but fed at tables which claimed other masters: this thought will be an excellent preservative, and thy table shall not be thy snare whilst this one thought is inculcated. What moderation, temperance, and sobriety, yea, what bounty and liberality would this single thought give birth unto? let thy plenty incite thee, to recollect his penury, and thy convenience bring his inconveniences to remembrance. When thy family is convened around thee in safety and peace, either to feed or worship, call to mind that dismal night on which all his disciples forsook him and fled; on which he trode the wine-press * of divine wrath alone, and of the people there were none

with

---

* *Trode the wine-press.*—Treading of the wine-press by Jesus undoubtedly refers to the victory he gained over his enemies;

but

with him. Thus dip thy morsel of domestic tranquillity in the vinegar of his personal disquiet; lying down in bed, safe and secure beneath the covert of divine protection, confident that God is thy shield of defence; forget not how Jesus, who had not where to lay his head, was wont to wrestle in prayer whole nights for thy salvation. Instead of retiring as we do to rest, we find the loving Saviour retiring to a mountain to pray; to pray for us, being pure, perfect, and holy in himself; to pray earnestly, even in an agony, that he might obtain eternal redemption for all that should believe in him in every part of the habitable world.

Once more, are you fed with the bread of sorrow, and drink of the waters of affliction? by all means dip thy morsel then in the vinegar; plunge thy personal sorrows into those of the friend of sinners, and death shall remove from thy pot; even the bitterest waters shall become sweet and salutary; the seeming curse shall change into a sanctifying cross, and the apprehended indignation into fatherly chastisements. Bring all thy griefs unto Calvary, and hang them on the arms

---

but when could the heavenly Conqueror be more fitly represented, as dipping his garments in the blood of his enemies, than when he bruised the serpent's head, spoiled principalities and powers, and made an open shew of them, and that was when he fell under their seeming superiority.

of that accursed tree where hung the great Immanuel, and however thick and threatening the cloud may be, thou shalt see everlasting love beam through its darkness; every present sorrow, the prolific source of future joy, and glory arising from every sigh and groan. Thou shalt see the once slain Redeemer faithfully collecting thy tears, thy groans, and sighs, and treasuring them up in heaven till thine arrival, that he may by them give an additional lustre to thy future glory.

SERMON X.

Ruth ii. 14.

And she sat beside the reapers, and he reached her parched corn, and she did eat, and was sufficed, and left.

IT having been attempted, in former discourses, to illustrate the name and character of this generous husbandman; also the damsel invited, in her character and former connections; likewise to enlarge upon the invitation itself, we shall trace the agreeable and consistent conduct of Ruth on receiving such generous treatment: *She sat by the reapers—she ate what was given to her—she gleaned until even—she beat out that she had gleaned—all that she had gleaned she carried home to her mother Naomi.* These five things attended to, we shall have a more clear view of the exemplary conduct of this young Moabitess, and shall see how by small things the Lord is pleased to teach his people knowledge. As he is pleased by this damsel to instruct even the most grown and advanced among his people; so that, as Paul observes,

serves, he chooses things that are not, to confound those that are; and, as Jesus observes, perfects praise to himself out of the mouths of babes and sucklings, when the wise and prudent are left to perish in ignorance of the great salvation. The conduct of this amiable Moabitess was, in all respects in character, agreeable to her needy, humiliating circumstances. For,

1st. She is said to have sat by the reapers at meal-time. She knew herself to be a stranger in a strange land, and having found a friend in the person of Boaz, she embraced his invitation with gratitude, and for safety convened with his labourers. It is good for *you* also, who know yourselves to be aliens from the commonwealth of Israel, and strangers to the covenant of promise, to abide by the labourers of your Lord. If you would glean your living, you must follow the reapers: if you would eat your dipped morsel in safety, you must sit by the servants of Boaz. It is dangerous to depart into other fields, and sit in the company of strangers. What canst *thou* have to do in the way of Egypt, to drink the waters of Sihor? or, what hast *thou* to do in the way of Assyria, to drink the waters of the river? Thine own wickedness shall correct thee, and thy backslidings shall reprove thee, if thou followest after the ways of strangers.

Are you strangers and pilgrims, conscious of your urgent necessity? let your necessity prompt you to cast yourselves upon the mercy of your heavenly Boaz; for he is the friend of the destitute, and the patron of helpless strangers. Embrace his invitation, come hither at meal-time, and eat of the bread; who knows but he may reach unto thee the parched corn, and thou shalt be sufficed, and leave: at all events keep close to his reapers, and thou shalt see if at last he will finally cast thee out. Know, if a sinful Israelite could have such compassion on a friendless stranger, much more the friend of sinners, who laid down his life even for his enemies: trust in his mercy, leave the issue to him, for it *shall be well.* If thou hast no hope, no Saviour besides him, thou hast his salvation in thy heart, as certainly, though not as fully, as if thou wast already in the region of felicity: he is the hope only of the hopeless; the Saviour, the all-sufficient Saviour, only of the necessitous.

She was needy, and pressed by want, gladly accepted of the invitation given her; notwithstanding she did not consider herself in any wise equal to the maidens of Boaz. Necessity alone makes the gospel invitation suitable and welcome, removes from the mind all needless scrupulousness: before our necessity becomes absolutely urgent and indispensable, we are apt to frame
many

SERMON X.

many excuses, why we should not embrace it. We are too vile, too depraved and unworthy to venture upon privileges so great and distinguishing: we must stay yet a little longer, and remove from the leopard, at least some of his spots, clear the polluted heart from some of its filthiness, and in some measure abridge the power of sin before we can venture to make use of gospel provision; because we are not like the saints of the Lord; our spots are different from their spots; and our character is far inferior to theirs: for under first awakenings, poor sinners are apt to consider the believer as a perfect character, and the church below as little inferior to *that* triumphant, however much the contrary appears in future experience. But when the hungry beggar appears at the gate of the rich man, when shall we see him refuse an alms because of his unworthiness, or make any mortifying comparisons between himself and the domestic servants within. We are not aware how much pride discovers itself in that impious modesty of ours, which makes us say with Peter, *Depart from me, O Lord, for I am a sinful man: Lord, thou shalt never wash my feet.* Little considering that the more sinful we are, we have the more need of the Redeemer's approach unto us; or, that unless we submit to be washed by him, we have no part in his great salvation.

Necessity will make the sinner run to the Saviour's embrace; however secure the Israelite might have dwelt in time past, the moment he commences manslayer, and hears the avenger of blood at his heels, he flees with full speed to the city of refuge, nor dare he slacken his pace till safely lodged within its environs. In like manner, whilst the sinner apprehends himself innocent, or at most no more guilty than others, he may rest very secure and easy; but when sin becomes exceeding sinful; when the clamours of a guilty conscience become loud and alarming; and the voice of condemnation sounds louder and louder, he will, he must flee to Jesus for relief: unworthiness and sin are no longer impediments in the way; but he casts himself at the wounded feet of Jesus, saying, *Though he should slay me, I will trust in him;* if I must perish it shall be here; it shall be crying out for mercy, for there is salvation in none other.

Ruth kept fast by the maidens of Boaz, and was not found in any other field; nor was her departure at all necessary, seeing handfuls were dropped on purpose for her, and none might reproach her for gathering of them. It is good for believers to glean only in the gospel field, to abide fast by the virgin churches, for in wandering abroad there lacketh not danger. Curiosity, if gratified, may lead us into temptation and a snare, and into diverse hurtful lusts, which drown men in perdition. It had been well for Jacob's daughter had she confined her curiosity to the tents of her honoured parent, and his family, and not rambled abroad to see the daughters of the land, to the entire pollution of her person, and dishonour of her character. That is a good direction given by him who possesseth all the treasures of wisdom and knowledge, *If thou knowest not, O thou fairest among women, go thy way forth by the footsteps of the flock, and feed thy kids beside the shepherds' tents.* What can be expected but peril and jeopardy, when we depart from God's appointed way? when itch lays hold of the ear, and curiosity presides in the heart, the erring feet are likely to tread the steps of danger, where foul comfort shall be blasted, and destruction come upon our pleasing sensations. It is good to watch against whatever tempts us to vacate our seats in church assemblies; whatever would induce us to forsake the assembling of ourselves together on the day of the Lord; set the example of the prudent Moabitess before you, and abide by the reapers of our heavenly Boaz.

IId. She ate what was given to her; *he reached her parched corn, and she did eat.* She ate corn —the corn she ate was parched—this parched corn was reached to her—though reached to her by the hand of another, there was enough to suffice her, and still to be left for fresh comers.

At meal-time she ate corn in the field of Boaz; not chaff or husks, as the sinners eat in a strange land; what she ate was healthful and nourishing, not debilitating, and apt to gender disease. Such is the food of the faithful soul, the corn of heaven drawn from the granaries of God; such only can feed the immortal mind, and nourish up the human soul to life eternal. Grace, sovereign grace, reigning through righteousness to eternal life, is corn proper to the flock of Jesus; but that doctrine which centers in self, and exalts the creature, is light and insipid chaff, which never did, which never can administer suitable nourishment. Where the great trumpet is blown, and a free salvation is published, thither resort, for that is parched corn provided for the hungry sinner, the friendless stranger: parched corn, a proper emblem of the believer's food, which hath all passed through the fire, before reached to us by our generous husbandman. The Redeemer's obedience includes the whole of the Christian's nourishment *; upon this he lives throughout his life; on this he lives in his dying moments; and only upon this shall he live within the regions of light and happiness. This is fitly represented by parched corn, as every part of it has passed through the fire, and that

* *Nourishment.* The idea which the author has of the Redeemer's obedience, always includes his death and sufferings, as well as the rectitude of his conduct.

too heated to the utmost. It hath passed the fire of human malice, and hellish rage, as the Evangelists abundantly witness: he was tempted of the Devil, he endured contradiction from sinners against himself, and heard the malicious cry, *Away with him, crucify him, crucify him.* It passed the fire of the burning mountain, which none with safety could touch; the fiery curse of a broken law, which would have pressed any other subject down infinitely lower than the grave; notwithstanding he rose superior to it, in virtue of his indwelling divinity. This holy obedience, the food of the Christian, passed through the fire of divine anger heated to the uttermost, as must clearly appear from that alarming summons given to the sword of justice by the indignant Father, Zech. xiii. 7. *Awake, O sword! against my Shepherd, and against the Man, my fellow, saith the Lord of Hosts: smite the Shepherd, and the sheep shall be scattered.*

Here the adorable Jesus is considered as the Shepherd of his people Israel, called and appointed to office by the eternal Father, and therefore owned for his own Shepherd; my Shepherd. But although the relation and appointment is owned; yet, considered as the sinner's substitute, no mercy is shewn him, but he is treated with the utmost legal severity: divine justice is roused; not the rod of a father, but the sword of a judge is employed againſt him: the rod is for chaſtiſement, but the ſword is for bloody execution, and it awoke in all its fury againſt the perſon of our holy ſubſtitute; ſo that our food is corn of heaven in the earth, and parched by ſufferings the moſt intenſe.

This parched corn was reached unto her; *he reached her parched corn*, before ſhe could have an opportunity of eating: a fit emblem of the conduct of our heavenly Paſtor, who hands forth the bread and the water of life to his humble followers. What we gather, he gives; our induſtry however great, doth not in the leaſt impair his bounty: he reacheth to us the corn of heaven, and we do eat. There are two ways in which the corn of heaven is reached to us; by the public miniſtry, and in private means; but both of theſe in the hand of the Holy Ghoſt, and the former as neceſſary as the latter; and the firſt of theſe is as much his gift as the laſt. It is by faith that we eat; but how can we believe without a preacher; and how ſhall they preach unleſs they be ſent? Now we have heard, becauſe he hath ſent forth his preachers into all the earth, even to the ends of the world: hence it has reached Britain and her Colonies; we who are by nature ſtrangers of the Gentiles, eat more delicate food than that by which elect angels are ſuſtained; becauſe his goſpel hath not come to us in word only, but in power, in much assurance by the Holy Ghost: this is the way in which he reaches it home to our cases, and satisfies the hungry with good things. Indeed experience shews that not only the invitation, but the power to eat; not only the power to eat must come from him, but his hand must reach us every morsel of mental food and refreshment. She ate what was reached to her; unlike to Peter in his mis-judged humility, saying, *Lord, thou shalt never wash my feet: depart from me, O Lord, for I am a sinful man.* She knew that she must either eat or starve, and deemed it better to live upon the bounty of a stranger than to perish by famine: just so will it be with every humbled sinner, who is hunted from all his subterfuges and lying refuges, he will be glad to cast himself entirely upon the goodness of the Saviour, and willingly be beholden to him for salvation: whereas, whilst unmortified to self and sin, you will have many excuses, all seemingly the fruit of humility, and therefore the more soothing to legal pride. For instance, the Saviour's holy person shall never be defiled by the sins of such a wretch as you are: you have too much esteem for him to murder him by your guilt and sin; you would not defile the precious fountain of his blood by washing in it such a polluted and filthy heart as yours: Lord, thou shalt never wash my heart; it is so vile it would defile thy heavenly hand but so much as to touch it. Thence it is that you cannot think of coming to Jesus, till you can do something worthy of his acceptance; or of washing in his cleansing fountain till you have at least purged away the grossest part of your filthiness: thus it is that legal pride assumes the garb of the deepest humility, and imposes itself even upon the dear people of God themselves. But in Ruth you have a very proper example set before you; she ate whatsoever was reached to her, asking no questions either for the sake of conscience or delicacy; go then sinner and do likewise.

Her food was reached to her with a bounteous and liberal hand, for though she ate till nature said it is enough, she left. *She ate, and was sufficed, and left.* Many, long before our day, fed upon the corn of heaven; our fathers did eat bread in this wilderness till they were sufficed, and yet they left enough for their descendents, enough even for us: we also may eat freely and plenteously; for in our Father's house there is bread enough and to spare; therefore, when we have eaten till we are sufficed, there will still be enough for all comers. Though but an handful of corn is cast into the earth, and that too upon the tops of the mountains, so exceedingly fruitful is it that it shall shake like Lebanon, and scatter fruit sufficient to feed all nations, peoples, kindreds, tongues, and languages. Every thing

thing in Christ is plenteous and abundant: with him is plenteous redemption, abundant pardon, and more than conquest: with him are riches of every good; riches of grace, of mercy, and glory; all the treasures of wisdom and knowledge. Therefore there can be no straitness with Christ: all contractedness is in our own bowels, and not in the fulness of the Lord of glory. We have not because we ask not, or because we ask amiss, upon some selfish consideration: if we ask, we must expect what we ask, not in the least on account of any thing in our asking, or of any personal qualification whatever, but merely in a way of independent, sovereign grace. When you and I are filled with his fulness, and quite absorbed in his personal glories, there will be just as much for new comers as there was for us, an inexhaustible fulness still to be entered upon. You see that the natural sun every day irradiates innumerable objects without decreasing its own effulgence: much more the Sun of righteousness, the spring of whose light and life is entirely in himself, and not in another; when all the redeemed hosts shall have lived infinite ages upon his fulness, we shall then find that his stores are undiminished.

IIId. She gleaned until even, notwithstanding she was so plenteously regaled at noon; the plenty with which she was fed had not the least tendency to hinder her diligence: she ate, she was sufficed, and left; yet she arose and gleaned diligently. As the pious Herbert says, "Much would have "more." The adage is true with respect to the things of this life, as the greatest increase in no way tends to abate the thirst of getting. So in divine things, feeding increaseth hunger, drinking serves to inflame our thirst, and feeding plenteously makes us more industrious in gleaning, as is shewn by the history of this Moabitess.

The bounty of Boaz prompted her industry, and plenteous feeding invigorated her for gleaning. If any of you are favoured to-day with a liberal repast, it will not in the least abate either your necessity or diligence; your wants will return in their season, and therefore though you eat now, you must yet glean in future. What Boaz gave to Ruth, she gathered; handfuls were scattered; but as observed in another place, the scattered handfuls must be gathered before she could use them for food. The blessings of grace also are scattered abroad in the gospel field in the greatest abundance; but they must all be gathered in a diligent use of the appointed means. Sovereign grace could, if Infinite Wisdom saw meet, save its objects without the intervention of means; and so might Boaz have given Ruth the handfuls unscattered, but he did not choose to do that, neither does grace choose to do this. God
has

has therefore bound his people to as strict, as conscientious a use of the means, as if upon them only salvation was entirely dependant. And although he hath reserved to himself a sovereign and undeniable right to work by, without, above, or even contrary to them, when he sees meet, we may not expect any blessing without the most diligent attendance upon the ordinary means. What he gives in a way of sovereign goodness, must be gathered in the way of the strictest diligence.

Handfuls of corn were scattered on purpose for her, but scattered no where except in the field of Boaz, therefore she found her account in abiding fast by his houshold maidens. In other places, and under other ministrations, your ears may be tickled, and your fancy delighted, by the pleasing sallies of wit, and lively displays of genius and imagination; but under a pure gospel ministry alone, may you hope to enjoy the plenteous blessings of new covenant grace. Pleasing the ear with that which has little or no tendency to affect the heart; to tickle the fancy, and flatter the imagination, without informing the judgment and enlightening the understanding, will answer no valuable purpose. Were preachers inflamed with all the oratorical powers of Demosthenes or Cicero, unless Jesus Christ, and him crucified, be their theme, they are not likely at all to profit the Lord's people.

This accounts for it why people, even of good parts and taste, are contented to sit under the plain preaching of that gospel, which cautiously avoids the enticing words which man's wisdom teacheth, notwithstanding that thereby they risk their reputation for judgment and taste: not barely contented with the simplicity of the gospel, but holding in comparison of it, all philosophy, by whomsoever taught, to be vain and contemptible; contemptible as the insignificant dross; contemptible as the basest dung. The believer strays not abroad after strangers without suffering loss; he finds his account in abiding fast by the maidens of Boaz, and gleaning in the field of the blessed gospel.

When believers have gleaned till the evening, they never find that they have store laid up for futurity; in this therefore there is a palpable difference between them, and the self-sufficient Pharisees: the latter may sing a requiem to their own souls on account of the goods which they have laid up for many years; but the former set out in emptiness, experience emptiness all their days, and even finish their course in total emptiness. So, from day to day, from his first outsetting in religion to his dying moments, the believer never has store laid up, but lives upon Christ for every hour's supply; nor do I know a better or more lasting evidence of grace, than such a consciousness

ness of nothingness as glorifies Jesus as our all in all. How groundless then are the fears of many who mourn their situation, and at the same time bear about them the best evidences of the Christian life? evidences that they would deem solid and substantial if found in another; but which they pass over unnoticed as found in themselves. I come now to a

IVth. Particular in the conduct of Ruth, which also demands our serious attention. She not only gleaned till evening, but *she beat out that she had gleaned* before she carried any part of it home to her mother-in-law. Corn, even the finest kidney of the wheat, grows encompast with chaff, and therefore must be beaten out and winnowed before it is fit for use. Hence in ancient times the threshing instrument having teeth was in use, and in ages more modern the flail and fan. To explain what the meanest peasant must necessarily be acquainted with, might well be deemed superfluous. I shall therefore proceed immediately to the application; and would observe, that the word is preached by us ministers, so that the infinitely wise God can and doth make it the power of God to salvation. The true word is indeed preached, and perhaps the whole counsel of God is from time to time delivered to you; but,—but it is mixed with much of our own chaff: I speak not this in disparagement of any minister; I hope I can say with Moses, *Would to God all the Lord's people were prophets;* and I think I can even add to it, *Would to God all the Lord's people were successful prophets.* But I speak of others as I feel in myself, and he that knows my heart will witness, that I feel much ignorance, pride, and hypocrisy in my ministrations.

Paul, that incomparable preacher, freely confessed that he saw and prophesied but in part: if he in part, surely we in a very little part; consequently, much of our own chaff is mixed with our Redeemer's wheat; and that you our hearers are called to beat out what you glean, by a diligent search of the Scriptures, by meditation and prayer.

They are noble and ornamental hearers, likely to grow and profit by what they hear, who receive no doctrine upon the preacher's testimony, but diligently search the Scriptures to see whether these things are so. This was the practice of the Bereans, and for this their character is ennobled by the Holy Ghost; and extolled by his amanuensis. Searching the Scriptures is indeed indispensably necessary, in order to distinguish the voice of Jesus from that of Antichrist, and avoiding the paths of heresy and error, as well as to profit by what we hear. This searching of the Scriptures, and comparing of spiritual things with spiritual, will divide between the chaff and wheat, and will

will lead to that meditation that will digest the word you have heard, and render it food for the immortal mind. Amongst beasts, under the legal dispensation, only those were chosen as clean which parted the hoof and chewed the cud; an animal action which figures that contemplation upon the word we have heard, that will make it useful and nutritive. When we hear a sermon with ever so much attention, and think no more of it afterwards, there is but little prospect of its being of much use to us, in animating our frame, and making sin still to be more detestable.

Touching prayer, it has been observed, that it is always seasonable, and in many cases indispensably necessary; necessary prior to our hearing the word, that we may hear with attention, and mingle faith with our hearing; after sermon, that we may profit by what we have heard; that the word preached be not to us like the seed sowed among thorns or stones which cannot grow to maturity; so that he who would reap advantage by the word preached, must pray over it with earnestness.

The word is preached in a mystery, which mere unassisted reason can neither understand nor receive. God manifested in the flesh, is such a mystery of godliness that will require the instructions of the heavenly Prophet himself, in order to subdue our enmity against whatsoever transcends the unassisted efforts of natural wisdom to

P 3   comprehend,

comprehend, and to make us willing to embrace God, and the Father, and Christ, as revealed in the gospel of mysterious grace. How necessary then is prayer, meditation, and searching the Scriptures to our feeding upon the divine testimony? for want of these many are almost famishing amidst the greatest plenty; crying, my leanness, my leanness; whilst the corn of heaven lies in handfuls around all our camp. How diligent will people be about the things of life? things that are comparatively of no consideration, can administer no pleasure in the prospect of dying; and ought not we who have an eternity in view, an ever-during existence to hope for, much more to be diligent in the use of all appointed means to obtain the enjoyment of God and Christ, whilst we are training up for the kingdom of peace and felicity.

Once more, there is yet a

Vth. Part of the conduct of Ruth which deserves the believer's imitation, and which I would a little touch upon before I dismiss the subject. We have already heard that she embraced the generous invitation, and came hither at meal-time—that she sat by the reapers—that she ate the parched corn which was reached to her, till she was sufficed, and left—that she rose up after feeding and gleaned till evening—that she laboriously
beat

beat out what she had gleaned—and now we have to observe,

That having beaten out and cleansed her corn, she carried it all home to her mother Naomi; yea, even when Boaz loaded her with as much as she could carry, as we find in the subsequent part of the story, it all went to the mother: an example, how rarely followed, though so truly worthy of imitation! This intercourse and communion which this young Moabitess kept with her mother-in-law, is capable of improvement very profitable to believers as members of gospel churches.

God bestows gifts and graces upon each of you according to your measure, but not entirely upon your own personal account, the leading and public design of the whole is the building up of the saints, and edifying the body of Christ. It is a mean, ignoble, Antichristian spirit, that leads a professor to live only to himself; yet many such professors there are from whom you hear nothing either of their troubles or comforts: they have no share in the internal communion of the church; they bear no part of the common burden further than assisting in outward things; their hearts have no share, no feeling in the burdens of their brethren. These unsocial spirits walk alone in the midst of company, and live selfish lives even under a gospel profession: but it ought to be considered

dered that the gospel spirit is a social spirit; mutual good is the great end of Christian society, and that the more extensive a man's privileges and gifts, the more he is called to usefulness in the church of God.

The church is our mother, whom we are called to serve and comfort; therefore every comfort you glean ought to be brought home to her; so disposed of and applied that she may share in your pleasure. It is unknown what delight it would afford an assembled church, to hear how the Lord had visited and spoken kindly to any of its members; it would be upon the whole as a token for good, that the Almighty hath neither forsaken nor forgotten them. Every degree of fresh information you receive from the unerring Prophet in the knowledge of himself; every ray of divine light by which the treasures of Scripture knowledge are opened to your understanding, bring directly the first opportunity to your venerable parent for her edification; for the whole community are edified by knowledge imparted to individuals.

The day of the Lord is in a particular manner appointed for a gleaning season, whatever is your success on that day, ought to be imparted to the church in her retired and mixed assemblies. If the Man is pleased to look kindly upon thee, permit thee to gather even among the sheaves, and
cause

cause handfuls to be dropped on purpose for thee; if he invite thee to the bottles, and reach thee food at meal-time, inform thy mother of it all, it will rejoice her heart, and open her lips in praise and thankfulness on thy account, and she shall share in all thy delights, whilst thus she breathes her fervent gratitude, *Blessed be he that did take knowledge of thee; blessed be he of the Lord, who hath not left off his kindness to the living and to the dead!* If it should so happen that the man come not into his field that day, or that thou shouldst not see him, or hear any thing from him; or if he should chide thy unguardedness in venturing into any other field, for not keeping fast by his maidens; or take offence at thy sinful modesty, in not gathering the handfuls dropped on purpose for thee; tell it to the church, tell her every tittle of what passeth between him and thee. Ruth told her mother all that the man said unto her without any reserve. Happy would it be for the church of God, could we with freedom communicate to her all that the Man says unto us whether good or bad. O what love, what delight would glow in every bosom! and how near should we approach to the state of the blessed?

Give your good old mother the church, a taste of the food with which your beloved Bridegroom is pleased to entertain you at meal-times; so shall you have her prayers for the continuance of his bounty

bounty to you, and for wisdom to enable you diligently to attend his field, and go forth with his virgin train. Ruth ate, was sufficed, and left; what she left she brought home to Naomi, and she also shared by this means in the bounty of Boaz.

One thing in the account must by no means be omitted. When Ruth came home from gleaning, Naomi inquired where and with whom she had spent the day; and thus the favour of her love, and the meanness of her circumstances, did not at all lessen her parental authority. No circumstances how dark and distressing soever can deprive a gospel church of the authority of inquiring into the conduct of its members, where, how, and with whom they glean; nor can any thing excuse a church from this as their immediate duty. It is injurious to members to be left at liberty to glean where their fancy may lead them, whether in the field of Boaz or in another field.

Ruth's answer is truly becoming; she sustains the subordinate character of a daughter to admiration. The mother says, *Where hast thou gleaned to day? and where wroughtest thou?* Some saucy, self-conceited young woman would have replied, " What is that to thee? sure I am of age to judge " for myself, and am wise enough to know what " field is most profitable for me." But Ruth, with
becoming

becoming submission replies, *The man's name with whom I wrought to day is Boaz.* When truth and integrity direct our steps, there is no need of the least evasion: we may give a minute account of our conduct. That a gospel church hath authority to inquire into the conduct of all its members, is a truth that cannot be denied; yet there are members who will murmur and complain if a church exerts its authority, and with a sullen air, ill becoming a follower of the meek and lowly Jesus, will dare to reply, " Sure a church is no " prison: have not I a right to go where I will, " so that I neglect not the worship of God?" This unbecoming treatment of a church discovers the greatest ignorance of the principles upon which society is founded.

The end of all society, civil or religious, is that we should be helpful to one another; but if after I am become a member of society, I should consider myself as having a right to break through its fundamental laws with impunity, it would shew that I have neither inclination to, nor knowledge of its leading design. Such treatment of a church evidently discovers an impious neglect of that solemn engagement we entered into with the church, when at first we commenced its members. Then we covenanted before God and man to give ourselves up to one another in the Lord, to strengthen each others hands, and to walk together in all the ordinances of the Redeemer, as far as enabled, without blame. I have indeed remarked, that for thefe twenty years paft, in which I have been converfant with Chriftian people, that I have never heard church authority fpoken lightly of, but by thofe whofe confciences laboured under a ftruggle between guilt and pride: guilt, from a confcioufnefs that their conduct could not bear the ftrict examination of a gofpel church; and pride, which prompted them to feek by every evafive means to conceal their infamy.

But when I fpeak of church authority, I am by no means to be underftood as intending the authority of the minifter; who, in my opinion, can do nothing but as he acts by the power of the church, as their delegate; and has no more power in church government, than any other of its members. A ruler and a preacher are two different characters, and a man may have every quality requifite unto the firft, and be very inadequate to the laft. As to the miniftry of the word, no man is to be his dictator; but as a member and ruler, he is entirely the church's fervant, under their direction, and to them accountable, as much as the moft private of all their members: if the minifter himfelf is accountable to the church, what muft be its authority when acting fimply by a divine warrant over the reft of its members?

Now,

SERMON X.

Now, to dismiss this text, permit me to ask you, my dear hearers, with what weight these things lie upon your mind? whether you really see your necessity of living upon the bounty of Jesus for life and salvation? Know this of a truth, that all who are afar from him shall perish, for the words of eternal life and salvation are only in his possession. Needy sinners, do you consider that the man Jesus is our near kinsman, to whom the right of redemption belongs, and who will not fail to take care of you and yours? Put then your cause into his hand, and so shall you prosper; and drink of the well spring of life and consolation. Let all see with what spirit the ordinances are attended; whether you come to them as those that need assistance, and really seek the blessings of grace; if you do, you will be sure to find, for that is his promise, to which you shall do well to take heed.

SERMON XI.

RUTH iv. 9.

And Boaz said unto the elders, and unto all the people, ye are witnesses this day that I have bought all that was Elimelech's, and all that was Chilion's and Mahlon's of the hand of Naomi.

HAVING briefly treated of the daughters of Naomi, and consequently their different dispositions and conduct, the retrograde motion of Orpah, and Ruth's firm attachment to her mother-in-law; having noted her humility, obedience, and industry, in assiduously gleaning throughout the day in the field of Boaz, we shall now treat of her enlargement, and reward in that dignified station to which she was raised, and the renown conferred upon her by the people of Israel, as one of the honoured mothers of the transcendently illustrious Redeemer. This honour, this reward, consisted in her being owned as near of kin to Boaz, and as such united to him in the bonds of marriage, according to the institutions

of

SERMON XI.

of the Israelitish legislator: concerning which connection some things are to be considered as preliminary before we can come at the union itself; as, on Naomi's part; on the part of Ruth; and on the part of Boaz.

1st. On Naomi's part, some things are to be considered as preliminary to the marriage of Boaz and Ruth.

(1.) The good woman's heart was set upon seeking rest; a comfortable and honourable settlement for her daughter Ruth, who had voluntarily become partaker with her in her afflictions; that she might have no reason to say, that the God of Israel was to her as a barren wilderness, after she had forsaken her kindred and native gods for the love she bore to a mother in Israel. *Shall I not seek rest for thee, my daughter, that it may be well with thee.*

How solicitous was the mother church of the Jews for the poor Gentiles then uncalled, Cant. viii. 8, 9. *We have a little sister, and she hath no breasts; what shall we do for our sister in the day she shall be spoken for? If she be a wall, we will build upon her a palace of silver—if she be a door, we will inclose her with boards of cedar.* Prophetic of that purity of doctrine by which the New Testament church is sustained, and that profitable and pleasing code of discipline by which it is governed and defended: likewise descriptive of the spring from whence we derive thefe bleffings fo eminent, and privileges fo exalted; as derived from the Jews from whom all falvation flows. Jefus himfelf, that foundation and corner of the beauteous fabric, was a Jew in lineage, and fubject to the Jewifh law of circumcifion, notwithftanding the law of ordinances was abolifhed by his myfterious death. The mafter builders who laid the foundations of this palace of filver; thofe fkilful artifts who inclofed the door of the gofpel church with boards of cedar, were all of them Jews, members of that mother church, which fo early interefted herfelf in behalf of her younger, her minor fifter, whom fhe forefaw, by the fpirit of prophefy, would be fpoken for in the time appointed.

In one thing indeed, the analogy will not hold: it was the decline of life with good Naomi when fhe thus fought reft for Ruth her daughter; but the Jewifh church was in the beauty, glory, and vigour of her youth when fhe cared for the Gentiles, *I am a wall*, faith fhe, *and my breafts like towers*. It was when vifion was in its brighteft fplendor, when the word of God was plentiful and abundant. And fuch were the tender fentiments of the fpiritual among the Jews at that time, however thick and gloomy the cloud of ignorance, error, and enmity became in after times amongft them.

Naomi's

SERMON XI.

Naomi's carefulness of her daughter's welfare, is farther analogous to the tender sentiments and solicitous conduct of a gospel church toward those damsels, those virgin souls, who have forsaken all for the sake of Christ and a good conscience, and who have as yet no visible settlement, no visible inheritance in Israel. Jerusalem is always tender towards her daughters, the spouse is solicitous for the happiness of her companions, and the church in this case will use Naomi's words, and say, *Shall I not seek rest for thee, my daughter, that it may be well with thee?* Shall I not bow my knee to the Father of mercies, and make earnest supplication for thee before our common Goel, our near kinsman? shall I not point out before thee the footsteps of the ancient flock, that thou mayest apprehend the good, old, and perfect way.

(2.) She revealed unto Ruth the nearness of relation subsisting between herself and Boaz. Little did Ruth know, when the good man treated her with so much unexpected kindness, that he was her near kinsman, and that she had a legal claim of marriage upon so honourable and excellent a man. How distant from her mind, on receiving the parched corn at his hand, the thought of the nearest alliance which possibly can take place, commencing between her venerable host, and a poor helpless, desolate Moabitish damsel, and less still,

still, if possible, that a race of kings should spring from this alliance; and least of all, that from her womb should proceed the great Messiah, the Saviour of the world. But Naomi tells her, *the man is near of kin to us*, and no doubt had instructed her in the Mosaic law, in reference to the obligation upon the near kinsman to raise up seed to the deceased, prior to her approaching unto Boaz in the threshing floor.

The gospel church, in virtue of the ministry of the word in her assemblies, reveals to seeking souls —to strangers come to glean in their Redeemer's field, his affinity by blood to the children of men, especially those who are divorced from a legal hope. Mahlon's widow may always assure herself that Boaz is her near kinsman: the sinner who is dead to the law, who can no longer hope to live upon his own *well doing*, may assure himself also that Jesus is his Goel, his friend and brother, born on purpose for the adversity of the soul.

But O! little does the poor, trembling, self-condemned and hopeless sinner know, that he has a personal claim upon Jesus as the near kinsman of the perishing. That a guilty convict may warrantably plead consanguinity with the Holy One of Israel; that a dying thief may solicite a seat in the Redeemer's throne: even when informed doctrinally of this affinity, how difficult is it to give credit to a truth so mysterious, and yet so indispensably necessary?

necessary? how strongly unbelief will remonstrate against an appropriation of this blessed truth none can say, besides the man who has endured the personal conflict. But unbelief is the offspring and the parent of error, and publishes nothing but the counsel of the enemy: such is every thing that tends to discourage the helpless and needy from trusting in the Redeemer's perfect and finished salvation. If any sinner ever had room to question the efficacy of the grace of Jesus, surely the thief on the cross was the man: yet he questioned it not, but preferred his petition to the dying Jesus, *Lord, remember me when thou comest into thy kingdom.* Jesus remembered him whilst yet on the cross, and that same day introduced him to the assemblies of paradise, as a trophy of his victory and conquest upon earth.

(3.) Naomi directs her daughter to seek out his retreat, and to come privately to his feet, ver. 4. make confession of the identity of her person, prefer her supplication to him, and even to put him in mind of his duty to her as the near kinsman, under whose shadow she was come to trust. Such instructions are likewise exhibited by the church to her followers and attached friends, as yet unprovided for with comfort in Israel. Seek him in private when no eye but that of Heaven is upon thee, come secretly to his feet, and lay thy helpless, desolate state open before his seat of

mercy;

mercy: freely confess the baseness of thine original; he will not despise thee on account of the hole of the pit from whence thou wast digged. Acknowledge thy former marriage to the legal covenant, but be sure to inform him of the death of thy hope and comfort in thy first husband. Tell him that Mahlon is dead, and that thou art seeking an inheritance in Israel: tell him plainly thou art Ruth, the Moabitess; that thou hast left thy kindred and thy country gods; that thou hast no pleasure in those things of which thou art now ashamed: that if he should reject thee, thou shalt be miserable in both worlds; that thou hast now no possession in the land of Moab, and must be destitute for ever if thou findest not favour in Israel.

Make supplication to him: say to him, *I pray thee spread thy skirt over me,* for I am naked and exposed to the inclemency of the weather. See that wretched infant, Ezek. xvi. how helpless, how hopeless its state! But he passeth by, not with the unconcern of the priest, or of the Levite, but with bowels of compassion, like the good Samaritan: his eye is fixed on its wretchedness; they sparkle with love, and drop with sympathy: he stands fixed, and can proceed no farther: his holy hand stretches forth the crimsoned mantle, and covers all its pollutions. This is Jesus thy friend; Jesus thy dear Redeemer, thine adorable

kinsman:

kinsman: let thy prayer be preferred to him, he will not forsake the poor and needy: plead thy relation to him, for he is the seed of the woman, and the son of man: tell him that thou art bone of his bone, and flesh of his flesh. Art not thou he who was born of a daughter of Adam? who lived and died in the room of such sinners as me? who, with thy dying breath, didst pray for thy murderers, and for me amongst the rest of the bloody train.—Have mercy upon my apparent nakedness, and spread forth thy robe of righteousness over me—regard my pollutions with a pitying eye, and wash me in thy cleansing fountain—suffer a poor, helpless, desolate sinner to be beholden to thy beneficence for life, pardon and salvation. Such words are doctrinally put into the mouths of young converts by the church, careful for their present and eternal welfare.

(4.) Naomi encourages Ruth patiently to wait the issue of the enterprize, assuring her, that it would finally prove to her advantage, chap. iii. 18. *Sit still, my daughter, until thou knowest how the matter will fall: for the man will not rest until he have finished the thing this day.* Probably Ruth might be restless and uneasy about the event; might even deem it scarcely possible that it should terminate so happily as her mother-in-law had encouraged her to hope. But Naomi, better acquainted with the laws of Israel, and with the integrity, rectitude and benevolence of her kinsman, assures both herself and daughter, that he would take care to act the part of a kinsman to them, and that he would not rest till the thing was accomplished.

Young converts are apt to be jealous of the Redeemer's love, and exceedingly to fear that he will never condescend to such misery as theirs: especially if permitted to wait for some length of time under the ministry of the word, without receiving sensible comfort; how prone are they to fear that comfort is not designed for them; and, in a word, that it is not to such as them that he will shew the plenitude of his mercy. But the church, better acquainted with the way of the Lord, assures them, that those who ask, shall receive; who seek, shall find; and that of all that come to him he will in no wise cast out. That although Infinite Wisdom may not seem meet to answer as soon as we call, invariable truth hath assured us that the needy shall not always be forsaken, nor the expectation of the poor perish for ever. And therefore although the vision may seem to tarry, in a manner very discouraging to their view, the spouse encourages her companions to wait for it; assuring them, that in the end it shall speak, and not lie; shall speak good words, and comfortable words unto their souls; as Jesus cannot see a poor sinner perish at the footstool of his throne, whilst it is in the power of his arm to help him out of his misery.

IId. The conduct of Ruth herself, prior to her exaltation, may not be unworthy of our present notice, as it naturally tends to the end proposed.

(1.) She considered herself as a poor ignorant Moabitess, unacquainted with the laws of Israel; therefore she resolves implicitly to obey her mother in all things, *All that thou sayest to me, I will do.* It is remarkable what simplicity attends the young convert on his first setting out in quest of a kingdom; how low his opinion of his own, how high his esteem of the wisdom of the church! He also is ready to say, *All that thou sayest to me, I will do.* He expects scarcely any thing short of perfection, in doctrine and discipline, in the spirit and conduct of the church, till sad experience teaches him from his own feelings, that this militant state is at best a state of imperfection; and that Christ's own sanctified ones are apt to halt both in doctrine and discipline.

(2.) She risked her personal reputation in order to obtain a settlement in the Lord's inheritance; and has been censured for her conduct by many of those who love to cavil at Scriptural characters, and at Scripture itself. But even those pretenders to reason and delicacy ought to consider, that the simplicity of those ancient times admitted of things in common life, which would in these times of rampant luſt, be indelicate and dangerous: that human nature was then univerſally depraved, and in enmity againſt God, will not be denied; nevertheleſs, it cannot be proved that lawleſs love, and wanton luſt, were arrived at the ſtate in which they appear in modern times.

Beſides, it is plain that Boaz, the party moſt intimately concerned in the affair, was far from conſidering her conduct ſo much as indiſcreet, much leſs bordering upon indelicacy; yea, that he conſidered the ſtep ſhe had taken as virtuous and praiſe worthy, Chap. iii. 10. *Bleſſed be thou of the Lord, my daughter: thou haſt ſhewed more kindneſs in the latter end, than at the beginning, in as much as thou followedſt not young men, whether poor or rich.* ver. 11. *And now, my daughter, fear not, I will do to thee all that thou requireſt: for all the people of my city do know that thou art a virtuous woman.* After ſuch a teſtimony of Ruth's virtue from this venerable Hebrew, the party moſt nearly concerned, one would ſuppoſe that *little critics*, at the diſtance of three thouſand years, would bluſh to cenſure this amiable Moabiteſs.

In this, however, ſhe is not alone; for who ever yet ſought a ſettlement in Iſrael, a kingdom of glory and felicity, but at the expence of their reputation. That Jewiſh Rabbi could not put in a word in favour of Jeſus and his religion, but

he

he is instantly branded with coming out of Galilee. Saul was in great esteem whilst he was mad with rage against the church, but as soon as brought to the feet of Jesus, and become a preacher of salvation, he is held to be a seditious person, a disturber of the people, a man who turned the world upside down. The moment your soul is laid low at the feet of Jesus, and your cry is for free mercy, you commence fanatics and enthusiasts in the esteem of the wise and prudent, from whom the mysteries of the kingdom are concealed: agreeable to this, our blessed Lord tells his hearers, that *if any man will be his disciple, he must deny himself, take up his cross daily, and follow him.* Yea, he denounceth a curse upon those who are spoken well of by all men, and beloved by the world. So that if you would win Christ, you must be content to part with your reputation for sense and prudence, and be willing to be a fool in the eyes of the intelligent worldling.

(3.) When Ruth lay at the feet of Boaz, she declared who and what she was, *I am Ruth thine handmaid*, a woman made drunk with affliction, desolation and sorrow. So freely does the poor sinner make confession at the feet of the Saviour. I am Ruth, the poor Moabitish damsel, drawn away by the good report I have heard of thy land and country: I am a guilty descendant of apostate Adam;

Adam; one who juftly merits thy wrath and indignation, yet look up unto the feat of mercy: one who may juftly be fent down to hell to take up my abode with devils and damned fpirits, but would fain obtain an inheritance with thy fanctified ones: one who has deftroyed myfelf by tranfgreffion, yet looks up unto thee for help and pardon: Lord be merciful to me a finner. Like unto Ruth, you will make fupplication to Jefus, whilft you lie in fufpenfe at his feet faying, I pray thee, fpread thy wing over thy handmaid, and caft not out a poor helplefs finner, who is come to truft in thy fhadow: cover me with the robe of righteoufnefs, and clothe me with the garments of falvation.

As farther directed by Naomi, fhe pleads his kindred, *thou art a near kinfman;* and fo may the finner plead with Jefus, and ufe his relation as an argument to win his regard: for Jefus is thy Goel, thy kinfman, O fenfible finner! and thou mayeft as warrantably afpire to the bleffings of his grace, and complete falvation, as fhe might afpire to this honourable relation. She had the word to warrant her conduct; thou haft the fame. Thy Jefus will take thy trufting in his falvation as much a kindnefs as Boaz took the conduct of Ruth, and he will do all that thou requireft of him. Allow me to fay, that in feeking after the bleffed Jefus, and defiring to be found in him, thou

SERMON XI.

thou art aspiring to the greatest honour which God can confer upon a mortal worm; and by so doing thou pleasest and honourest him; for he is glorified by giving rather than by receiving.

(4.) Ruth renounced all other society for the sake of Boaz, even before she knew that he would act the part of a kinsman towards her; and in this she shadows forth the poor, convinced, sensible sinner. At all events he is necessitated to forsake the vain pleasures, and uncertain honours of this transitory world; *the lusts of the flesh, the lusts of the eye, and the pride of life;* the sins to which he has been addicted, and company with which he has been connected. Should he even be miserable in the future world, he can no longer live in the sinful practices and changing customs of this; and whatever becomes of him hereafter, he will choose religion now, even upon its own account. The things in which he formerly delighted, are become his shame and burden; every past pleasure is become the parent of present pain: the company from whom he could not refrain, are now quite disgusting to him: all of which are to others, if not to himself, so many convincing evidences, that the Spirit of God has begun the work of sanctification with power in the soul; and are to the church a manifest insurance of the enlargement of the captive from his prison and fetters.

(5.) Once

(5.) Once more: Ruth told Naomi all that the man faid to her, fhe withheld nothing from her; if good, that fhe might rejoice with her, and, if otherwife, that fhe might fympathize with her in her diftreffes. How open and free are many young converts in communicating their experience? they are apt to tell all that the adorable Man Chrift Jefus faith unto them; till having unhappily caft their pearls before fwine, they fee the pearls trampled under foot, and feel themfelves rent, they become as referved as ever they were free: and being deceived by fome under a profeffion, they fufpect the whole, and will have no manner of confidence in any. But, as obferved in a former difcourfe, it were well if every daughter of the church could find freedom to tell her mother all that the Man fays unto her, whether in a way of reproof or confolation. And happy were it for individuals if fuch were the general temper of the church, that this might be done with fafety to our own peace. Having thus confidered the fpirit and conduct of mother and daughter, I fhall,

IIId. Attend to the conduct of Boaz, prior to his union with the fair Moabitefs, and fee how far it may tend to lead us to contemplate the ways of Jefus towards his people.

(1.) He acted the part of a prudent and vigilant hufbandman, who overlooked his rural affairs

fairs in his own person, and left not the winnowing of his grain solely to his servants. He went into the threshing floor, and attended to the winnowing of his barley himself *. *I also*, saith Jesus, *went down into the garden of nuts, to see the fruits of the valley; to see whether the vine flourished, the pomegranate budded* †. Yes, the heavenly husbandman is at the head of his own affairs, and suffereth none of his servants, how skilful soever, to act but by his direction. He comes into his church, his threshing floor, to inspect the labours of his servants, and to examine thoroughly the grain to be laid up in his granary. When any pretended servant of his shall take upon him to act independently of Jesus, or, which is the same thing, to act without his authority, he becomes Antichrist, and so far an enemy to the Redeemer's power, as sole proprietor of the threshing floor.

Whenever the Redeemer, our exalted Lord, condescends to come into his threshing floor, it is usually to winnow his wheat from the chaff. It was so at his coming in the flesh, according to that of his forerunner the Baptist ‡, *I indeed baptize you with water unto repentance; but he that cometh after me is mightier than I, whose shoes I am not worthy to bear; he shall baptize you with the Holy*

* Chap. iii. 2. † Cant. vi. 11. ‡ Matth. iii. 11, 12.

Ghost

Ghost and with fire. Whose fan is in his hand, and he will thoroughly purge his floor, and gather his wheat into his garner: but he will burn up the chaff with unquenchable fire. In what an astonishing manner did the conduct and doctrine of Jesus divide between man and man, separate the self-sufficient, and the helpless sinner; between the proud Pharisees, and harlots and publicans. The parable of the Pharisee and Publican will be held in everlasting remembrance by the church of God; and blessed shall they be who shall enjoy the Publican's portion, and come down justified from the divine tribunal.

When Christ came in the Spirit, and preached his gospel by the mouths of his apostolic legates, it was still the same; still produced the same separation. To hear one part of a multitude crying out, on one hand, under extreme anguish of soul, *Men and brethren, what must we do?* and on the other hand, another part of the same multitude raging against the preachers, as men drunken with new wine, morning drunkards, which are the worst of all, must need give us a very affecting view of the winnowing and dividing quality of the preached gospel: yet this influence, so amply manifested at the feast of Pentecost, has invariably attended the preaching of the gospel from that time down to the present; and in what age soever, or where soever the gospel

has

has been preached, it has proved a favour of death to the self-sufficient, and foolishness to the wise in the world, as well as the favour of life, and the power of God to the salvation of all who believe. Blessed are they, and only they, who are not offended with the person, grace and righteousness of Jesus.

When Christ comes into the soul, in a convincing and converting way, it is still the same; his business is to winnow. By the breath of his fan to disturb the chaff, and draw forth our latent corruptions to view; to put our hope to the trial, and manifest its foundation to be but sand: to discover the emptiness and insufficiency of all creature dependence and delights, and bring the soul to an entire submission to the righteousness of God. How stripping this season? when all heart goodness, integrity of intention, sincere endeavours to please, strong resolutions to amend, and supposed capacity to will and do, flies before the word, in the hand of the Spirit of God, as chaff before the wind of the fan. Nothing is left but a mass of sin and wretchedness. The self-sufficient, the man of virtue, and self-esteem, must excuse me if I plan my doctrine here according to my own experience; and let him believe, that if he has not sustained these winnowings of gospel truth, they have been familiar to me; and I have most certainly as good a right to proclaim my
own

own wretchedness, as any man in the world can have to talk of his own personal excellence. But from my very heart, I pity those who are strangers to these winnowing influences of the gospel, which I consider, upon good ground, as essential to final salvation. But to return to the history of Boaz, it is recorded of him

(2.) That he took up his lodging for the night by the heap of corn; which, without any force put upon this transaction, may lead us naturally enough to contemplate the presence of Christ with his people. If ever you would see Jesus; if you would obtain any favour at his merciful hand, you had best look for him by the heap of wheat; seek him in the threshing floor amongst the assemblies of his people. His presence is promised in a peculiar manner to his assembled church, *Wherever two or three are met together in my name, there am I in the midst of them to bless them*, are the words of the true and faithful Witness. Here are no stipulated conditions; but the promise is absolute, and the grace is certain. As sure as you meet together in the name of Christ, so sure is he present with you to bless you, either in one sense or other: only then examine well into the motives of your meeting, whether you indeed meet in the name of Christ; if you do, there is no more reason to doubt his spiritual presence with
you,

you, than there is to doubt his corporeal presence being now in heaven.

It was with his eye upon this truth, that the Apostle thus cautions the believing Hebrews in his epistle to them *; *to hold fast the profession of their faith without wavering, not forsaking the assembling of themselves together, as the manner of some was.* And why this care to keep up a conscientious assembling of yourselves together, if there was not some peculiar privilege connected with it? and what privilege can there be abstracted from the presence of Jesus with his assembled people? It is vain and absurd; it is even fanatical, to hope for the comforts of his love but in his own appointed ways. To meet conscientiously, to meet constantly with his assembled church, is his appointed way, and where, therefore, ye may warrantably expect his presence, and hope for the blessings of his redemption.

(3.) She lay at his feet, she waited till midnight, dark midnight, before he spoke to her: this is frequently the case with those who seek to Jesus for life; he puts their faith, hope, and patience to the fullest trial, before he is pleased to manifest his lovingkindness, the more effectually to bring them off from every sandy foundation, and to endear his own person, blood, and righte-

* Chap. x. 25.

ousness more to the heart. When the Syrophœnician woman came crying after him in behalf of her daughter, he answered her *not a word:* on her persisting in her suit, he was requested by his disciples to send her away, because *truly* she was troublesome to them. He answered her with a seeming repulse, *It is not meet to take the children's bread, and cast it unto dogs:* and after all, having put her to the trial before all the people, he highly commends her faith, and treats her with uncommon regard.

The blackest cloud was drawn over Joseph's fortune just before his advancement to government. The hand of oppression was most severely felt by the Israelites just at the eve of their deliverance from bondage. So it is most commonly midnight darkness with the soul, when we are favoured with an interview with Jesus, either at our first enlargement from bondage to the law, or subsequent manifestations. It was at midnight God visited Jacob at Bethel; at midnight he condescended to be wrestled with by the same patriarch at Peniel. In the night of darkness, light shines forth; on the mount of straits, deliverance is revealed. When brought to his feet, Boaz

(4.) Makes Ruth explain herself. Who art thou? what dost thou want with me? I am Ruth; Ruth the produce of incestuous contact; Ruth an helpless Moabitess. What dost thou want? speak plain,

plain, and shew me thy request. I want that thou shouldst act the part of a kinsman towards me: spread, I pray thee, thy skirt over me, for I am come to seek a settlement in the Lord's inheritance; for the sake of which I have left my father's house, and the idols of my native land. Jesus also brings his people to an explanation of their base original and native connections; of their personal misconduct, and heart alienation from God; of what they deem most valuable for time and eternity; and what for this purpose they require of him: for he will be inquired of. Although all blessings are laid up in him, he will have his blessings sought for by earnest prayer and supplication. Good reason indeed that we should lie low at those blessed feet, for they once were pierced for our salvation. And, O sinner! with what freedom mayest thou open thy case to the friend and confident of perishing sinners, for he is an Israelite indeed, in whom there is no guile. O, my soul! make Jesus thy confident, so shalt thou have a friend in the time of need, like Ruth the Moabitish damsel. Go to him alone as she did, and according to his own direction, so shalt thou prosper in the suit preferred. For,

(5.) Having brought her to an explanation, Boaz dealt honourably with her, and spake to her only the words of kindness and compassion. Far from blaming her confidence, or rashly censuring the step she had taken, in thus exciting him to his duty, he highly applauds her for the honour she had done him *; *Blessed be thou of the Lord, my daughter, thou hast shewed more kindness in the latter end than at the beginning, in as much as thou followedst not young men whether rich or poor; and now, my daughter, fear not, I will do to thee all that thou requirest.* From which it is plain, that Boaz took it as kindness that she should glean in his field, rather than that of another man's. But a greater kindness still, that she should take this method of putting him upon obeying the institutes of his God. Jesus is also far from upbraiding the soul that comes to him for life and salvation: he never once upbraided the dying thief with his former villany, nor penitent Magdalene with her former ways however unclean; but of all who come to him, he by no means casteth out. The dying villain no sooner solicits his remembrance, than he obtains this gracious promise, *This day shalt thou be with me in paradise.* The only instances which look any thing like upbraiding of the sinner by the Redeemer, are those of the woman of Samaria and Paul. To the first he said, *Thou hast well said I have no husband, for thou hast had five husbands, but he whom thou now hast is not thy husband.* But does he not immediately reveal himself to her, and send her into the city

* Chap. iii. 10.

SERMON XI.

to preach his gospel? To Paul he said, *Saul, Saul, why persecutest thou me?* and also reveals himself to him immediately; sends him forth to preach that gospel which he had hitherto persecuted.

(6.) Boaz gives her encouragement to wait in expectation of what he would do for her. *And now, my daughter, fear not, I will do to thee all that thou requirest.* This is also an emblem of the conduct of Jesus towards his people. It is not always, perhaps very seldom, that he is pleased to manifest himself to them on their first application to him; but usually he gives some staying, encouraging, supporting word, before he makes himself fully known to his people as their own Jesus, their all-sufficient Redeemer. There is a set time to favour sensibly, and Jesus must do all things decently and in order. According to the customs of Israel, must regulate the dispensations of his grace by the purposes of Infinite Wisdom, and take his Moabitess honourably to his bosom. But, O seeking soul! he will go about it, he will not be at rest till he has finished thy deliverance; and in the mean while thou shalt live upon his benefits, and his bounties shall sustain thee.

Thus I have cleared the way to the intended marriage, by considering its antecedents, or preliminaries as they lie with the mother, the daughter, and with Boaz, and shall make the marriage itself, God willing, the subject of another discourse.

SERMON XII.

RUTH iv. 9, 10.

And Boaz said unto the elders, and unto all the people, ye are witnesses this day, that I have bought all that was Elimelech's, and all that was Chilion's and Mahlon's, of the hand of Naomi. Moreover, Ruth the Moabitess, the wife of Mahlon, have I purchased to be my wife, to raise up the name of the dead upon his inheritance, that the name of the dead be not cut off from among his brethren, and from the gate of his place: ye are witnesses this day.

THE second head of discourse on this subject at first proposed, was to speak of the purchase made by Boaz, and of his marriage to Ruth the Moabitess. Under which general head we shall consider, Ist. The manner. IId. The matter of the purchase which he made; and IIId. The rites of the marriage itself. Each of which we may accommodate to gospel purposes, and, if duly attended to, may serve to display the excellent lovingkindness of our gracious redeeming Kinsman.

Ist. The

1st. The manner in which the purchase of Ruth and her inheritance was effected, falls, according to our plan, first under our consideration. And we find it

(1.) To have been openly transacted in the gate of the city before the elders of the people. The upright intentions of this honourable Israelite had no need of private and clandestine means for their accomplishment; the law of his God being his rule, his conduct was able to bear the most public scrutiny. Those actions are to be suspected which require the aid of darkness and privacy; as none besides evil deeds need to shun the searching light. Although convinced of his near alliance with this daughter of Moab, of his own duty as a kinsman, and now, by her endearing conduct drawn to affect her tenderly, he would avoid whatever might seem to be but an appearance of any ground of reproach upon either of the parties concerned; and therefore transacted the whole in the public gate of the city.

When Jesus, our excellent, our most holy Redeemer, was about to redeem his church out of the hands of her enemies, about to purchase to himself an everlasting possession, and bring home the daughter of the Gentiles, the younger sister to his dwelling, he does all things in the broad face of the open day, before men and angels: in such an open and public manner as to render heaven, earth,

earth, and hell, the witnesses of his unparalleled transactions. Without the gate of his city he paid down the price of our redemption, whilst the sun that enlightens our horizon beheld with horror the amazing deed, and the rifting rocks proclaimed, *We are witnesses*. Men and angels; angels celestial, and angels infernal, witnessed the dying agonies of our expiring Kinsman. When he weds the soul to himself in the day of calling grace, it is the same; it is by the public ministry of the word, in the hand of his Spirit, that he brings her to his feet, to solicit redemption through his blood, the forgiveness of her sins; and when he speaks kind and affectionate words to the heart, the very countenance will tell all that he hath said unto you; he even brings to an open separation from the customs and company of the world, and adherence to his people and ordinances in a way of profession.

When he espoused the Gentile church to himself, it was as it were by the sound of a trumpet, so very open and public, that the voice of his heralds *went into all the earth, and their words to the ends of the world*; so that all heard, and had notice of the gracious design. And it shall still be so, when at the last day, he *shall come the second time without sin, to the salvation of his people*. He shall openly acknowledge them for his own; in the face of heaven, earth, and hell, shall espouse them

them to himself for ever in faithfulness and loving-kindness. Whilst hell trembles with horror, burns with indignation, and rages with malice, heaven shall resound with acclamations of praise over the Bridegroom and his beloved bride; and he, more tender of his love than the turtle of her young, shall rejoice over her with eternal delight, shall rejoice to feed her for ever out of his own personal fulness of grace and glory. Thus, believers, whatever debasing thoughts of yourselves ye may indulge, your infinitely amiable Lord is not ashamed of his attachment to you, is not ashamed to call you brethren, to call himself the Bridegroom of your souls. O bless the Lord, ye souls of his people! let heart and hand be devoted to him whilst existence endures!

(2.) In the redemption of Ruth and her inheritance, every thing must be transacted with decency and order; therefore as there was a kinsman nearer than Boaz, who consequently had the prior right of redemption, it was necessary that every thing should be settled with him before he could proceed in the work intended.

It was so with respect to the church, there was a kinsman who had a right prior to that of Christ. According to the order of things in the œconomy of revelation, the law was our first lord and wedded husband. The law, in its covenant form, is that way of life to which the soul naturally adheres,

heres, and upon which it founds every expectation of future good; nor can it ever be won over to the way of grace, till all hope of being justified by works is slain. Then, and not before, the soul will be brought to the feet of Jesus, saying, *Spread, I pray thee, thy skirt over me, for thou art a near kinsman.* But Jesus must have the consent of the law, in order to which he must consult its honour, fulfil its tenor, and endure its penalty. God, in the character of a lawgiver, being as tenacious of his honour as in that of the God of mercy. And surely this honourable Israelite, in whom there is no guile; this adorable Kinsman, designed the righteousness of his people, will do that which is right, and will therefore never wish to indulge the mercy and benevolence of his own compassionate heart, at the expence of the honour and veracity of the law, even in its covenant form. Before, therefore, the heavenly Bridegroom could take his betrothed bride home to his house, he was under a necessity of settling every thing to the entire satisfaction of the law, that he might obtain its permission to take his Moabitess to himself to be his wife.

Boaz went up to the gate, and sat him down there, and behold the kinsman of whom Boaz spake came by; unto whom he said, Ho, such a one, turn aside, sit down here, and he turned aside, and sat down. And he said unto the kinsman, Naomi that is come again out of the country of Moab, selleth a parcel of land which was our brother Elimelech's, and I thought to advertise thee, saying, buy it before the inhabitants, and before the elders of my people. If thou wilt redeem it, redeem it: but if thou wilt not redeem it, tell me that I may know; for there is none to redeem it besides thee, and I am after thee. And he said, I will redeem it. Then said Boaz, what day thou buyest the field of the hand of Naomi, thou must also buy it of Ruth the Moabitess, the wife of the dead, to raise up the name of the dead upon his inheritance. And the kinsman said, I cannot redeem it for myself, lest I mar mine own inheritance.

The nearer kinsman probably having children of his own, deemed an accession to his family by another wife, of dangerous consequence by confounding his seed, and injurious to his present children, therefore refused to act that part by Ruth for which, as the nearer kinsman, he was qualified, and delivered up his pretensions as such to Boaz.

The law, in its covenant form, had the prior right and claim upon mankind, but could not redeem the alienated possession. It is said to be weak through the flesh in this respect: and what ever becomes of the ruined race, no delinquent may hope for redemption, or even favour from that covenant: it has an inheritance of its own

which

which muſt not be marred on any account: its holineſs, truth, and juſtice are inviolable, and conſiſtent with which it can ſhew favour to no criminal whatever. Redeem the inheritance who may, the law will have its own inheritance unmarred; have its honour maintained inviolable, as holy, juſt, and good: have the purity of the precept, and the equity of its penalty, maintained beyond controverſy. Indeed, when it is conſidered that the law is none other than a tranſcript of the infinite Mind, as ſoon may Jehovah part from his perfections, and ceaſe to be the juſt and holy One, as the law give up any of its prerogatives. Therefore not to redeem, but to condemn the guilty is its province. Yet being duly honoured by a perfect obedience either in perſon, or by ſubſtitute, it demands no more; it allows the ſinner to eſcape under the ſhadow of his repreſentative, and delivers up its future authority into the hand of Jeſus. *Redeem thou my right.*

The right delivered up to Boaz, the other claimant muſt have his *ſhoe pulled* off in token of loſt authority, and to ſhew that thenceforth he had no juſt right ſo much as to ſet his foot on the inheritance in queſtion. In like manner, the *law* being magnified, honoured, and ſatisfied, it delivers up all its authority into the hand of Jeſus, diſclaiming all right whatever ſo much as to approach the purchaſed poſſeſſion in its covenant capacity;

capacity; and renouncing all claim upon those who lie at his feet as the near kinsman. How great, O believer, is this privilege to them who have no might or power to perform duty, to be delivered from that covenant which can be satisfied with nothing short of perfect obedience! which denounceth death for the smallest defect! but thy deliverance is complete and eternal. The law otherwise than in the hand of Jesus has now no more to do with thee, than if it had never been given, or if thou hadst never offended against the purity of its precept.

When the first claimant, or nearest kinsman, refused to marry the widow and to raise up seed to his brother, it was appointed that she should pluck off his shoe in token of disgrace, and spit in his face, as finally renouncing all connection with him; from which time he was called in Israel, him that hath his *shoe pulled off*.

It is with all reverence I speak of a point so delicate, when I have to do with a law which is holy, just, and good; yet there is something not unlike to this takes place, when the soul is first driven from the legal to the gospel hope. He hath long lain at the bottom of mount Sinai, looking up to the burning throne, imploring patience to be exercised with him, and time to turn his hand, promising finally to make good his payment, and satisfy its strict demands. But still it is to no purpose; the law is inexorable; it knows not how to shew mercy. Meeting with nothing but bitter reproaches, heavy accusations, and tremendous curses from that quarter, hope sickens, and at last perisheth, from the moral impossibility apprehended of doing any thing acceptable and pure in its sight. But when Jesus speaks words of kindness to the soul; when he makes the fulness of his grace, and plenary satisfaction known, with what alacrity does the soul reject its authority, and appeals to the Redeemer totally and finally, renouncing all allegiance to it as a condition of acceptance with God, and of our enjoyment of eternal life. This is a delicate proposition, and I beg to be heard attentively on it. I mean not a renouncing of the law in any sense, which can give countenance to libertinism; for the very man who, to take up his rest in Jesus, renounceth the moral law, as a covenant of life, on obedience to which depends his everlasting all; I say, this very man most heartily approves of, and most cordially embraceth it, as the best and the only rule of conversation ever exhibited, considered in the hand of a mediator. Indeed, the profane use which has been made of this truth, and the extreme to which some men of evil minds have carried this renounciation of the law, to the encouragement of all manner of licentiousness, has intimidated others from that candid disquisition

tion which the importance of the subject requires; so difficult is it to escape one extreme when we labour to avoid another.

The middle way is most commonly the path of judgment, and in this case it brings the greatest honour to the law, as the most perfect rule of obedience that ever was, or ever will be exhibited to either angels or men; whilst it rejects its covenant form as inadequate to every purpose of grace, and design of everlasting love. But this is as different from the doctrine of modern ranters and Antinomians, as light is from darkness; this is the very doctrine delivered by Paul, Rom. vii. and for which he himself was deemed an enemy to holiness and good works, notwithstanding he maintained the justice, goodness, and holiness of the law as a rule of conversation: and thus the fruit of good works is raised up to the honour of the law, notwithstanding it is dead to us, and we to it, as a covenant of works.

We shall now pass from the mode or manner of the purchase, to the things purchased, which was designed as the

IId. Head of discourse, and to which we shall now attend.

The description here given of it is very comprehensive, *All that was Elimelech's, all that was Chilion's, and all that was Mahlon's.*

(1.) *All*

(1.) *All that was Elimelech's.* His sole property descending to Naomi and Ruth, upon his demise, and that of his two sons, upon Orpah's rejection of the inheritance of Israel, and all that descended from him to them, was now the matter of the present purchase.

Elimelech, as I told you in a former discourse, signifies, " My God the King," therefore to accommodate the history to gospel purposes, the doctrine will be " Jesus, our near Kinsman, re-
" deemed and purchased all that belonged to our
" God the King." Redemption by Christ supposeth the state of its objects to be that of slavery; therefore can have no reference to sinless angels, because they were never enslaved : and as it is confined to those who in a special and peculiar manner belonged to Elimelech, it will fix the bounds of redemption to the chosen of his love, and the preserved of his grace. Jesus addressing his heavenly Father in the behalf of his people, thus says, *Thine they were, and thou gavest them me.* His by his own sovereign and free choice of them in his Son, to be the adopted of his grace. Having thus chosen them in, he also preserved them in Christ when fallen in Adam, and with him exposed to wrath and ruin.

All the chosen being the property of God, all the chosen were given to Jesus for redemption when fallen; and actually redeemed in the day of saving power: not one left unnoticed, unransomed, and unprovided for, but all that was Elimelech's were purchased for the Redeemer's own inheritance: not one besides, for the business of the kinsman here, was only with what peculiarly belonged to the Father. What their number is, or what proportion they bear to those that shall be left, is no part of my concern: nor what reasons induced the Almighty Father to choose some, and to leave others; it is enough for me to see it one of the fundamental truths of revelation, and I rest satisfied that God, who worketh all things after the council of his own will, can well justify himself to his creatures: moreover, that the same justice which might have left the whole, when become sinners, cannot be impeached for having left some unprovided for by that salvation which is the object of their natural aversion. The business of Boaz on this occasion was not what should become of the possessions of other men, but to redeem and secure the property of Elimelech to the family. Neither was it the business of Jesus in this world to inquire what should become of the children of the Devil, but redeem his Father's property, and everlastingly secure their inheritance unto them; so that all who were chosen in him, should finally enjoy the pleasures and immunities of paradise.

(2.) The

(2.) The matter of the purchase under consideration was all that belonged to Chilion the son of Elimelech. Chilion, signifies *perfect*, and how remote soever he himself might be from being any figure of the blessed Jesus, the name in this sense of it is very applicable to the person of the Son of God, who is white and ruddy, the chief among ten thousands, and altogether lovely; whose ways are all integrity, and whose words are inviolable truth; which makes the spouse to say of him, *his mouth is most sweet, yea, he is altogether lovely*. Chilion's property here referred to, is perfectly answerable to the state of the elect, considered in union with the adorable Immanuel. Perfect, spotless, and pure must the members be, because such was their head in whom they were chosen. Christ and his church, in the original choice, were not considered in that situation into which the latter fell in Adam, but in all the resplendency of that glory, and the brightness of that perfection, in which they shall appear in the paternal kingdom. This need not seem strange when it is considered, that being in Adam as their old covenant head, they were considered just what he had made himself; in like manner what the Son of God himself was, such were, and such are they who are considered in him. All then who were chosen in Christ from everlasting, were considered as perfect, all fair, and without spot in him: all thus perfect in him were the matter of his purchase.

Chilion also signifies *wasted*, and is truly descriptive of the awakened sinner *. He was once alive without the law, but the commandment coming in the day of divine power, slays his legal hope, and revives sin in all its defilement and malignity. He feels himself wasted, ruined, and undone: stript of his primitive integrity and innocence; stript of moral capacity to do the will of God, and yet without strength to abide the penal consequences of his disobedience: wasted with respect to the goodness of his heart, and rectitude of conduct; his beauty withers as the fallen leaf, and his glory fades as the flower that is cut down. His former foundations of hope are razed, and every refuge of lies cast into a general ruin; the whole world is to him as a waste, howling wilderness, in which he can have no pleasure, and is yet destitute of hope in another. Yet a sense of being thus wasted by reason of sin, is a sure and infallible evidence of your being the Redeemer's purchase. All that was Chilion's; all that are sensibly wasted, and brought, with the dying thief,

* I am so far from thinking it an impropriety to apply the name Chilion to Christ, and his members, that there appears to me a real beauty in it, seeing the same word is at once expressive of the perfection of the Head, and the personal ruin of the members.

to supplicate his favour, who alone can be a refuge to the dying sinner, and such every saint shall find himself when he comes to give up the ghost. Though you should live as saints, my dear friends, you must lay your account for dying as sinners; and, if I do not exceedingly mistake, you will find as much need of Jesus, and fresh communications from his fulness in your dying moments, as ever you did in your lives, or may do at this present moment; and whatever yours may be, I am sure that my necessity is great.

There is yet another sense in which the word is used by some, which is, *like a dove*. How far the Holy Ghost might intend this history as adumbrative of the blessed gospel, I have more than once told you that I pretend not to say, but surely there is something here which is truly analogous to that blessed scheme. Here we first view the elect as standing perfect in Christ from eternity, even when fallen in Adam; in their fallen state as ruined and wasted by sin, and as recovered by grace. In a fallen state, the souls of even the elect lie in the ruins of humanity, as among the pots of Egypt, of sin, and affliction. But by calling grace, the soul is made as the wings of a dove, covered with silver, and whose feathers are yellow gold.

The fruits of the Spirit are truly ornamental, and produce this effect wherever they are wrought.

SERMON XII.

They are wrought in every converted soul; for he is become the subject not only of the Spirit, but of faith, hope, and charity, &c. as his blessed fruits and graces. Hence when we read of the King's daughter, we hear of her being all glorious *within*, as well as being clothed in wrought gold: or of the church, we shall find her clothed with the garments of salvation, as well as covered with the robe of righteousness. Holiness ever becometh the house of the Lord; and uprightness of heart those who stand in the courts of our God; so the fruits of the Spirit will ever adorn the subjects of grace; and faith, hope, and charity shall abide in the heirs of heaven and happiness.

(3.) Boaz, on that day, purchased all that was Mahlon's. This was the husband of Ruth, and his name signifies *infirmity:* exactly agreeable to the heirs of grace, purchased by our heavenly Kinsman. They feel their infirmity, and groan under an afflicting sense of it, till set at liberty by the Spirit of Jesus: they are like him whose hand was withered; they cannot work out their own salvation; the sick of the palsy who could not walk; no more can they in the ways of righteousness and true holiness: they are like the man born blind, and cannot see, therefore their daily cry is, *Lord, that I might receive my sight:* and like the deaf adder, they cannot hear to edification. In a word, they are the very people described in the parable, as *poor* and *maimed, halt* and *blind*; so that they cannot do the good that they would.

How helpless is the state of the convinced sinner! how wretched and miserable the condemned criminal, when the horrible sentence is denounced upon him! such is the state of that sinner in whose heart the sentence of death is passed, till the word of salvation present him with a full and free pardon; yet such is his infirmity, that could pardon and salvation be obtained by performing any, the slightest condition, he must die in despair of ever fulfilling the terms, incapable of a truly good thought of himself. Possest of an evil heart of unbelief, an heart deceitful above all things, and desperately wicked, yet cannot of himself control it in the least, nor wash away the smallest of its stains; the poor believer in seasons of darkness and distance, is apt to conclude that his case is singular, and his spots different from those of God's children: yet this discovery of pollution, this sense of incapacity either to will or do, only proves you to be the Redeemer's purchase; for he purchased all that was Mahlon's, all the sons and daughter's of infirmity.

Mahlon, also signifies a *song*, which may lead us to reflect on the believer's character. For, although they have their days of mourning and nights

nights of anguish here below, they have also their short seasons of singing. On the back of some sore temptation, or some deep affliction, when God appears to them, and says unto the heart, *Behold me*, how is the heart filled with gladness and the lips with praise! Israel, although in a waste, howling wilderness, could sing, when God had brought them through the deep, and delivered them from the hosts of Egypt. There are seasons, how short, and how seldom soever, in which the believer says, *I will greatly rejoice in the Lord, my soul shall be joyful in my God, because he hath clothed me with the garments of salvation, and covered me with the robe of righteousness.* And eternity is coming, in which they shall sing the song of Moses and the Lamb for ever and ever, so that the purchase of our holy Redeemer may be called the sons of music, or the children of Mahlon, or a song.

From these remarks, you may see who are the people purchased by Christ for his own possession and inheritance.—All who were chosen in him by the Father from everlasting—all who stood perfect in him when fallen and ruined in Adam—all who feel their sore, and seek unto him for help; who know themselves to be ruined and wasted by sin, and apply to him as the repairer of the breach—All whose state is hopeless and helpless, and desire to be saved by Christ alone
—such,

—such, only such, are they who may hope to have a new song put into their mouths, even salvation to our God and to his Christ.

Thus much for the mode and matter of the purchase; which we shall understand as now accomplished, and proceed

IIId. To the marriage itself, and the several rites used in its celebration, which we shall also find to be significant and instructive.

As to the marriage itself, it was public and before witnesses, which indeed is essential to that institution; for there is no such thing as a marriage private and without witnesses. People living in fornication may, to quiet their own consciences, soothe themselves with a notion that their private engagements are equivalent to marriage, but in reality it is no such thing: an union of heart and affections, as necessary to an happy marriage state, is readily granted; but that it is any part of the essence of marriage, must be denied. Domestic and social happiness being the ends proposed in this institution, care has been taken to have its celebration public before witnesses, the better to ascertain the end proposed.

It has been observed, that the purchase which Jesus made of his people was public and open; and it may now be observed, that his marriage with his church does not take place in a corner. The banns are proclaimed by the sound of the great

great trumpet, which found has reached to the remoteſt bounds of the habitable world. The creation has been invited to come and fee the bride; and the confummation of the nuptials fhall be before affembled worlds. O God, may I on that day be numbered among the righteous! then fhall it be a day of feſtivity with me, and this poor, fin-oppreffed foul, fhall then rejoice in God my Saviour.

Touching the rites of the marriage, it may be obferved that

(1.) The bridegroom took a cake of bread, and brake it, or a fmall parcel of corn, and divided it betwixt the bride and himfelf, to which it is thought Hofea alludes, Chap. iii. 3. where he tells us, *that he married his wife for an homer and half of barley.* This rite among the Jews was truly fignificant, as pointing out the onenefs of their union, that by marriage they became one, even as the cake was before it was broken. Believers, as married to Jefus, are faid to be one bread, probably in allufion to the bread ufed in the Lord's fupper. No union can be more near than that of Chriſt and his myſtical body; the head and members are bone of each others bone, and fleſh of each others fleſh.

Moreover, a onenefs of intereſt is here fhadowed forth; fuch a onenefs as no circumſtance can alter, being immutably fixed in the laws of neceffity.

cessity. There is a moral impossibility of a man and wife having two separate interests: to admit a possibility here, would charge defect upon the relation which constitutes the parties one flesh, and no longer twain.

This unity of interest most beautifully agrees with that endearing relation betwixt Christ and his church, with whom his interests are common. Nothing can be to the Redeemer's glory but what tends to the advantage of his church; and nothing can be to the advantage of the church, or of individuals, but what has the glory of Christ as its ultimate object.

The breaking of the cake, signified the dependance of the bride upon the bridegroom for food and raiment, and every supply. Consistent with this in all civilized countries, especially those called Christian, the eye of the wife is to her husband for supply; a law from which only barbarous nations and barbarous people have departed. This most loudly preaches the gospel to us, and points out our constant, eternal dependance upon the fulness of our heavenly Husband.

Yes, believer, you are indebted to Jesus, for all, for every part of your supply. Whatever gifts, whatever graces ye are the subjects of, they are all derived from his personal fulness. Your clothing is his; your robe of state is your husband's property; you live upon him daily; daily
derive

derive from him mercy to pardon, and grace to help in every time of need. This is agreeable to the eternal purposes and transactions of grace, which have laid up all fulness in him; to the injunctions of Holy Writ, which direct us to be strong in, and live upon the grace of Christ. This dependance of the church on Jesus the Bridegroom, effectually secures all the glory of salvation to grace alone: lays the foundation in grace; in grace raises the beautiful structure, and brings forth the head-stone with shouts to grace.

This dependance is warranted even in the meanest believer, by the same rite of breaking bread in the marriage; and when broken, sharing it between the parties married; for by this he endowed her with his property: the same union which rendered her dependant on her husband, gave her a legal title to his possessions and property. With holy reverence, and the warmest gratitude, let it be said that the Heir of all things, the adorable and faithful Bridegroom of his church, hath been pleased to endow her with all his property, notwithstanding her uncomely appearance and base original. Yes, my friends, he hath endowed you with all that he has; his holy obedience, all-sufficient atonement, heavenly Spirit, and unsearchable riches. Is he the Son of God, and only Begotten of the Father? ye also are the sons of God through him; for ye are all

the

the children of God by faith in Jesus Christ. Is he the Heir of all things? ye also are heirs of God, and joint heirs with Jesus Christ. All the grace that is in him; all the glory he is heir unto, and even his death, and life, are all the believer's property, in virtue of union with him, as his spouse, glory, and fulness. I know not but his breaking bread between himself and his disciples, in the first institution of the supper, might have an allusion to this rite used in Jewish marriages; thereby leading the believing church to consider him and themselves as one bread, one mystical person, having eternally one common, indivisible interest, and reciprocal possessors of one common property.

(2.) Another rite, which, according to Mr. Weemes, was called *Tebhignoth kedushim*, was the bridegroom's putting a ring upon the fourth finger of her hand, saying, " Be thou my wife, " according to the law of Moses," was very significant; expressive of the perpetuity of the relation commenced, and probably designed to lead the church of God to contemplate an union more answerable to the figure. A ring with the ancient Magi was an *hierogliphic* of eternity, being one continued line without an end or beginning. In every thing, as far as it could be done, God hath graciously accommodated his way to human customs and the received doctrines of men, the

better

better to penetrate the mind with things that are heavenly and spiritual.

It is beyond a doubt, that one great end of natural marriage was to shadow forth the relation between Christ and his church; and may not that rite of the ring, that hierogliphic of eternity, be improved in such a way as may lead us to contemplate the eternal relation between Christ and his church. That it was designed for some spiritual improvement, I think is pretty clear from the parable, where the returning prodigal is said to have had a *ring* put upon his hand, as well as otherwise ornamented, seeing it is universally agreed that the application of that parable is spiritual.

Some people, indeed, affect to deny the eternity of this union betwixt Christ and his church, alledging that it commenceth at conversion, or when the soul by grace closes with Christ as the only desirable way of salvation; they will even be ready to treat the doctrine of eternal union as Antinomianism, as if it produced some evil effect upon the morals of men. If these gentlemen mean no more by union, than the unity of our hearts and affections to Christ, I readily grant that this takes place in conversion, and not before. But if they mean that an elect soul is never considered by the eternal Father as in Christ till he actually believes, I must reject their doctrine as absurd

and

and preposterous. They themselves talk of the elect as chosen in Christ before the foundation of the world, and of being preserved in him from the beginning; of his being set up from everlasting as their federal head and representative: as if they could be chosen in him, without being considered as any way united to him; or that the Son of God could be an head without any manner of relation to that body of which he is the head.

One of the characteristics of truth, is to be consistent with itself; this therefore cannot be a truth, because of its inconsistency.

But it is consistent enough to believe, that although our hearts and affections are never united to Christ till effectual calling, the persons of all the elect were united with his person in the act of choosing or election, by which they become God's property, in a manner different from the rest of creation. In the settlements of grace, all was laid up in Christ, not for himself, but for them; which shews that grace still considered them as in relation with him, as members with the Head. In a word, as the spring of this union is in the Deity himself; it must follow, that it is eternal as himself, and that what takes place in regeneration and conversion, is only the effect of that union secretly subsisting from everlasting. But as my business is not now to defend this truth, so much as to hold forth from the history that which may be be profitable to the fouls of God's people, I pafs on to a

(3.) Ceremony ufed in Jewifh marriages, which was their putting a crown firft upon the head of the bridegroom, and then on the head of the bride: which ceremony feems to have been performed by the bridegroom's mother, if alive, Cant. iii. 11. *Go forth, O ye daughters of Zion, and behold King Solomon with the crown wherewith his mother crowned him in the day of his efpoufals, and in the day of the gladnefs of his heart.*

I thought to have finifhed the ceremonies of the marriage in this difcourfe, but time being fo far elapfed, muft beg your attention for another on the next opportunity.

SERMON XIII.

RUTH iv. 9, 10.

And Boaz said unto the elders, and unto all the people, ye are witnesses this day that I have bought all that was Elimelech's, and all that was Chilion's and Mahlon's of the hand of Naomi. Moreover, Ruth the Moabitess, the wife of Mahlon, have I purchased to be my wife, to raise up the name of the dead upon his inheritance, that the name of the dead be not cut off from among his brethren, and from the gate of his place: ye are witnesses this day.

WE have been discoursing of the rites of the Jewish marriages, the

(3.) Of which was the coronation of the married couple; not indeed with crowns of gold, but of laurel, or bays, or flowers, very common on ancient solemnities, and used even in modern times on jovial festivals, especially as an ornament to the queen of the May. The sacred penman of the Canticles seems to allude to that ancient custom,

Cant.

SERMON XIII.

Cant. iii. 11. *Go forth, O ye daughters of Zion, and behold King Solomon with the crown wherewith his mother crowned him, in the day of his espousals, in the day of the gladness of his heart.*

Much has been the pains taken by commentators to adjust the sense of this text, and a very practical improvement of it has been given by Doctor Gill, in his excellent exposition of that mysterious book; but I must say, that I cannot help thinking that the sense of the text has been but slightly touched upon.

To me it appears that the mother here spoken of, mystically understood, is the Jewish church, of whom the Saviour descended. The Jewish church may be said to have put the crown upon the head of Jesus in a twofold way: by type, and by prophecy.

1st. Every type figured forth, and centered all in him, from the destined bullock, down to the flour sprinkled on the altar *. More especially,

2d. By prophecy, perfectly describing his person, character, and work; ascribing all salvation to him, and shewing the confluence of the redeemed Gentiles to his standard; fully describing the glory of Christ and his church in the gospel day of gracious visitation.

The day of his espousals may intend either his bringing of the Gentiles to the knowledge of him-

* Lev. ii. 2.

self, or the glorious day of salvation, when the whole church shall be gathered into one, and join him in the kingdom of glory. The latter of which I should prefer to that of the day of his crucifixion, which does not appear to me to be so properly called the day of the gladness of his heart. The crown of salvation thus prophetically put on the head of the Redeemer, it follows

That the crown of glory is first put upon the head of the Bridegroom, as of old; but as sure as the crown is put upon the head of Jesus, it shall also be put upon the head of the bride: for as the head and members were loved by the Father with the same love, they shall, according to the tenor of the Redeemer's prayer, be crowned with the same life and glory. The interval between the coronation of the one and the other may to us seem long, but that of the former insures this of the latter. Christ died not for himself, but for his people as their covenant representative, and in the same character he has entered into the heavenly world, the sure pledge of their certain arrival, and his coronation the earnest of theirs. O Sirs! when we hear these things, how diligent should we be to know for ourselves the real ground of our hope, whether it is founded upon Christ and grace; whether his assumption of our nature is the spring of our consolation; or we have some other hope distinct from him. Be this your care, for diligence here is sure to meet with its proper reward; and this only is worthy of our studious attention. How vast the glory to which the believing church is predestinated! to sit on the same throne, and to bask in the same glories with the Son of the Father! There is yet a

(4.) Circumstance attending ancient marriages which must by no means be omitted; which was, the bride brought no dowry with her to the bridegroom, but on the contrary the bridegroom himself gave the dowry to her relations, when at the same time she brought nothing but the paraphernalia, which consisted of some presents from her father and near relatives. The practice of hunting fortunes commenced in latter times, when luxury, voluptuousness, and dissipation became more prevalent, but was by no means requisite in those days of ancient simplicity. Instead of demanding a fortune with Rachel, Jacob agreed to serve for her the space of seven years; and instead of giving them a portion, Laban exacts with severity upon his son-in-law. In like manner the son of Hamor, enamoured of Dinah, proposes to give, and not receive money with her, *Ask me never so much dowry, and I will give it.*

This is perfectly applicable to Christ and his church; he gives, but receives not: he, like Jacob hath won his bride by servitude; and well might complain that he was made to serve with her sins, not seven only, but three and thirty years, before he could remove every impediment to his taking his betrothed to his embrace. He finds his people destitute of all personal excellency and comeliness, besides what he himself is pleased to put upon them. When we come to Jesus by faith, we are wretched, miserable, blind, and naked, friendless and helpless, cast out to the loathing of our persons, by father and mother forsaken in point of salvation: yet we, like another Rachel, although made willing to follow him from Haran to Canaan, would treacherously be for carrying our gods with us; and it may be long before we are entirely weaned from the works of mens' hands. Yet notwithstanding he receives nothing along with his spouse but guilt and defilement, such as to purge it required the efflux of his own precious blood; behold what a jointure! what a dowry the heavenly Bridegroom has settled upon his bride! *I give unto them eternal life, and they shall never perish, neither shall any pluck them out of my hand.*

His obedience is made yours for justification, his blood for pardon and sanctification, his grace for support, his house for a dwelling, and the fruits of his Spirit for ornamental attire; all that grace, life, and glory, laid up in him, are settled upon the believer: verily thy lot is cast in pleasant places, and thou hast a goodly heritage. The Father

SERMON XIII.

Father of Chriſt is thy Father through him; the throne of the Redeemer is the ſeat of thy reſt; his unſearchable riches are thy portion for ever. Let thy hand then put the crown of ſalvation on his venerable head, which once bowed under the weight of thine enormities; let his glory be the object of thy pleaſurable purſuit, his will the law of thy choice.

Theſe obſervations made concerning the marriage itſelf, we ſhall now proceed to the

IId. General head of diſcourſe, which is to ſpeak of the ſubſequents of the Jewiſh marriages, and particularly of this of Ruth and Boaz. Under which head, we ſhall ſee how far the ſpiritual things of the gracious kingdom are ſhadowed forth by the natural inſtitutions amongſt men.

(1.) The elders and all the people bleſſed the bridegroom and bride, in ſinging the *epithalamium*, or marriage ſong, as was cuſtomary among the ancients of Iſrael. Ver. 11. *The Lord make the woman that is come into thine houſe like Rachel and Leah, which two did build the houſe of Iſrael.* This was the manner of bleſſing among Iſrael: *The Lord bleſs thee: the Lord lift up the light of his countenance upon thee: the Lord make this woman like Rachel and Leah*, &c. What honour was here conferred upon this Moabiteſs! to rank her in this benediction with thoſe two mothers of Iſrael! but infinitely ſuperior is that honour conferred

ferred on the stranger brought into the house of Jesus; she stands at the right hand, and is numbered amongst the honourable of his court. To see the church of God, although the descendants of a guilty and apostate parent, and children of wrath, even as others by nature, ranked in a station superior to the thrones and dominions of heaven, must astonish every beholder, and clearly shew that their advancement is of grace.

1st. But why like Rachel and Leah? because they followed Jacob their husband into Canaan from Haran, to the forsaking of their father's house, former connections, acquaintance, and native customs. In this respect the Lord, by his grace, makes every true convert like Rachel and Leah, willing to forsake all for the sake of the heavenly Bridegroom. Many would go with Christ, if they could but carry their father's house and former connections along with them, and incorporate his religion with the customs of their country, but have not an heart to part with all for his name's sake. But this is the call: *Hearken, O daughter, and consider, and incline thine ear, forget also thine own people and thy father's house:* * expressed yet in terms less figurative by the heavenly Bridegroom, *If any man will be my disciple, let him deny himself, and take up his cross, and follow me.* The Lord make you, my hearers,

* Psal. xlv. 10.

like Rachel and Leah, who followed Jacob out of their own into a strange country: the Lord make you to follow Jesus from earth to heaven, for the love you bear to his dear and precious name.

2d. But why like Rachel and Leah, rather than Bilhah and Zilpah, for they also followed Jacob from Haran? The answer is plain: Rachel and Leah were the lawfully wedded consorts of the Patriarch; the other two were bondmaids. We would never wish for the servile spirit of a slave to attend any that come into the house of Israel: we would always wish to see a spirit of adoption encouraged amongst the people of God. You have probably, my friends, experienced the bitterness of a spirit of bondage: the Lord make you like Rachel and Leah, the truly betrothed of our gracious Patriarch. the Lord set the doors of your prison open, and bless you with a spirit of liberty, that ye may cry, *My Father, my Father; who wast the guide of my youth.*

3d. Why is Rachel put here before Leah, seeing Leah was the elder both in years, and in the marriage relation? Leah was less beautiful than Rachel, being tender eyed; somewhat like the Jewish dispensation, which was dark and cloudy, the highest of whose privileges were far inferior to the immunities of the church under the gospel dispensation. Hence, on a comparison of the two dispensations, our blessed Lord represents the least of his true followers, in point of privilege, as greater than the greatest of the Old Testament prophets.

Rachel was most favoured and beloved, notwithstanding her sterility and long barrenness: her womb being shut up hindered not the fond affection, and warmest regard of the patriarchal lover. It is in some measure so with Christ and his Gentile church: for although, with respect to the emanations of everlasting love, there is no difference between Jew and Gentile; yet in regard to the visible fruits and effects of this love, the difference is great. The immunities enjoyed by, and blessings long reserved for the gospel church, are unspeakably great in a comparative view; notwithstanding which superior excellence was intended for her, the Gentile church, like favoured Rachel, was long barren; four thousand years of the world's age were elapsed, ere it pleased God to gather the Gentiles under the shadow of his gracious wings. But when the set time to favour was come, barren Rachel brought forth beloved, renowned Joseph; the Gentile church brought forth that man child, who was a terror to the bloody dragon. The Lord make thee, O believer, like beloved Rachel, precious in the sight of thy husband, and beautiful to every beholding eye!

4th. Why

SERMON XIII.

4th. Why like Rachel and Leah rather than like Sarah and Rebekah, who also were the renowned progenitors of Israel? The reason of this is plain: because from them also proceeded the Edomites, who were not of the church visible, but a people unblest and rejected; a people to whom the Almighty shewed no peculiar favour. But the descendants of Rachel and Leah were all of the church visible, and numbered amongst the chosen of the Lord.

The Lord make you and me in this respect like Rachel and Leah, that our seed be numbered amongst the chosen and redeemed of the Lord; and that we ourselves may dwell in the house of the Lord all the days of our lives, to behold the beauty of the Lord, and inquire in his temple.

The elders and people having poured out their benevolent blessings upon Ruth, turn the subject upon Boaz the bridegroom; *Do thou worthily in Ephratah, and be thou famous in Bethlehem.* Ephratah and Bethlehem are different names for the same city, now the city of Boaz, afterwards the city of David, and, lastly, famous for the nativity of Jesus. Bethlehem signifies *the house of war*, and may have reference to that horrid massacre of the infant martyrs, subsequent to the birth of the Redeemer. Herod, that monster of cruelty, like a bloody dragon, waged war against the infant Saviour, to make sure of whose destruction

struction all the babes of Bethlehem, and its environs, fell victims to his brutal ferocity. Cursed be his wrath, for it was cruel; and his anger, for it was fierce.

But Herod is not the only enemy who has risen up against the Lord and his Anointed; by nature all men are full of wrath against him, as the only way of salvation and life. Jesus is born into the world a man of strife and contention unto the whole earth; every man's hand is against him, notwithstanding the benevolence of his disposition, and holiness of his whole conduct. In a special manner in Bethlehem, the war upon Satan's kingdom began; that war, the final issue of which is not only decisive victory by the heavenly Christian, but the entire destruction of the powers of darkness. From this mountain the little stone, which destroys the image, was cut without hands; and upon whose top the handful of corn was sown, the fruit of which has shook like Lebanon.

Bethlehem, signifies also the *house of bread*, perhaps, because the bread of God, which came down from heaven to be the life of men, was first revealed in that city. Ephratah, intends abundance, or plenty; the house of abundance of bread, which must be true of the city of Jesus, for *in this mountain, the Lord of Hosts hath made for all people a feast of fat things, full of marrow,* &c. and his kind invitation is, *Eat, O friends! drink, yea,*

SERMON XIII.

yea, drink abundantly, O beloved! What plenty of every good! what adorable riches and righteousness have poor believers found in him! and O what depths of undecaying comfort do the saints in glory find in him! blessed means by which the soul is brought to live upon the unsearchable riches of Christ. Do thou worthily in Ephratah, and be thou famous in Bethlehem.

If we apply this blessing to Jesus, it will be replied, " He hath done worthily in Ephratah, " and is famous in Bethlehem."

He hath done worthily in Ephratah, in the abundance of his goodness, fulfilling the legal covenant as the substitute of perishing and undone man; restoring its lost honour, magnifying the holiness of the precept, and submitting to the severity of the penalty, as deeming it just and righteous. It was worthily done to place himself betwixt the burning mount and his chosen people; to lay his own neck beneath that sword of justice, brandished to cut them down as cumber-ground sinners.—He hath done worthily, in spending his whole life going about doing good to the bodies as well as the souls of men. He thought no fatigue too great; no suffering too intense to pass through, that he might minister relief to his distressed contemporaries: wherever he went, he pointed out the way of life, and diffused blessings all around. It may well be said of him, that no needy sinner ever perished at his gate; for he was eyes to the blind, ears to the deaf, and limbs to the maimed: he was all to every suppliant that the most extreme misery could possibly want. He did worthily in Ephratah, in dying in the room and stead of his avowed enemies; and, with his dying breath, to pray for his bloody murderers. This is an instance of unparalleled love, and unbounded beneficence, for which his character will be extolled on the harps of saints and angels to eternity. He hath done worthily in Ephratah.

Be thou famous in Bethlehem. He is famous in Bethlehem. That famous, that only infant, who being the Heir of all things, having heaven and earth at his command, was content to put up with a manger for his cradle, and with a stable for the place of his nativity; that only babe, whose praises the highest order of heavenly choirists delight to sing, who, notwithstanding, condescended to be brought into the world amongst beasts of drudgery, as oxen and asses. This amazing stoop in Deity, this astonishing condescension of the blessed Immanuel, will render the name Jesus, in the highest degree, famous for infinite ages still to come.

He is that famous infant, who struck terror to the heart of Herod the tyrant, whose dignity tottered at the account, even of the history of his birth. This dread it was which instigated him to send forth his murderous ruffians to massacre

sacre the hope of Bethlehem. But he is that famous, that awful Judge, whose lips shall at last denounce the definitive and irrevocable sentence against all the persecutors of his person and people: that awful Judge from whose presence the heavens and earth shall pass away! and to shun whose wrath, the wicked shall seek to hide themselves, were it even in the very depths of hell!

He is that only famous sacrifice appointed by the Almighty to take away the sins of guilty man; that only sacrifice whose virtue and efficacy is for ever; for of none other it is said, *that by once offering up of himself, he hath for ever perfected all that believe.* None was ever known upon earth, none in heaven, who was in himself priest, altar, and sacrifice, besides the Son of God. His divine person is the altar; his human nature the sacrifice; and in the union of his two natures, as the adorable God-man, he is our priest, the high-priest of our mystical Israel.—He is that famous Prophet who spoke as never man spake, his very enemies being judges; whose words penetrate the dullest, and enlighten the most ignorant understanding: that famous King, who lives to be a father and fountain of blessing to his people, who levieth no tax upon his subjects, and who is the everlasting terror of all who would make inroads upon their peace and felicity; a famous sanctuary in this house of war, whose precious name is the only refuge known in the palaces of Zion.

In his blood poured forth, is opened that fountain so famous for its transforming quality, its cleansing efficacy, as instantly to wash the scarlet or crimson sinner as white as the fleecy snow; to restore the flesh of the most confirmed leper like that of a tender infant. What numbers of defiled Syrians have here washed and been cleansed! what numbers of blind beggars do daily wash in this pool, and as they wash have their sight restored to them! this famous fountain stands open night and day; it is free to all comers; a sense of pollution makes its virtue necessary to you, and assures you of a welcome; and without a sense of pollution, none could be welcome to come to it, could they even come. No pollution is of too deep a dye, no stains are of too deep a tinct for its power to cleanse, for the blood of Jesus Christ the Son of God cleanseth from all sin.

Who, like unto our famous Jesus, delights to give power to the faint, and increaseth strength to them who have no might? who, like him, binds up the broken in heart, and becomes the famous rest of the weary? who delights to visit the dungeons where prisoners dwell, or to enter the domains of slavery for the redemption of captives? of whom can it be said, *In him dwelleth all the riches of wisdom and knowledge?* who so extolled

extolled for wisdom as this servant of the Lord? what power in heaven, on earth, or in hell, can match with that which bores the jaw of leviathan through with a thorn, and plays with the prince of monsters as with a bird? and oh! his benevolence surpasseth all description, exceeds the utmost limits of human thought! Gabriel's pencil, or the eloquence of the brightest seraph, would here faulter and egregiously blunder. Those lofty tribes who surround the heavenly throne, the happy recipients of his favour, could say much, but when they have said what they can, must still leave the description scarcely begun! heaven, with its thousands of tongues, and eternity, with its innumerable ages, will not be adequate to the stupendous, the wonderful task! May it be thy employment, O my soul, to dwell for ever on thy Redeemer's beneficence! this will be heaven for thee sufficiently sublime! Such are his riches never to be counted over! unsearchable in the most proper sense! Exert all thine own powers; call in the assistance of elect angels and men; claim an ever-during existence; let every moment of that existence be employed in counting the Redeemer's riches, and still shall they be left unsearchable! Delightful work for an eternity yet to come, even after numberless ages are rolled away. How inexpressible the bliss of the glorified! how delightful the work of the

inhabitants

inhabitants of heaven! through all whose regions the name Jesus shall be famous for ever!

Let thy house be like the house of Pharez. Why like the house of Pharez, rather than that of Shelah? &c. Because that of Pharez was the first family of the house of Judah, as appears from the chronology of Israel. Pharez was one of the line of Christ's ancestry, and recorded as such by Matthew and Luke, the genealogers of Jesus. But who is this Pharez, thus honoured, thus preferred to his brethren? He is the son of incest, born to Judah by his daughter Tamar, widow of his sons Er and Onan. Surely nothing meritorious or alluring seems to appear in the descent of this Jewish chief, which should induce the great Governor to give him precedence. O how brightly does divine Sovereignty here shine in its radiant beams! how emphatically does it here assert its right! Shall Shelah, lineally descended from lawful embrace, be neglected in the chronology of the Jews; and Pharez, the fruit of a stolen, an incestuous amour, be recorded with honour? What less can we say than that the conduct of God, in a way of grace, is altogether independant on human virtue. It is not to be wondered at, that men of mere natural principles should stumble at conduct so mysterious, and contrary to human maxims.

Let

SERMON XIII.

Let thy houſe be like the houſe of Pharez.
Pharez, *diviſion,* or *a breaking forth.* There was a time when the houſe of Jeſus was like the birth of Pharez, a breaking forth; it broke forth upon the right hand, and on the left. The light of the goſpel broke forth from Judea, and darted to the ends of the world; and how low ſoever the work of God in our day may ſeem to be, there ſhall be a ſeaſon when the houſe of Jeſus ſhall again be as Pharez, and break forth upon every quarter of infidelity.

> Haſte, haſte old time! the tardy moments draw
> Which intervenes between me and that day!

Pharez, *diviſion,* which figures forth the diviſion of Chriſt's houſe from the ſynagogue of Satan, the houſes of the world, and dwellings of the wicked. This diviſion began in the family of Adam, and hath continued ever ſince; and ſtill I may ſay, ye are not, ye who have known the grace of God, I ſay ye are not of the world, that world which lies in the wicked one. The ſame diviſion ſhall continue to the end, and indeed when time ſhall be no more, even to all eternity. But though foreign to this benediction, the houſe of Chriſt is divided in a regular, and in an irregular manner; in a regular manner, by divine appointment into fathers, young men, and children, which diviſion is profitable to the whole:

in

in an irregular manner, into various opinions, perfuasions, and sects, who unbecomingly militate against one another, and who might be of the greatest mutual disservice, according to the natural tendency of those divisions. But such is the wisdom of the great Governor, that those things which in themselves tend to the ruin of the interest, are made subservient to the best purposes, by making them all expert in the knowledge and defence of sacred truth; as the friction of iron upon iron will infallibly brighten both, and in some cases will endure with a magnetic and attractive quality. Thus out of the greatest seeming evil the Lord can, the Lord doth bring forth good to his church and people, to his cause and interest in general.

2d. Another subsequent of the ancient Jewish marriages was, the bridegroom brought the bride into the marriage chamber, which was called Beth-hillel, *the house of praise;* the time of marriage being in ancient times, as well as modern, a season of festivity and mirth, whatever the consequences of marriage may be in these latter times of voluptuous licentiousness. When Isaac married Rebekah, he brought her into his mother Sarah's tent, and he loved her, and she became his wife. Here the mate of the son's choice became successor to the venerable mother. In the case before us, Boaz took Ruth into his house,

house, as appears from the 11th and 13th verses compared.

The heavenly Lover also brought his spouse into his banqueting house, displayed over her the banner of his love, and made her partake of his richest blessings. His Gentile church was brought into the tent of her Jewish mother, notwithstanding she is of the old olive by nature; yet being now ingrafted into the living vine, her privileges and beauty far exceed those of the other. But shall we from hence have one elated thought? God forbid! by the grace of God we are what we are: far from being high-minded, let us fear offending against that goodness and love from which spring all our advantages; and being brought into Sarah's tent, may we by grace walk becoming our dwelling.

Jesus has a marriage chamber, a *Beth-hillel* into which he brings the soul on the day of espousals, and which upon those occasions is generally *an house of praise*. It is indeed said that there is joy in heaven amongst the holy angels when a sinner repenteth, forsaketh all, and cleaves to Jesus; and much more may there be in the believing church which is so nearly concerned. In a particular manner, it makes the hearts of gospel ministers rejoice, because therein they behold the travail of the Redeemer's soul, and are satisfied that the pleasure of the Lord prospers in their hands

hands. Every lively experimental member must rejoice to behold poor sinners plucked as brands from the burning; brought out of darkness into marvellous light. Being really a spiritual member of the gracious church below, introduceth the soul into such an affinity and alliance with the triumphant in heaven, as would surpass all human credibility, were it not so plainly testified in Scripture. It would be well if believers could consider themselves as minor heirs of heaven, training up to a meetness to join the enthroned church in glory.

3d. A third subsequent of marriage was, the next day after the celebration of the nuptials, the bridegroom brought forth his bride and presented her unvailed to the guests, which might not be done before; the custom being for her to wear her vail till after the marriage was consummated. This vailing of the damsel prior to her marriage, however it might be designed in providence, is certainly very expressive and picturesque of the state of Christ's people before their conversion. They are vailed; their relation to Jesus lies concealed from every eye beside that of Omniscience: they lie in the common ruin of the human nature, and cannot be distinguished from the children of the Devil, till grace brings them forth to the light, and makes their adoption manifest by faith and repentance.

But

SERMON XIII.

But on the day of calling grace, when the trembling soul gives her heart and hand to Jesus, the husband of its choice, the vail that formerly disguised the heir of promise is taken away, and the Bridegroom presents the believer to his church, as the choice of his affection, and purchase of his blood. All glorious within, in virtue of grace infused, or the indwelling of the Holy Ghost, and clothed with wrought gold. Now, without a vail, the queen stands at the right-hand of the King himself, clothed with the gold of Ophir, and she and the blessed Bridegroom can talk with delight of their reciprocal affection, and rehearse the transactions of their mutual loves: now the Redeemer says, *Thou art all fair my love, there is no spot in thee.* And now says the bride, *His mouth is most sweet, yea, he is altogether lovely; this is my beloved, and this is my friend, O ye daughters of Jerusalem.*

If ye, my brethren, are the children of light and of the day, ye are in some manner made manifest. The child of grace is born alive, and will discover itself by its crying; so the bride of Jesus will be known by the ornaments he hath put upon her, and clothed in his own attire he will present her to his friends now, and to his Father blameless in the day of his appearance.

4th. Fruitfulness was the issue of this marriage between Boaz and Ruth. *The Lord gave her conception,*

ception, says the text. By which it appears, that fruitfulness or conception is the gift of **God,** entirely dependant on his sovereign will and pleasure; which ought to quiet the minds of those to whom it is denied: had it been duly considered by Rachel, she had never addressed her husband in the unbecoming manner she did, *Give me children, or else I die:* seeing children were not Jacob's gift, but that of his God.

Fruitfulness will always be the result of marriage to Jesus: the bride, the Lamb's wife, is represented as a woman travailing in birth, and bringing into the world a man child, the dread of the dragon, who therefore sought his destruction. And so will every soul united to him, in virtue of that union, be fruitful in every good word and work, bring forth fruit unto holiness, and have his latter end life everlasting: not that you shall be able always to do the things that ye would; on the contrary, you will always find that the flesh shall lust against the spirit, and that when ye would do good, evil is present with you; yea, when you stand before the Lord, that Satan shall stand at your right hand to resist you: but this conflict shall not hinder the fruits of faith; rather shall it tend to promote its fruitfulness and enlargement.

5th. Once more, for I hasten to a conclusion. Perpetual cohabitation is another fruit or subsequent

quent of this marriage relation. Boaz took Ruth into his houfe, and Jefus takes the efpoufed foul in his houfe alfo; the houfe of reft and habitation of his holinefs. In all her wildernefs warfare, and fojourning below, he gracioufly condefcends to vifit, and to dwell with her, how black foever the curtains of her tent may be. This is his gracious promife to his believing church, and whilft below, his people may expect his prefence. When her warfare is accomplifhed, when fhe hath finifhed her militant courfe, he will take her to his heavenly kingdom, that fhe may be ever with the Lord, and behold that glory which he had with the Father before the world began: but as to her happinefs and glory when thus taken home, what fhall we, what can we fay? Eye hath not feen, nor ear heard, neither hath it entered into the heart of man to conceive what glories are prepared for thofe who love the Lord, and who have by grace made choice of Jefus as their only, their all-fufficient Saviour and Redeemer!

SERMON XIV.

A GENERAL IMPROVEMENT OF THE WHOLE.

AS the great end of our hearing the gospel is soul-profit, and as our profiting in a great measure depends in God's ordinary way on the manner in which we hear, it may not be amiss to examine ourselves upon the premises delivered, and see what grounds of encouragement arise out of the doctrines deduced from the history of Ruth and Boaz. The

Ist. Head of improvement I propose, is examination. Examine yourselves.

1. Whether Moab or Israel is your choice? whether you delight in the kingdoms of the world, or in the commonwealth of Israel? whether our hearts are fixed on earth or heaven? This is one of the grand questions to be attended to; a question of the last importance, and which enters into the very state of our soul concerns. Is alienated Moab our choice? then Israel is not: if earth is your delight, there can be no such thing

SERMON XIV.

as a defire after heaven in your bofom. It is not difficult to fee whether we worfhip idols or the true God; cannot any one determine whether his heart is running upon riches, pleafures, and honours; or whether thefe things appear all as vanity, and the heart is fet upon higher pleafures? Let thefe things engage the attention of my hearers now; for there is a day coming, a long expected day of final retribution, when every thing earthly muft appear in its own identical emptinefs, and nothing fhall appear valuable befides the very things which we are now moft prone altogether to neglect, or to treat with indifference.

Admitting that everlafting happinefs is your concern, and to flee from the wrath to come your fupreme defire, afk your own hearts, whether ye are wedded to Jefus or to the legal covenant? There is fuch a thing as feeking falvation in a way that will never fucceed, as it were by the works of the law; or the doing of fome good thing with a view to obtain eternal life. That young man in the gofpel who came to Jefus, appears to have been very defirous of eternal life, but he fought it only in the way of doing, *Mafter, what good thing fhall I do that I may inherit eternal life?* But when he found the way to life unanfwerable to his own inclinations, he went away forrowful, and for any thing faid about him in Scripture, never returned. Orpah alfo, who wept to part with her mother-in-law, but notwithstanding parted with her, rather than part from her kindred and country. If your hearts are wedded to the legal covenant, and you hope for heaven by your own personal holiness, your disappointment must finally be dreadful; for by the works of the law shall no flesh living be justified, all that are under the law being under the curse. How sad then must the state of those be, who being ignorant of God's righteousness, go about to establish their own works as the grounds of their acceptance, and title to happiness!

If your souls are wedded to the Lord Jesus, and you really do prefer the land of Israel to that of Moab, it may further be asked, Are you wedded to him only? there are some who would intermix the customs of the two nations: even Rachel was for carrying her gods along with her. There are who would be called by the name of Jesus Christ, yet eat their own bread, and clothe themselves with their own raiment; and there are who would join themselves to both him and Moses, as well as others who would serve both Christ and the world. If you can even say, that you have renounced the legal covenant as the ground of your hope, the customs of the world as the objects of your choice, there is yet a possibility of your being joined to your frames and feelings, as well as to Jesus Christ. It is truly desirable to have an

agreeable

agreeable frame of soul; but this frame is not attainable till you have learned to live above all the changes of your own minds upon Jesus only, and that fulness that is in him. When indeed taught to approach him not as a saint, but to live upon him as a perishing sinner, you may have those frames which are truly evangelical; and leading the life of faith, you shall enjoy the pleasure of believing; which can never be your case, till you yourselves are reduced to your own proper state of nothingness, and Christ is become your all in all.

But farther, if you are married to Jesus only, and have such experience of heart deceitfulness, and the instability of your frames, that you dare place no dependence upon them, permit me to ask you, Has your Bridegroom, the beloved of your souls, brought you into his banqueting house, into the church, the tent of his mother? Isaac brought Rebekah into his mother's Sarah's tent; Boaz took Ruth into his house; and Jesus brought his spouse into his banqueting house also. Perhaps you will say, as some do, I must wait the Lord's time, when that comes I shall be inclined to give up myself to his church. But having the written law of Christ in our hands, it is absurd, and to the last degree enthusiastic, to expect some farther manifestation to induce us to be found in the way of duty. The Lord's time is
now:

now: *now is the accepted time; now is the day of salvation.* If not embraced now, you may never have an opportunity of glorifying Christ in the ordinances of his house.

I knew a dear saint, whose memory will ever be precious to me, who from a deep sense of her own nothingness and unworthiness, could never prevail with herself to embrace the privileges of God's ordinances; who, when she came to a death-bed, and could even meet death with a smile on her countenance, had nothing that disturbed her, though leaving husband and children more beloved by her than life itself, but her having neglected to honour Christ in his house and ordinances. Her pathetic lamentations will never cease, at times, to thrill through my heart, till I meet the beloved spirit within the confines of eternity. O Sirs! duty neglected, is sin committed; sin which may one day lie inconceivably heavy upon your hearts, and be the matter of the most bitter lamentation; and whether you may choose to hear and obey, or be offended with me for disturbing your repose and putting you on thinking, this is one part of my duty which must by no means be neglected.

Now, believers, I would in a particular manner address myself to you concerning the marriage of Jesus with his church; but how sublime the subject! how far surpassing the power of description!

scription! how infinitely then must it transcend the feeble efforts of my unequal pen! Christ and his church are the children of one Father, as were Abraham and Sarah: he is the only Begotten of the Father, full of grace and truth; she is his daughter, all glorious within; daughter of the Eternal King by adoption and grace. The match determined upon in the paternal purpose, the Father presents his daughter to the intended Bridegroom, who views her with rapturous delight, and in the endearing language of fervent love expresses his approbation of her, *Thou art all fair my love, there is no spot in thee.* The approbation of the Bridegroom thus expressed, the Father in council engages for the consent of his daughter, *Thy people shall be a willing people in the day of thy power:* this is the betrothment of the church to Jesus, by which she becomes the bride, the wife of the Lamb.

In the gift of his church, the Almighty Father and the co-equal Son enter into solemn covenant upon her account. On the part of the Father, all grace, glory, and happiness is settled on her, as the chosen of the Son for his fulness and glory: on the part of the Son, he engages to use her as his beloved consort, to pay whatever debts she should contract; to bear what sins she should commit; to deliver her from whatever evils she should expose herself unto; and, in all respects, to use her as bone of his bone, and flesh of his flesh.

Preliminaries thus settled, nothing remained but the celebration of the nuptials, or the becoming one flesh with his people, being already one spirit, or married in the intention of the mind. There being a moral impossibility of the bride assuming the nature of the Bridegroom, he graciously condescends to humble himself, in the assumption of her nature, with all its sinless infirmities. Thus he became man, became bone of our bone, and flesh of our flesh, and thus in open marriage he gave his hand to his betrothed.

But still the consent of the bride is wanting, till the day of divine power, when the Father says to her by his word and Spirit, " Wilt thou have " this man to be thy wedded husband, to have " and to hold for better and worse?" Then the soul, renouncing all other lovers, gives her heart and hand unto Jesus only, is become a partaker of the divine nature. Here is now an intermixture of natures; he, as the bridegroom, appears clothed in our nature; and the believer appears as having received, and acting under the influence of his spirit. Now can the soul survey the unsearchable riches of Christ as legally her own, in virtue of his marriage endowment, and may say, " My Be- " loved is mine, with all his fullness and glory ; " and I am his, with all my imperfection and sinfulness :"

"fulness:" which leads me to take notice of a few things, which naturally result from this marriage relation, more particularly than has been done in the former discourses.

(1.) A mutual participation of property, naturally and legally results from your relation to the Redeemer. In marriage all that the husband has becomes the property of the spouse: yes, believer, all that the Lord Jesus has, or is heir unto, is your own property; his righteousness so spotless in itself, and so acceptable to the Father, is all your own; he hath made it over to you in marriage contract. Yours is the efficacy of his atoning blood, which would be useless with regard to himself, for he never offended: yours is the Spirit of his grace to lead, to guide you whilst here, and to bring you to his glory, which also is yours. His heaven, his glory, his fullness, and unfathomable depth of comfort, his unsearchable riches, and his God and Father, are all your own. Whatever Jesus is heir unto, you are joined with him in his expectations; if he is heir of all things, ye are heirs of all things through him, joint heirs with Jesus Christ.

But, O believer, what an exchange is here! our sole property is sin and wretchedness, and even that he graciously takes off our hand; he freely acknowledges all that is ours, to have become his own, in virtue of his relation to his people

people: hence, because they were sinners, *he was made sin;* because they were rebels, he died the death; because they had merited stripes, the stripes fell upon him. Good Lord, we have all thy glory and grace, and thou all our guilt and shame! We may well say each of us, "O what "shall I do my Saviour to praise; so good, and "so true, so plenteous in grace!"

(2.) A oneness of interest results from this relation; and the longer we live, the more we know of the Christian life, the more we shall see the propriety of this proposition. Our true interest lies in promoting the interest of his gracious kingdom: they mistake exceedingly who think that believers may have an interest separate from Christ's, or an interest which has no immediate connection with his manifestative glory: no, my friends, as Christians you can have none, whatever you may have as men in common with others. If ever you pursue profit or pleasure where his interest is not concerned, expect to meet, at one time or other, a lion in your way, and an adder in your path: if you consult his interest, you will be sure to find your account in it; for he will take care of yours, whilst you are endeavouring to pursue that which is obviously to his honour and glory.

On the other hand, his interest as man and Mediator lies in securing the real advantage of his church

church and people, against all the attacks of hell and sin, of foes without, or lusts within. The reason of this is evident, because the church as such, is his fullness, and his glory. What would an head be, if ever so perfect, without a body? or a sun, if ever so radiant of itself, without beams? what would a bridegroom be without a spouse? or indeed the Lamb without a wife? In short, nothing can be to the Redeemer's honour, which is not for his church's good in its several members; nothing can be for the good of the church in general, or of individuals in particular, which is not for his honour. If so, I infer

(3.) That here is a ground laid for the certain safety, and undoubted perseverance of every believer in the blessed Jesus.

If it is for the glory of Christ that believers should persevere, they certainly shall, for he will not give his glory to the Devil, that head of all Antichrists. A loving husband will never suffer his beloved consort to despair in prison for debt, whilst it is both his interest and inclination to deliver her. What should we think of such a brutal, unfeeling husband as a member of society, who would let the wife of his choice perish in a jail, rather than redeem her from the cruelty of her creditor, notwithstanding he had it in the power of his hand to set her at liberty? we should certainly hold him as an execration, and the pest of society who could act so insensibly to his relation. But our adorable Bridegroom has given the utmost demonstration of his love, in laying down his life for his people, when in a state of enmity against him; and will therefore not leave them to perish when sin has actually become their burden. As thy Husband, O believer, he is the guide of thy youth, the defence of thy person, through all the vicissitudes of life, and in death itself; for thou hast his word for his being with thee for ever, having said, *I will never leave thee nor forsake thee.* Thy marriage with the Son of God insures thee safety in, and a comfortable issue from death, a welcome admission into the splendid society above, where, clothed with gold of Ophir, thou shalt stand at his right-hand and behold the excellency of his beauties, for thy very death is precious in his sight.

(4.) Many special privileges arise for the present from this desirable alliance, of which the following is a specimen.—You become dependant upon him for all things: from him you derive the food and nourishment of your immortal spirits; only Jesus hath the hidden manna in store to impart, and what he has is become thine own. On him is thy dependence for clothing and ornament for thy whole person, both for ordinary and extraordinary

extraordinary occasions; the fruits of righteousness which adorn thee before men, are of the operation of his Spirit; and the robe of state in which thou appearest at court, proceeds from his perfect and complete obedience. As your Husband and Lord, you are dependant on him for wisdom to direct your steps in the difficult mazes of this wilderness state; he is given as a leader, and to him you are directed to apply for direction. if any man lack wisdom, let him ask it of God (in Christ) who giveth liberally and upbraideth not (our ignorance.) Moreover, as the betrothed of his affection, you have the nearest access unto his private affairs, for he does not keep the door of his lips from her that lieth in his bosom, but openeth the secret of his ancient kindness, and sheweth the plenitude and stability of his gracious covenant unto her.

(5.) Behold the dignity to which ye have attained, O believers! dignity far transcending the station of angels! Your Maker, the Lord of Hosts, is your husband. To what degree of nearness are you brought? to be nearer is not possible. Thy Maker is thy husband; *bone of thy bone, and flesh of thy flesh*, Eph. v. 30. How much, my brethren, are you indebted to free and sovereign grace? See a wretched infant nursed up in the hospitable bosom of everlasting love, dandled on the knee of providence, and married to the King of kings, and Lord of lords. See a condemned criminal freely pardoned, taken into favour, made a courtier of the King of univerfal nature, and fitting on the bench with the Judge of all worlds, and own falvation by grace alone! But then let this

(6.) Be our concluding remark. If it is only by the grace of God that we are what we are, under what obligations are we to feek his honour in all we do or fay? He calls us away, *Hearken, O daughter, incline thine ear; forget alfo thine own people, and all thy father's houfe, fo fhall the King greatly defire thy beauty.* In return for love fo vaft, for condefcenfion fo unfpeakable, be ye his; he is your Lord, and worfhip ye him; let his will be your only law. It behoves the fpoufe to fubmit to the mild government of an hufband who loves her fo entirely: Sarah owned no lord but Abraham; the fpoufe no beloved but the faireft among the fons of men; own ye no authority befides that of your own wedded Lord.

Let it be your pleafure to ferve him, for he took delight in faving you, though at the expence of his own precious life; and he loves cheerful obedience and willing fubmiffion; if therefore you would honour him, do all things without murmuring, make the peace and profperity of his house the principal study of your lives; let the language of your conduct, as well as of your lips, be *peace be within thy walls, and prosperity within thy palaces.* Whilst there is a possibility of saying without doing, cautions of this sort can never be unseasonable.

His interest is your interest, his cause your own; as well may the interest of man and wife be divided, as that of Jesus and his church in its individual members. It is altogether vain to set up a personal, or family interest, as separate from that of Christ in his church. It was Ephraim's great sin that his heart was divided, and the fruit he brought forth was to himself. Where God has the person, he will have his heart; where he has the heart, he will also have the hand: ye are not your own, ye have nothing that can be called your own; therefore let Jesus be glorified with what he hath dearly purchased. Let nothing tempt you abroad from his house; dwell in his land, and verily ye shall be fed. If a famine should come upon Canaan, let it not drive you into Egypt as it did Abraham; he had like to have suffered fatally by his conduct, if God had not mercifully preserved Sarah whilst in the house of Pharaoh. Bad as the church at any time may seem to be, it is the land of promise, and therefore ought to be preferred to Egypt. If Dinah's

curiosity

curiosity had not prompted her to visit the daughters of the land, her virgin purity had not been invaded: her example is a suitable warning to all to guard against vain curiosity. Abraham's rebuke in the loss of Sarah should teach us to wait with patient diligence in the house of prayer, even when under the greatest discouragements, for the set time to favour, when God shall again send rain upon the earth, and himself become as the dew unto his Israel.

END OF BOAZ AND RUTH.

THE
NATURE AND END
OF THE
LORD's SUPPER.
A
SERMON,
Preached December 5, 1779.

WITH AN
APPENDIX
BY A FRIEND.

SERMON XV.

1 COR. xi. 24.

This do in remembrance of me.

GOD having created man in a state of holiness, and endowed him with all possible happiness, constituting our first parents the head of a progeny that should be called by his blessed name; and which progeny he also constituted declaratively as his family, according to the administration of grace. Thus established, or rather, created in honour, man abode not; but became a breaker of the law, a transgressor against his very Maker; and in so doing brought down the just curse of the Lawgiver upon himself, upon the earth for his sake, and upon the whole extent of his posterity. Amongst the posterity of our Eden-head, the Lord having chosen to himself a peculiar people, predestinated in due time to be called by grace, and made comformable to the image of Christ; (not merely to re-instate them

into

into the happiness which they had lost, as some have said, but to exalt them to the dignity of sons and daughters of the kingdom, co-heirs and fellow companions with the Son of his love for ever and ever;) it behoved him to take such measures as infinite Wisdom dictated, in order to bring about his own purposes consistently with the perfections of his nature. And in the very first family that ever was upon earth, divine sovereignty begins to beam forth on the one hand, in the election of grace; and the antipathy of the natural man discovers itself on the other hand, in a spirit of persecution. Cain, the first man born into the world, being of that wicked one, became the first founder of a city of the world, and consequently an adversary to Abel the first founder of the kingdom of Messiah; and in the issue as a virulent persecutor, subtilly and secretly murdered him; but the murder could not be hid from the all-seeing eye of Jehovah. From Abel downward, it appears that God had reserved to himself witnesses chosen, and in due time called to the knowledge of his name, taught to put their trust in him, and to act the part of the righteous man, that we have been hearing of in the former part of the day *.

But how should God have reserved to himself a people in the fallen world, without satisfaction

* From Psal. cxii. 6, 7.

being made to the juſtice of his nature, and the diſhonour that was offered unto his law being fully repaired? he could not do it, omnipotent as he is! juſtice required ſatisfaction; the law required due honour; for every affront that was offered unto the law, was offered unto the Lawgiver; therefore God himſelf appoints the way, and begins to diſcloſe the plan of grace, in the promiſe of the ſeed of the woman.

No ſooner did human neceſſity call for aid, than aid was given; no ſooner was the breach made between God and man, than a healer is revealed. Man ſinned; a Saviour is promiſed; but the viſion was long before it ſpake. Near four thouſand years were elapſed ſince the promiſe before God appeared incarnated in the fleſh. But in the fullneſs of time, in the ſet time to favour, in the time foretold by all the Prophets, who gave witneſs to him that was to come, the Saviour appeared in his own proper character, he comes as the divine Meſſenger with a ſpecial meſſage to the children of men. He comes in due time, to work out that redemption that had been *eternally* the object of Jehovah; a complete, a full, a plenteous redemption unto every elect veſſel of grace, even unto all that ſhould believe. The Saviour came in the fleſh unto his own; he was deſpiſed, he was rejected of men: no one, till grace touched their heart, would own him, believe in him, regard

gard him, as one that came down from heaven; but on the contrary, the popular clamour was, *Away with him; crucify him, crucify him.*

Perfectly acquainted with the work which he had to perform for the sake of man, and the sufferings he was to endure for the redemption of his people, he bore the contradiction of sinners against himself; he turned not away his face from shame; he did not even screen it from spitting. He was reviled, but he reviled not again; he was buffetted, but his wrath was not kindled; he was vilified to every intent and purpose, but at the same time he conducted himself like unto his own proper character, as the Lamb of God that taketh away the sin of the world. One point his heart was fixed upon, the completing of the work that was committed unto him; he longed, he had as it were an anxiety upon his mind, until the work should be fully completed. *I have a baptism*, saith he, *to be baptized with, and how am I straitened until it be accomplished!* He knew it would be a bloody baptism to him; but his blood was the atonement of his peoples' transgression. He knew that God would frown upon him; but he chose that God should frown upon *him*, rather than to frown upon the people of his love. He knew that he should be contemned and scorned; in his last moments, and dying agonies,

nies, reviled; but he would endure this to rescue your souls, my friends, from the torments of hell.

Having passed through the work for which he came into the world, and finished the ministry that the Father had committed unto him, he comes to take farewell; farewell of his associates, of those that had been sharers with him in his hungerings and fatigues; sharers with him in the infamy that was poured upon him; and in doing of which they sat down to supper. When supper was finished, desirous still as it were to commune with them, desirous to maintain an intercourse with his faithful followers, whom he was now about for a season to depart from, he only commits unto them one token of remembrance. He could not go away without he had, as it were, an assurance that his people, for whom he had performed such wonderful works, should bear him in remembrance, and not forget that there was such an one as Jesus of Nazareth once amongst them; not forget him, as though they had no concern with him, or interest in him.—Wherefore he institutes this very ordinance, which, if God will, we shall attend unto this day. And the manner of the institution is clearly and explicitly laid down by the holy Apostle, quite distinct from the pompous pageantry of the church of Rome; but in its own proper native simplicity: for divine religion needs no ornaments that human wisdom

wisdom can devise:—*The Lord Jesus, the same night in which he was betrayed, took bread; and when he had given thanks he brake it, and said, Take, eat, this is my body which is broken for you: this do in remembrance of me. In the same manner also he took the cup, when he had supped, saying, This cup is the New Testament in my blood, this do ye, as oft as ye drink it, in remembrance of me: for as oft as ye eat this bread, and drink this cup, ye do shew forth the Lord's death till he come.*

Now you will observe, before I enter upon the remarks I have in view, that during the whole of this institution there is not a single hint of *consecration;* there is not a single hint of *transubstantiation;* there is not a single hint of *consubstantiation;* but the bread still remains simple *bread,* the wine in the cup remaineth simple *wine;* so that the doctrine of transubstantiation, so greedily swallowed by the votaries to free-will, hath no manner of foundation in the original institution of the Supper.

But as it is not my view to combat the Papists on the present occasion, I would attempt an application of the words to practical purposes, among the real lovers of a loving Redeemer. And in the

First place, I would, for my intention is barely to analyze the words, take notice a little of that monosyllable, *do.*

To

To *do*, you know, is directly the opposite to inactivity, or not doing; from whence we gather, that the Lord Jesus Christ never did call any one of his people to an idle or an inactive life. Nay, the very contrary is the case; and there is an awful threatening against that man who has done no good amongst his people. It is not enough that people are inoffensive, and do no harm. A man may do no harm, and yet he may fall under the threatening: he that hath done no good, is liable to the threatening, as well as he that hath done evil. Now for men to be in an inactive state in a life of profession, they prove themselves to be burdens unto society. None but them that live for the public good, answer the end of either their creation as creatures, or their calling by grace as new creatures. A philosopher can say, " Man is a public creature not made for himself; " not made merely to live and to act *for himself;* " but to have the good of society in view." And, if philosophy can thus refine upon the duty of man, what must Christianity do, that binds men to the horns of the Redeemer's altar with every possible tie of gratitude? The voice of the Redeemer is, *do.* Awake, thou that *sleepest*, and *do.* It is the property of divine faith to be active. Faith in exercise can be no otherwise than active, and this activity will always have a respect unto

its

its proper object. So that the doctrine of faith, or of sovereign grace, which is all one, I cannot distinguish them, instead of confirming people in a way of indolence, it is the only thing that calls a man to proper, rational activity.

Well, but a man may be doing all his life, and be doing nothing; there is a vast deal of labour and pains taken to do-nothing at all; nothing that can answer any valuable end to society; nothing that can bring comfort to the departing spirit; nothing that can bring the smallest revenue of glory unto our heavenly Creator, from whom we have received all things; therefore the Lord points out the *way* of doing; *do this*. Do what you will, let not *this* be omitted. It is as if the Lord in this little word *this*, concentered every other article of duty; and yet, to the shame of many let it be spoken, that they will do every thing but this. Does the cause of Christ want support? they will *do:* they put their hands in their pockets and do; they will give (from what *motives* I ask not, but) they will be *doing*. Is the word to be preached? they will do, they will go and hear; they will attend to all the duties of religion, personal and social, so that they are doing; but alas! whilst they are doing every thing, they leave that undone which the Redeemer principally fixes their attention unto. *Do this*, saith he.

SERMON XV.

Now this was not so difficult an injunction as Elisha laid upon Naaman the Syrian. Naaman was a most loathsome leper; he was universally so; he goes into Israel for a cure; he comes and stands at the door of the Prophet, as the fittest man to cure him; the Prophet points out unto him the means, as much as to say, "Without "the use of the means, great as you are, Naaman, "expect not the end." He was sent consequently to wash in Jordan, as the means that God had appointed.

Now many are walking with their hands upon their loins, their doleful cry is, "O my leanness, "my leanness! my distance from God, my con- "tractedness of mind! Oh the hardness of my "heart! the wandering of my imagination, the "earthliness of my disposition!"—And well they may; for can people expect the blessing without the use of means? *means* and *end* are intimately connected. If you will therefore hear a favourable word from Jesus, hear what he says to you, and *do this*. Is the command grievous? that was well said of Naaman's servant of old, *Father, if the Prophet had bid thee do some great thing, wouldest not thou have done it?* So, if instead of saying, *Do this*, the Lord Jesus had put you upon the meritorious works of the Papists, to build chapels, and endow them when you have done; to give your all to the church, and the like, why

Y you

you would have thought there is much depending upon such an act as this, and therefore have looked upon yourselves bound to fulfil the commandment, grievous as it is; but here, all that he requires is, to eat a morsel of bread, to drink a cup of wine in remembrance of him. Sure there can be nothing grievous in that commandment.

But it ought to be further observed who he speaks to; and they are recited through the whole context by *ye*. He does not speak this to every man and woman in a Christian land, or where the gospel is preached; and consequently the admitting of *all* promiscuously to partake of the ordinance of the Supper, hath no warrant, no foundation at all in Sacred Scripture. *Do* YE *this—As often as* YE *eat this bread, and drink this cup,* YE *do shew forth the Lord's death till he come.* And who were the *ye*'s so distinguished by the Master? why, those that he had called by grace; called to be saints; called to put him on by an open profession: those in fact that had no other way of getting to heaven but by him. And you will observe, that there are no *if*'s and *and*'s in the way. He does not give them time to wait till they are grown whole, till they think themselves in a proper frame for attending upon such an ordinance; but the command is absolute—*Do ye this*, as much as to say, if you have no other dependence for salvation but me, this I require of you, that you will bear my name in remembrance, and do this in abfolute fubjection to my authority; *Do this*, faith the Lord. Do this, do ye this, though to this grand end, in a way of remembrance.

There are many do it from form, mere cuftom; their fathers did fo, they follow their fathers' example: their religion is hereditary; they cannot deviate a fingle hair's breadth from the faith and practice of their anceftors. As to faith they have none of their own; and as to practice, it is dictated by cuftom, or the eftablifhed forms of the land. There are others that do it with a view to wipe away the fcores of guilt from their confciences. There are many to be found that will go on pleafantly and cheerfully in the ways of fin for the beft part of the month, and when the ordinance-day comes about, they will prepare themfelves, as they call it, by mumbling a few prayers extraordinary every day; and behold! they come and receive what they call the facrament, and come away as clean as Naaman, when he rofe out of the flood of Jordan; and their confciences are quite at eafe! nay, it is much if God is not now their debtor! But thefe are not the ends Chrift hath in view in this inftitution, *Do ye this in remembrance of me.*

Now you will obferve, that when people come together, in order to eat bread and drink wine in the name and in the prefence of God, they have nothing to do with any object whatfoever befides Chrift and him crucified. I have often thought of the ftupidity of too many (and it is a ftupidity, I am afraid, that will long continue, let minifters, let others and others do all they can to remove it); "Why, I am offended with that brother, or "that fifter, and therefore I will not fit down." What! did the Lord call me to *do this* in remembrance of any brother or fifter whatfoever? I have nothing at all to do with who fits down. Might not Peter, that refolute lover of his Mafter, before he knew his own weaknefs, having been informed that one of the twelve difciples was a devil, might not he have faid in his zeal, "Then, "Mafter, I cannot fit down till that devil is caft "out." He had as juft grounds to refufe fitting down with that fecreted devil, as any brother in any church upon the face of the earth can have to fitting down, according to the Lord's commandment, with the proper body to which he belongs: but, in fact, it argues an entire ignorance of the true end of the inftitution when this is the the cafe. Brother and fifter are out of the way; we have nothing to do with this man or that woman; our whole bufinefs is with the Lord that bought us. If you do this in remembrance of your bleffed Mafter, there is nothing will, nothing can turn your feet afide from the path of duty in

this

this particular. *Do this in remembrance of me.* O happy, happy were it for us, if we could come upon all occasions, thus having Jesus in our eye! and when we come not having Jesus in our eye, alas! Sirs, it is no wonder that we go away without the blessing, because we act not according to the precept, *Do this in remembrance of me.* There is enough here to be thought upon: instead of looking at the faults and failings of our fellow men, we may be taken up with the glory of an exalted Redeemer; we can hardly forget his dying groans and bloody sweat; the agonies of his departing spirit! We can hardly need a crucifix to be held up before us to keep us in mind that Jesus died the just for the unjust: true faith wants no such stimulus as this. Divine faith will be attracted by these signs of our suffering Lord: *Do this* then in remembrance of him who loved you, who washed you in his blood, and gave himself for you, a ransom to be testified in due season. It is as if the Lord had said, Remember that there was such an one as me sojourning amongst you; remember me, remember the time when I called some of you from your fishing boats, and your nets, and made you fishers of men; when I called others of you from the receipt of custom; called you out of an ungodly world, and placed you as under shepherds at the head of my flock. Remember me, who all the time that I was with you, spent no part of it in idleness; spent no part of it in a useless way; but went about doing *good*, not *evil;* went *continually* about doing good. Remember what you have seen of my sufferings: remember what you saw in the garden; a sight that never was seen any where else but in the garden of Gethsemane. Much grief many people have endured; but did you ever see the blood squeezed as it were through the pores of the skin by the anguish of the heart? great drops of blood falling down from a sinless being, and all for the salvation of guilty man!—Remember the distress you saw me undergo, when tied like a felon, and dragged to the merciless judgment seat of the high-priest. Forget not the loud clamours against the Son of God prior to his being nailed to the cross. Remember what you have seen—therefore this is the first end of the holy institution—remember me as a person that was once with you.

But remember me farther as a friend that hath departed from you. *It is expedient*, saith Jesus, *that I go away*. He did go away: the same eyes that beheld his sufferings, beheld his ascension from mount Olivet; they beheld him ascend up on high, leading captivity captive; they beheld the heavens open to receive him until the restitution of all things. Christ in heaven wants to be remembered upon earth, Sirs; can the man of faith help remembering him? can the man of love get him

him out of his heart, when he sees the symbols of his broken body and shed blood? no surely. Go therefore this day about this ordinance as your Master calls for, and when you *do this*, do it in remembrance of your departed friend.

But *do this in remembrance of me*, not merely as a departed friend, but as a departed friend that shall return; for he shall come a second time without sin unto salvation. The first time he came as the greatest sinner that ever was, or ever can be upon earth; for though he was clear of all defilement in himself, yet he had all the sins of his people laid upon him by imputation, according to that of Isa. liii. 6. *All we like sheep have gone astray; we have turned every one to his own way, and the Lord hath laid on him the iniquity of us all.* So that he came the *first* time with sin, but he shall come the *second* time without sin: he must come without sin, because sin is now no more. He hath finished transgression, he hath made an end of sin; he hath made reconciliation for iniquity, and brought in everlasting righteousness. It is true, the heavens have received him, but not for ever; it is only till the restitution of all things. The heavens have received him till the elect family are gathered in, and God hath amply made up the number; called them by grace, and prepared them for the heavenly kingdom; and then, behold your departed friend shall return again without sin unto your salvation!

HYMN I.
BOOK III.
Dr. WATTS.

I.
'TWAS on that dark, that doleful night,
   When pow'rs of earth and hell arose
Against the Son of God's delight,
   And friends betray'd him to his foes:

II.
Before the mournful scene began,
   He took the bread, and bless'd and brake:
What love through all his actions ran!
   What wond'rous words of grace he spake!

III.
This is my body, broke for sin,
   Receive, and eat the living food;
Then took the cup, and bless'd the wine,
   'Tis the new cov'nant in my blood.

IV.
For us his flesh with nails was torn,
   He bore the scourge, he felt the thorn;

And juſtice pour'd upon his head
  Its heavy vengeance in our ſtead.

V.

For us his vital blood was ſpilt,
  To buy the pardon of our guilt;
When, for black crimes of biggeſt ſize,
  He gave his ſoul a ſacrifice.

VI.

Do this, he cry'd, *till time ſhall end,*
  In mem'ry of your dying friend;
Meet at my table, and record
  The love of your departed Lord.

VII.

Jeſus, thy feaſt we celebrate,
  We ſhew thy death, we ſing thy name!
Till thou return and we ſhall eat
  The marriage ſupper of the Lamb.

APPENDIX.

APPENDIX.

TO what the Preacher hath advanced from pages 323, 324, and 325, in the preceding discourse, namely, that when "Members of gospel "churches come together, in order to eat bread "and drink wine in the name and in the presence "of God, they have nothing to do with any object "whatsoever besides Christ and him crucified— "that it is stupidity to say, I am offended with "that brother, or that sister, and therefore I will "not sit down—that they have nothing at all to "do with who sits down, their whole business "being with the Lord that bought them, &c."— I say, to this it may be objected by some, that our beloved Master says, Matth. v. 23, 24. *If thou bring thy gift to the altar, and there rememberest that thy brother hath ought against thee, leave there thy gift before the altar, and go thy way, first be reconciled to thy brother, and then come and offer thy gift.* And that it is the opinion of some very learned expositors, that " Though our " Lord here speaks according to that present state " of the church, wherein altars and sacrifices were

" in

"in use, yet it may teach us by proportion to "seek reconciliation before we come to the "Lord's table *."

But let it be observed,

(1.) That believers come not to the Lord's table to offer a gift (as the Papists in their unbloody sacrifice of the mass) but to remember the dying love of him who gave himself for them, *an offering and a sacrifice to God, for a sweet smelling savour* †: of him whose body was offered once for all; and by which one offering *he hath perfected for ever them that are sanctified* ‡.

(2.) That the connection of the words with the preceding verse manifestly shews, that the *offerer himself* is supposed to be the *offending*, not the offended party. *Whosoever is angry with his brother without a cause, shall be in danger of the judgment: and whosoever shall say to his brother, Raca, that is, empty, shall be in danger of the council; but whosoever shall say, thou fool, shall be in danger of hell-fire.*—Therefore, having offended against thy brother in any of these instances, *if thou bring thy gift to the altar, and there rememberest that thy brother hath ought against thee*, or any just occasion to charge thee with want of love and affection to him, or of rancour and malice towards him, *leave there thy*

---

* Assembly's Annot. on the place.
† Eph. v. 2. ‡ Heb. x. 10, 14.

APPENDIX.

gift before the altar, and go thy way, first be reconciled by confessing thy fault *unto thy brother, and then come and offer thy gift.*

So that this passage of Scripture, instead of countenancing an absence from the Lord's table, on account of any offence taken against a brother or sister, is rather a directory to *self-examination*, and a caution to take heed that we *give none offence, neither to the Jews, nor to the Gentiles, nor to the church of God* *. For *though it must needs be that offences come, yet wo unto that man by whom the offence cometh* †. But,

(3.) By *gift* here, we are to understand a *voluntary* offering: particular sacrifices were *commanded*. *Speak ye unto all the congregation of Israel saying, in the tenth day of this month, they* SHALL *take to them every man a Lamb* ‡, &c. *And he shall bring his trespass offering unto the Lord for his sin which he hath sinned* ‖. But gifts were *voluntary*, and therefore it is said, *If any man of you shall bring an offering unto the Lord,—let him offer a male without blemish; he shall offer it of his own voluntary will* §. And therefore they are called *voluntary burnt offerings* ¶, and *free-will offerings* **, and *holy gifts* ††. Hence, perhaps, it is that the Apostle makes that distinction in his ninth

---

* 1 Cor. x. 32.   † Mat. xviii. 7.   ‡ Exod. xii. 3, &c.
‖ Lev. v. 6.   § Lev. i. 2, 3.   ¶ Ezek. xlvi. 12.   ** Lev. xxii. 21.   †† Exod. xxxviii. 38.

chapter of the Epistle to the Hebrews, and the ninth verse, where speaking of the tabernacle he says, *In which were offered both gifts and sacrifices.* And these gifts as well as sacrifices were directed to be brought to the altar *. Therefore it is that our Lord here says, *if thou bring thy gift to the altar, and there remembereft,* &c. &c. But the Lord's table is never in Scripture called an altar; nor can *receiving* the bread and wine, with any propriety, be called a *gift*.

If therefore members of gospel churches feel resentment against any brother or sister, either on account of their disorderly conversation, or on account of any personal injury they may have received by them, let such persons see to it, that they follow the directions given them in the sacred oracles. Does a brother or sister walk disorderly? Hear the express command of Jehovah, *Thou shalt not hate thy brother in thine heart. Thou shalt in any wise rebuke thy neighbour, and not suffer sin upon him* †: which passage, perhaps, the Apostle might have in view when he says, *Brethren, if a man be overtaken in a fault, ye which are spiritual, restore such an one in the spirit of meekness, considering yourselves, lest thou also be tempted* ‡.

* Lev. i. 7, 8, 9. Ezra vii. 16, &c.   † Lev. xvii. 19.
‡ Gal. vi. 1.

APPENDIX.

Have you received a perfonal injury? hear the command of your Lord and Mafter Jefus Chrift: *If thy brother fhall trefpafs againft thee, go and tell him his fault betwixt thee and him alone; if he fhall hear thee, thou haft gained thy brother; but if he will not hear thee, then take with thee one or two more, that in the mouth of two or three witneffes every word may be eftablifhed: and if he fhall neglect to hear them, tell it unto the church; but if he neglect to hear the church, let him be unto thee as a Heathen man and a Publican* *. He is an offenfive member, and therefore though he may be as ufeful in the community as a hand, or a foot, or an eye is to the natural body, the church are commanded to cut him off, and caft him out, it being *better for them that one of their members fhould perifh, than that their whole body fhould be caft into hell* †.

* Mat. xviii. 15,—17.   † Mat. xviii. 7, 8, 9.

A
CAUTION
TO
GOSPEL CHURCHES
TO GUARD AGAINST
THE ACCURSED THING.
A
SERMON.

Z

SERMON XVI.

JOSHUA vii. 4.

So there went up thither of the people about three thousand men, and they fled before the men of Ai.

TO real Christians; to those who have tasted that the Lord is gracious, there can be nothing in history more agreeable than to hear of the success of the church, and her victories obtained over her enemies: if such, we naturally find ourselves interested in all their affairs. When their prospect is promising, pleasure glows upon our countenances, and joy sparkles in our eyes; but when the cloud of difficulty is drawn over the the pages of their history, we find the same cloud equally to vail our faces; hope declines, and fear ascends on high. To feel when we read is one of the finest sensibilities of human nature; to profit by what we read, is the great and unspeakable blessing of the God of heaven.

To allure us to the study of Scripture history, it may be observed, that there is nothing more edifying than the accounts we have of the failings, and discomfiture of the Lord's people in ancient times: these, as in a glass, we see our own weakness and folly, our weakness in ourselves, and personal need of divine assistance; our folly in naturally choosing the evil, and forsaking the good; choosing things which are seen, to the neglect of those that are unseen.—This is in part the use of Old Testament history, for *whatsoever was written of oretime, was written for our instruction.* This being the case, it might be asked, why we profit so little by reading Old Testament history? In answer to which it may be answered,

(1.) Because we have been accustomed to consider the books of Old Testament Scripture as mere history, and therefore seldom, if at all, have attempted to enter into the true spirit and meaning of them, as any way analogous to the gospel of our salvation; not considering that every incident in sacred history is very capable of spiritual improvement; and that Old Testament history is nothing short of the gospel of Jesus preached in a mystery.

(2.) We are very apt to be too disinterested, and very rarely make the cases of which we read our own; nor are we equally careful to improve so much by the historical, as by what we account

SERMON XVI.

the more spiritual part of divine revelation And, it must be owned, that both our own inclination, and the usage of our ancestors, but too much encourage our neglect of the true spirit of Old Testament history; and therefore some of the most interesting incidents are passed over without due regard, and such as this in our text shall rarely meet with any notice at all.

That three thousand men, flushed with a late memorable victory, should venture to storm a city, and that they should be overpowered by numbers and driven back by a superior force, has nothing at all of the marvellous in it. But when taken in its several connections, and the cause of their weakness and flight is inquired into, it will prove fruitful of instructive matter, and will shew itself profitable doctrine, as well as for correction of manners.

To enter into the spirit of the text, and to draw forth the instruction which it yields, be it observed in the

1st Place, that God was their covenanted God, and had pledged his honour and veracity that he would be with them and put out their enemies before them: but now his providence seems to thwart the gracious tenor of the promise. Moreover, he had actually come down in their behalf, and by a powerful hand redeemed them at the cost of their enemies from their bondage in Egypt. He had taken great pains to inspire them with

confidence

confidence in himself, by the wonders he wrought in their behalf, by leading them about, and instructing them in the knowledge of his name and worship, and keeping them in all their peregrinations in the wilderness as the apple of his eye. He shewed his works of mercy in their behalf in a variety of ways and on divers occasions. He preserved them from destruction in Egypt; he gave them light in their dwellings when all the land besides was covered with gross darkness; he caused the mighty waters to become their protector and avenger; he covered them with his cloud, and led them by his own Shekinah by night, and by day. At his command the heavens rained angelic food around all their tents, and the flinty rock poured forth living streams: their garments wore not away in the space of forty years, during all which period, in the barren wilderness, they were sustained by a continued miracle.

That they might stand in awe and fear before him, he also taught them his works of judgment partly upon their enemies, and partly upon themselves. The ten plagues which he sent upon Egypt were as so many preachers to teach them wisdom; to fill them with holy dread, and to inspire them with filial confidence. They saw their pursuers overwhelmed in the mighty deluge, were witnesses of the entire destruction of Sihon

and

and Og with their mighty armies; they beheld the punishment of Korah, Dathan, and Abiram, and were taught that even the fiery flying serpents were numbered among the armies of almighty vengeance.

God had, according to his own promise, brought them into the land of which he had spoken to their fathers, and happily begun their conquest for them in the destruction of Jericho by a very significant miracle; yet now, all of a sudden, they were deserted of their God, their arms were unnerved, their hearts melted, and they fell before the men of Ai. All these considerations joined to puzzle even Joshua himself, that he really knew not what to make of this unexpected providence; therefore in verse 8. you find him on his face, and thus expostulating with his God, *Alas, O Lord! what shall I say when Israel turneth their backs before their enemies.* From whence it is plain, that even the most highly favoured among the Lord's people sometimes meet with dispensations of providence which they cannot for the present unravel. How was this to be reconciled to the many promises which God had made to his people Israel? how could it be reconciled to the honour of his own great name? how could it consist with their destroying all the inhabitants of the land, seeing that they themselves had begun to flee before their enemies?

A general who feared not God, would upon this disaster have sent treple the force against Ai in a second attack, imputing the misfortune to the smallness of the number which went up at first: but Joshua knew that God could destroy by few as well as by many, and therefore from the flight of the people from before their enemies, he concludes that the Lord had a controversy with them, though as yet he knew not the cause. To come to the knowledge of which, he, and all the princes of Israel, lay on their faces before the Lord until the evening, when he obtained the following answer, as it is recorded, ver. 10, 11. *And the Lord said unto Joshua, get thee up, wherefore liest thou thus upon thy face? Israel hath sinned, and they have also transgressed my covenant which I commanded them, for they have even taken of the accursed thing, and have also stolen, and have dissembled also, and they have put it even among their own stuff.*

From which heavy charge solemnly brought home against enfeebled Israel, we may make the following practical remarks.

1st. The thing referred as accursed was the golden wedge, and the Babylonish garment; held to be so merely because it was forbidden. Whatever is forbidden in the law of God is accursed in the strictest sense; and so is that Israelite who shall dare to put forth his hand in defiance of divine authority,

authority, and take to himself that which the Almighty hath forbidden. This consideration ought to stir up Christians to beware how they venture to look upon interdicted pleasures; the eye may affect the heart, the heart may stimulate the hand to grasp the unlawful object, and we may, without the blessing of God upon a watchful spirit, bring home the accursed thing unto our own tents, to defile and render accursed all our other possessions. With what propriety then may we cry with the Psalmist, *O Lord, turn thou away mine eyes from beholding vanity.*

2d. This accursed thing was taken slyly, after the manner of the thief; therefore it is said, *they have also stolen.* The very manner in which the deed was perpetrated evinceth the unlawfulness of it; no work besides the works of darkness shunneth the light of day; but the deeds of dishonesty seek to be hidden; acts of uncleanness in general seek the aid of secresy, to cover themselves with the mantle of darkness, like the bird of night unable to bear the light. Hence it is said, Job xxiv. 15. *The eye of the adulterer waiteth for the twilight, saying, no eye shall see me; and disguiseth his face. But I know and am a witness, saith the Lord,* Jer xxix. 23. Ephraim may sin so slyly, and make his visits to the idols' temple with such well concerted secresy, that he may flatter himself, that in all his ways they shall find

find no iniquity in him that were fin, yet his iniquity shall find him out, and his sin shall cover him with confusion. O Sirs! it is in vain to dig deep, to hide our counsel from the Lord, or to keep our secret sins from the light of his countenance. Those actions which require darkness and secresy, will be found upon inquiry, for the most part, to be sinful and accursed; and it would be well for us by this rule to bring them to the trial.

3d. They dissembled also, still alluding to the son of Carmi, whose covetousness brought Israel into trouble. As it is said of the adulteress woman, Prov. xxx. 20. *She eateth and wipeth her mouth, and saith, I have done no wickedness.* So it might be with Achan, having got the golden wedge and the fine garment secretly and safely conveyed into the midst of his tent, he might bless himself in his own prudence and forecast; might appear to worship with as much fervour as the best of them, and as zealous for the law of the Lord as Joshua himself. Do we not find that masters who oppress their servants, and over-reach their neighbours all the week, shall sit and roll their eyes, and even shed tears, and in the depth of their hypocrisy seem to be mightily affected with the worship of God in the Lord's day. Yea, has it not been known, that the vile adulterer and the adulteress have come to the place of of worship together, and seemed as zealous for God as if no accursed thing had been transacted between them. Even Achan would give his lips to the Lord when his heart was burning with the golden wedge in the midst of his tent, and his mind was adjusting the fine garment to his person.

It is long since people began to sell their souls to the Devil, and their families to ruin for sensual gratifications. For the sake of a fine cloak, and a goodly sum of money, the son of Carmi brings down the vengeance of an offended God upon himself and all that were connected with him. He got an heavy wedge of gold, but he durst not convert it into current money; he had got a very fine cloak, but he dared not to wear it; so that still it answered not the end for which he broke the commandment of God. Those who deal in unlawful pleasures, have but a very partial gratification, and that too by stealth, like the thief in the night. The fear of discovery, unless hardened to all sense of shame, is like gall and wormwood mixed with their luscious, carnal delight; and, if conscience is not wholly silenced, what painful remonstrances must ring night and day in the ears of that soul who wilfully sins against the light of his own understanding.

This same Achan, this troubler of Israel, notwithstanding the high aggravations of his crime, seems upon his detection, to have acted more ingenuously

genuously than many of his kinsmen; he made a frank and open confession of the whole truth, verses 20, 21. *Indeed I have sinned against the Lord God of Israel; when I saw among the spoils a goodly Babylonish garment, and two hundred shekels of silver, and a wedge of gold of fifty shekels weight, I coveted them, and took them, and behold they are hid in the earth in the midst of my tent.* What man could make a more open and ingenuous confession? but how contrary is the conduct of most delinquent professors; what artful shifts, what evasive means are commonly used to elude the diligence of just inquiry? will not Achan the son of Carmi rise up in judgment against the duplicity of such professors of gospel religion? His confession was not only full and genuine, but, which is much in his favour, it was made in a very affecting manner, and ultimately refers to God whom he had offended: *Indeed I have sinned against the Lord God of Israel.* What congregation would not rejoice to hear such an honest confession from any fallen brother, how notorious soever the evils may be with which he is charged! but instead of an open, candid acknowledgment of sin, for the most part every low and unbecoming art is used in order to mislead the church in judgment, and to conceal the sin of the party himself; as if the delinquent were of opinion with the vile persecuting Lord Claverhouse, that if he can

can but manage his matters with man, he would very little mind his reckoning with the Almighty.

But now in order, through a divine blessing, to reach the callous consciences of proud and and unclean professors, I would make a few remarks further upon this subject.

1. Let those professors who trust to their own low, pitiful cunning, and craftiness, for the concealment of their unlawful ways consider, that here we find one as cunning and crafty as themselves, who notwithstanding was detected and brought to condign punishment. Achan was cunning enough to do what he did so privately, that it might be said his left hand did not know what his right hand had done. He trusted none with his secrets; he even kept the door of his lips from her who lay in his bosom. But he was baffled in one thing, and that proved his ruin; he could not hide his dishonest unlawful deeds from the Leader of Israel. He could have outwitted Joshua and his council, if that divine Zaphnath-paneah, that revealer of secrets, had not blowed him; but a crafty sinner will never be safe till he can outwit the Almighty, which is not to be done. The all-seeing, the ever-watchful eye of God was upon him, and saw the whole transaction.

Gehazi was wise enough to conceal his conduct from his disinterested master, and to conceal his fraud by dissimulation and lying, and might have

succeeded

succeeded in his mean and low artifice, if the Spirit of God had not revealed the whole affair to his master. He got the money and changes of raiment, and into the bargain a hereditary leprosy. Professors of religion may flatter themselves that they shall go on feeding their iniquitous desires undiscovered, but it would be much more rational and consistent in them to apprehend, that an offended Deity, an affronted Redeemer, will set their secret sins, their private abominations, in the light of his countenance, so as to bring them into judgment against them for their recovery, and not for their ruin, according to that of Psal. lxxxiii. For a time indeed, they may go on quietly and unsuspected, but in God's due time every hidden work of darkness, every private deed of dishonesty shall be proclaimed from the house top; for our God cannot possibly connive at iniquity.

2. Achan's transgression was personal, but its guilt was imputed to the whole of that community of which he was a member, involved the whole congregation of Israel in lamentable trouble. If one member sin in taking the accursed thing, the whole community is unnerved whilst that Achan is in their camp. If a hand or a limb is in a mortified state, an amputation is deemed necessary in surgery for the preservation of the body; and it is the very same in a body politic or religious:
one,

one Achan has brought ruin upon churches; one Achan has brought ruin upon a nation; being one of their number, a member of their body, it is said that Israel hath committed a trespass in the accursed thing; although, in fact, no Israelite besides himself had any manner of concern in the villany; and his wickedness was so far imputed to the whole, that they actually began to feel, and to bear the punishment of his transgression, and were for his sake treated as if even accursed.

Two things are taught as lessons very profitable to us, lessons which demand our attentive regard.

(1.) The great care which individuals should take to avoid the accursed thing, seeing by the hiding it in their tent they involve their innocent brethren in their punishment, notwithstanding they have had no share in the profits or pleasures of the delinquent. If a man lives merely to himself, he will pay but little regard to the circumstances of his brethren; but if the open, public, disinterested spirit of the Christian is prevalent in him, he will say, *For my brethren and companions' sake I will say, peace be within thy walls, and prosperity within thy gates, O Jerusalem!* He will say it practically, and use all means within his power to prevent any evil befalling the church upon his account. His morning, evening, and noon-day prayer will be, *O Lord, let not thy people be ashamed for my sake!*

(2.) We

(2.) We are here taught the great care that a community should take, that they have no fellowship with the workers of the unfruitful works of darkness, but rather to reprove them; to look diligently left any of their number fail of the grace of God, left any root of bitterness springing up, trouble them and defile many *. In order to which watchfulness, it is necessary that a church of Christ should have their eye up unto him as their Leader, Prophet, and Watchman; for his eyes see, his eyelids try all the actions of all his people, how deeply soever they may be hid from the eyes of our fellow creatures. Jonah lay very snug and secure, fast asleep in the sides of the ship, not one on board was acquainted with his rebellion, but the Lord from whom he fled took such measures with his fugitive Prophet, as to make them all acquainted with his wickedness. Let churches then wait upon Jesus as our divine revealer of secrets, by whose over-ruling providence whatever hurteth or defileth shall be brought to open view.

3. Achan's sin enervated the whole of the army of Israel, they turned their back and fled before the men of Ai. A very alarming and unexpected incident indeed! the times how changed! what an alteration in their circumstances! At the siege of Jericho, there was no need of battering rams,

* Heb. xii. 15.

of swords, or other engines of destruction. To level the walls, and lay their fortresses in ruin, it was enough that their trumpets were blown, and those too the trumpets made of rams horns; the trumpets of silver being reserved to uses more noble.—But now they are fearful and faint-hearted, and are not able to make head against the men of little Ai, even after they had laid proud and powerful Jericho in ruins. God was departed— God, who went out with their armies; and what are Israel more than any other people if left to go forth in their own strength against the Canaanites? God is departed, and assigns the reasons for his conduct, *Israel hath sinned in taking of the accursed thing.* And he can no more consistent with his own honour go out with their armies till this sin is purged according to the law; not that the Lord's hand was at all shortened, or his ear heavy that it could not hear, but their iniquities had separated between them and their Maker.— Sin cannot fail of bringing an unbecoming weakness on that professor who is entangled with it, and on that church too which shall connive at his iniquity. How unbecoming was it to see Israel, whose God is the Lord, flying before the idolaters of Ai! How awful to see Sampson led in triumph by the graceless Philistines! how is the mighty fallen! how are the weapons of war perished, O Sampson! hadst thou kept thy head from the lap of treacherous Delilah, thou hadſt preſerved thy ſtrength unimpaired, enjoyed thy two eyes, and not brought reproach upon the tribes of Iſrael.——Curſed Delilah—type of forbidden pleaſures—curſed Delilah can ſooner ſtrip Sampſon of his ſtrength, than all the giants of Gath and Aſkelon could have done. The ſoft and flattering careſſes of ſinful pleaſure are more to be dreaded than all the powers of external enemies, than all the aſſaults of Satan himſelf. When Delilah glances ſeeming affection, my ſoul reflect

> How vain are all things here below,
>   How falſe, and yet how fair;
> Each pleaſure hath its poiſon too,
>   And every ſweet a ſnare.
> The brighteſt things below the ſky
>   Give but a flatt'ring light,
> We ſhould ſuſpect ſome danger near
>   Where we poſſeſs delight.

4. There was an ill-timed and unſeaſonable confidence diſcernible among the Iſraelites. Fluſhed with the eaſy conqueſt of Jericho, and having but a feeble enemy next to encounter, they ſaid, *Let not all the people go up, but let two or three thouſand men go up and ſmite Ai*, ver. 3. They knew not that God was departed from them—and therefore they thought of nothing but ſmiting Ai, as they had done Jericho and her king. But ah! how vain their feeble efforts! God is
gone,

gone, and they are taught to know themselves to be but men. In vain does Sampson arise and shake himself as at other times after he is shorn of the repository of his strength; in vain does Israel attempt to fight whilst the accursed thing is in their camp; notwithstanding their enemies are doomed to destruction, they cannot stand before them till they are purged from their abominations.

We are never more apt to be too confident, than when we have the greatest cause to fear. The height of Peter's confidence was on the very evening before his fall. The Psalmist was never apprehensive of the firmness of his mountain, till God was about to leave him to militate with his trouble.—At all times we have need to make diligent inquiry if God be with us, before we make head against our enemies, yea, before we venture forth amongst them, and expose ourselves to their temptations and snares.—Had the Israelites inquired of the Lord prior to their going up against Ai, they had undoubtedly referred their expedition till a period more seasonable; and this had been their prayer, *Lord if thy presence go not with us, take us not up thence.*

SERMON XVI.

SECTION II.

Shewing the effects which Achan's sin produced on the congregation of Israel, and its analogy with gospel times, and the effects of sin upon particular communities, especially when the Lord is perceived to have departed, and Ichabod is written upon their doors.

HAVING considered their weakness, and traced it to its spring, we shall now attend to the immediate effects which their defeat produced, and practically improve it to the edification of gospel communities.

1st. They were filled with general confusion: *The hearts of the people melted and became as water; and Joshua rent his cloaths and fell on his face to the earth before the ark of the Lord until the even tide, he, and all the elders of Israel, and put dust upon their heads. And Joshua said, Alas! O Lord God, wherefore hast thou at all brought this people over Jordan, to deliver us into the hand of the Amorites to destroy us? would to God we had been content, and dwelt on the other side Jordan. O Lord, what shall I say when Israel turneth their backs upon their enemies! For the Canaanites and all the inhabitants of the land shall hear of it, and shall environ us round, and cut off our name from the*

the earth; and what wilt thou do for thy great name? verses 6,—9. So unexpected the fatal overthrow, they knew not what to make of the divine procedure, whether God was not turned against them for evil; in which case they repented of their former progress, and wished themselves safely on the other side Jordan, their present land instead of flowing with milk and honey being likely to flow with Israelitish blood.—— They knew not what to make of the power, the promise, and works of God. O Lord, what shall I say to thy power? Is thine arm shortened that it cannot save? what shall I say to thy promise, O Lord God? is thy word yea and nay? is this a putting out of our enemies before us according to thy word? is the Lord turned against his chosen people? is he in a confederacy against us with the people of the Amorites?—What shall I say of all the works he hath wrought for us? Did he redeem us from Egyptian bondage, feed us by a miracle in the wilderness, on purpose to reserve us for the sword of the Amorites? must all that he has done for Israel be accounted for nothing, and be wholly forgotten; be lost in our final overthrow?

O Sirs! to those who have been accustomed to their Maker's presence; to such as have been led for many years by him as their guide and leader, who have long fed upon his bounty, a sense of his abfence, in a feafon of difficulty and diftrefs, will caufe great fearching of heart; will excite many doubts and queftionings refpecting the divine conduct, its fprings and iffue.

Young converts on their firft entrance into gofpel liberty, having feen the powers of darknefs in their own fouls, fall before the power of gofpel grace, are apt to be flufhed with their victory, like the Ifraelites after the deftruction of Jericho, vainly fuppofing that they fhall go on now without any confiderable interruption; that fin is fallen in all its powers, and that the remaining Canaanites will be eafily fubdued, if not entirely eradicated. But oh! what confternation are they in, when by and by they flee before the men of Ai, and are beaten down by the lufts of their own hearts! when their hearts melt within them, and they are not able to make head againft their own corruptions and the temptations of the Devil! What confufion! what fearching of heart is there! what fears! what mifgivings of foul! Alas, O Lord! what fhall I fay to my former comforts! were they from thee, or from the enemy? what fhall I fay to the reality of my converfion; to the ftate of my foul! what fhall I fay to thy lovingkindnefs, and to my intereft in thee, when I feel my lufts fo vigorous, and their fuccefs fo terribly alarming? Thus were all the elders of Ifrael filled with confufion, whilft Achan, the caufe of all, was in his tent brooding over his ill-gotten wealth; even so it may sometimes happen that a whole church may lie in deep distress before the Lord, not knowing why his hand is heavy upon them, and that member who is the Achan in their camp, may be unconcerned in their calamity, brooding over his unlawful pleasures, until God shall bring him to shame, and visit upon him only his wickedness.

IId. It is evident they feared that the departure of God might be final and for ever; consequently to their ruin rather than their chastisement. *For the Canaanites and all the inhabitants of the land shall hear of it, and shall environ us round, and shall cut off our name from the earth.* They had not before experienced divine withdrawings, and therefore could not make a proper judgment of their present circumstances.—The young convert at his first defeat by temptation, when beaten down by his own corruptions, is ready to give up all as lost: now, to be sure, he shall come to nothing; he shall one day perish by the hands of Saul. If the Lord had been upon my side, if I had been a child of God, converted by the grace of Christ, it had not been thus with me; my heart would have been more clean; I should have had more strength to stand against temptations, and to subdue my own corruptions.—— Especially if drawn into wilful sin, and actual guilt is contracted on the conscience, there is nothing but fear on every hand without and within, of himself and of others. Fear of being discovered, for he cannot bear that his fellow creatures should know so much of him as is known to the Almighty—nor is he less afraid of repeating the action which has torn his heart with unexpected anguish—and oh! how does he fear that his heart has never felt the influence of renewing grace; never been quickened by the Holy Ghost; never brought to the knowledge of a crucified Redeemer; perhaps, he may hardly dare venture to hope that God will ever regard his wretchedness any more; any more shew mercy to such an ungrateful rebel, so vile an offender. When any wicked Achan has brought the community into a state of weakness and desertion, so that they cannot stand before their enemies; their fears also may be very alarming, and the general exclamation may be, "Surely the Lord hath forsaken us, "and our God hath forgotten us." Their hearts may melt within them, and tremble for the ark of the Lord, and confusion may vail every countenance on account of the sin of one delinquent.

IIId. The people of Israel were filled with deep distress, and lay in the lowest abasement before their offended God. *Alas! O Lord God! what shall we say, O Lord God! when Israel turneth their backs before their enemies?* They
pleaded

pleaded with him, and entreated the returns of his favour. What wilt thou do for thy great name, O Lord God? As if they had said, O Lord, as to us we are so rebellious and obstinate, so worthless and insignificant, it is but little matter what become of us; but thy glory, Lord, ought to weigh greatly with thee; thy glory is intimately connected with thy glory towards Israel. Thou hast gotten thee a great name by the deliverances thou hast wrought for us in times past: it is known abroad among the nations that thou camest down to redeem the seed of thy friend Abraham; that thou broughtest them through the deep, fed them miraculously in the wilderness, and dried up Jordan before them. What wilt thou do to maintain the honour thou hast gained? will not the Heathen say, that the Lord could not protect them any longer? or that thou hatedst thy people, and brought them hither to destroy them by the sword of their enemies? what wilt thou do for thy promise made to us and to our fathers, if it should at last fail, and Israel should not inherit the promised land? Thus they cried with rent cloaths, with dust upon their heads, and prostrate on the earth. They who know the presence of the Lord, are sure to mourn his absence in a season of distress and difficulty; for in his presence there is safety, and unspeakable pleasure have all they who walk in the light of his countenance.

It is not impossible that guilty Achan might be the only person unaffected with Israel's defeat, seeing sin is of an hardening, stupifying nature. If a person is gross enough to commit an enormous evil, it is not to be wondered at if he should be sufficiently hardened to deny, and industriously to conceal it, unconcerned at what evils his wickedness may bring upon that community of which he is a member. But, O Sirs! if sin thus affect others on account of their connection with a sinner, what must it be when it falls in its penal consequences upon the delinquent himself? he will then be convinced that it is an evil thing and bitter to have sinned against the Lord.

In this sad dilemma, in all this fervent supplication, Joshua insists chiefly on this; *What wilt thou do for thy great name?* First they plead their own danger to which they consider themselves exposed: *Our enemies shall hear, and environ us round, and shall cut off our name from the earth.* The name of Israel, O Lord, which is so dear to thee! the name Israel, which has been so great and formidable, is in danger, O Lord, of being brought into contempt, and cut off from the earth. From whence we learn that the best of men, the most holy of saints, are apt to suspect the worse, whilst under the dark dispensations of providence God is pleased to stand at a distance from them; which convinceth us that there is no such thing

SERMON XVI.

as perfection here below. But although Joshua's heart trembled for Israel, his principal argument was drawn from Jehovah's great name. *And what wilt thou do for thy great name, O Lord!*

Go thou trembling sinner and do likewise; plead with the God of salvation, and tell him all thy case: reason with him concerning the honour of his great name. Lord, what wilt thou do for thy great name, if I am left to perish? I am indeed but of small account; I deserve not the least of all thy mercies; I am less than nothing, altogether vanity: but if I die in my sins, Lord, thou wilt not have the honour of my salvation. If I perish, it will be said, There was a poor sinner came to Jesus, and could not be received, therefore was cast out. There was a poor guilty rebel perished before the throne of God, crying for mercy, but could not obtain it. Yes, my reader, you may warrantably plead this with your God; warrantably call upon him to have respect to his covenant, and bring his own gracious words before him in order to prevail for an answer; your fellow creatures would very probably be offended with you for putting them in mind of their promise, and the obligations they might have laid themselves under, especially if you seemed in any wise to question their honour and veracity; but our God takes it kind to be wrestled with,

and

and records them as princes who prevail with him.

They lay on their faces before the ark, till God was pleased to take notice of their supplicating posture. It was as if Joshua and the elders were determined to be heard, and to obtain an answer. Their extremity and danger made their petitions solicitous and ardent, and they could not depart without obtaining an answer of peace. The importunate widow will be heard; and poor Lazarus will either be relieved or perish at the rich man's gate. What examples these for our imitation! may we by grace do so likewise.

IVth. The discomfiture of Israel by the men of Ai caused a searching out, and an extirpating of the evil from which it proceeded. Their defeat and humiliation on account of it gave God an opportunity of revealing the secret cause of it. *Get thee up, wherefore liest thou thus upon thy face?* as if my ways were not equal; as if I had forgotten my covenant with Israel; or as if thou thyself wert the author of this evil; *Israel hath sinned, they have also transgressed my covenant which I commanded them; for they have even taken of the accursed thing, and have also stolen, and have dissembled also, and they have put it even among their own stuff.* This answer of prayer brought on that strict and impartial examination which issued in
the

the conviction of the criminal, and the purgation of the camp of Israel, by eradicating that sin which was the cause of their sorrow.

When the ship on board of which was Jonah, the Lord's fugitive prophet, was in danger of being wrecked, it brought on the like examination to find out the offender who troubled them, and the lot, under divine direction, fell upon the passenger Jonah, and the whole crew had safety as soon as he was cast over board.

When a church is in trouble, it is always a good sign that a spirit of inquiry is stirred up to find out the Jonah, that he may be cast out into the world, or be brought to repentance; to find out the Achan, that he may be treated according to his deserts, according to the trouble he has brought upon Israel; and still the better, when a spirit of jealousy is apparent, and every member is ready to say with the disciples, *Lord, is it I?* Not one disciple of Jesus, besides the traitor himself, but what discovered a godly jealousy over himself lest he should be the unhappy person, who should fall into this condemnation of betraying the Redeemer. Some you shall meet with who uniformly justify themselves on all occasions, and sin who may, they hold themselves to be righteous persons, and will even censure those who dare to alledge the contrary, let the proof be ever so flagrant: but these are that generation who are pure in their own eyes, who notwithstanding are not purged from their iniquity; a smoke in the nostrils of the Almighty, a fire that burneth all the day, and therefore to be avoided as the pests of Christian society: for the most part some hidden cause lies at the bottom of church afflictions, and one Jonah sleeping in the sides of the ship will work up the sea to a tempest the most terrible.

Vth. By this dispensation Israel were taught to know their own weakness, and brought to a sense of their need to rely only upon God. This was a lesson indispensably necessary for them to learn, which could not be taught them otherwise than by desertion on the day of battle; and God would not desert them without offence given on their part by a breach of his covenant. They might probably expect to make as easy a conquest of every city that they should approach, as they had done of Jericho; but God would teach them that the race is not to the swift, nor the battle to the strong; that it is not by might nor by power that men can conquer their enemies, but by the good Spirit of the Lord; in order to which they must flee before their enemies; and that too not before a very formidable enemy, but before the men of Ai, which was comparatively a little city. Sampson, who made nothing of slaying heaps upon heaps

heaps with the jaw bone of an afs, or pull down the gates of a city by the native ſtrength of his arms, muſt go out and ſhake himſelf as at other times before he knows that God is departed from him: and ſo muſt the ſinner be led converted by grace, be led about in the wilderneſs of temptation, and feel the power of the enemies he has to grapple with, as well as his own inability to ſtand before them, ere he is experimentally acquainted with that ſaving truth, *Salvation is of the Lord.* I ſay experimentally, for a man may be exceedingly clear in the doctrines of grace, ſtedfaſtly believing that the whole of ſalvation is by grace, and at the ſame time look into himſelf for ſtrength to ſuſtain his warfare, and live upon frames inſtead of the grace of Jeſus.

O Sirs! there goes much to a living upon God for all things, and yet thus to live unto God is indiſpenſably neceſſary to comfort, to uſefulneſs, to conqueſt. A man muſt be dead to the law to all intents and purpoſes before he can live to God; ſo ſays the Apoſtle, *I through the law am dead to the law, that I might live unto God.* Whilſt you dare venture abroad againſt your enemies in your own ſtrength, you are ſure to be baffled, as if you were already conquered: but when you once can do nothing but ſin of yourſelves, you will be forced to truſt in the grace that is in Chriſt, and find

find that you can do all things through the strength of grace. Jacob must be reduced to a state of weakness, must become even a *worm* before he can thresh mountains and beat them to powder. It is out of weakness that the Christian is made strong, waxeth valiant in fight, and turneth to flight the armies of aliens.

Permit me now to conclude this discourse with an address to those self-seeking sons of trouble, who look every man for his gain from his own quarter, without being concerned for the afflictions of Joseph. You promise yourselves much pleasure from the possession of the golden wedge and Babylonish garment, because your selfish, covetous hearts lust after them. But to procure those forbidden pleasures you must act the part of thieves, taking them secretly and slyly; saying within yourselves, *Stolen waters are sweet, and bread eaten in secret is pleasant*. You dare not avow your actions before the multitude; you dare not communicate your ungodly enterprize even to your most intimate friend, not even to your bosom companion. When you have obtained the object of your unlawful desire, you dare not use it, dare not put it on, it must be hidden in the midst of your own tent, and no man will esteem you the more for your ill-gotten riches; no man will wish to partake of thy pleasant, thy

poisonous

poisonous morsel.——But remember this, thou sordid wretch! that after all thy craft and cunning, after all thine underhand dealings, God will bring thee into judgment, and expose thy villany to all the congregation of Israel. Because thou hast brought his church into trouble, and been the occasion of such deep humiliation and sorrow to them, God shall trouble thee, and all Israel shall abhor thee, on account of the accursed thing which thou harbourest in thy possession. For although thou mayest be cunning enough, like the son of Carmi, to conceal thy ways from man, the God of Israel is thy witness, and will detect thee; is thy judge, and will condemn thee.

SOME

BRIEF REMARKS

ON

PAUL'S CONVERSION.

A

SERMON;

PREACHED

AT DEVONSHIRE-SQUARE.

SERMON XVII.

Acts ix. 3,—6.

And as he journeyed he came near Damascus, &c.

THIS history begins with our Lord's last instructions to his disciples prior to his ascension.—His visible ascension itself.—The choice of an Apostle instead of Judas.

(2.) Peter's sermon and the establishment of the first gospel church, with its form and order.

(3.) The cure of the lame man by Peter and John.—Peter's second sermon thereupon.

(4.) Their imprisonment—examination—and open avowal of their doctrine and mission.

(5.) The matter of Ananias and Sapphira.—Their second imprisonment; enlargement by an angel; preaching in the temple—further persecution.—The wise interposition of Gamaliel.

(6.) The choice of seven deacons.—Stephen's character—powerful preaching—and his persecution.

(7.) His masterly defence—and bloody death.

(8.) Introduceth Saul the tyrant and dreadful persecutor, on whose account the church was scattered.—Planting the church at Samaria.—Detection of Simon.—Conversion and baptism of the Eunuch.

(9.) Saul's madness and rage against Christ and his church—his conversion.

From all which it appears that the church is like the bush in the wilderness, *burning*—not consumed, because in her affliction the Lord divideth the flames of fire, Psal. xxix. 7.——That the church may have ravening wolves, like Saul of Tarsus, let loose upon her for her probation.

A taste of blood is necessary to quicken the scent, and excite the voracity of a blood-hound.—So it was with Paul; he breathed out threatenings and slaughter—from the taste he had of Stephen's blood; he spared neither age nor sex.—O turn aside and see a great sight!—A wonder of depravity in Saul; breathed threatenings.—A wonder of mercy on the other hand, that God should convert such a rebel—A wonder of divine sovereignty in permitting a vessel of mercy to run such lengths in sin.—His wonderful conversion: the wolf turned into a lamb; persecuting Saul into praying Paul—A monster in nature turned into a miracle of grace.

This conversion is recorded in several particular circumstances.

Time

SERMON XVII.

Time when—place where—manner how—witnesses thereof—things connected with it—the consequents of it.

Ist. the time when Saul was changed into Paul.—In the very act of his outrageous persecution; like that adulteress, John viii. 4. *In the very act*.

Some peoples' sins are brought to light purposely for their salvation.——Saul was permitted to run the greatest lengths, that he might be caught in the snare of grace.—Saul, *yet* breathing out rage and slaughter against the disciples of the Lord, *though Stephen was dead*—went to the highpriest, the prerogative court, and got his commission. But he had more need of God's bridle than the spur of the priesthood.—But he received his commission from the highpriest, and from all the estate of the elders, Acts xxii. 5.

What persecution has there been, and the priests have not instigated it? most profligate persons!

Learn hence,

(1.) Fine natural parts—consummate learning—education principles—zeal for hereditary religion—outward morality may all be perverted to the worst of purposes.

(2.) The awful lengths even the most accomplished characters may be left to run!—exceeding madness against the church.—Saul's religious oppression, was worse than Zaccheus's extortion, that was vile.

(3.) The gospel is highly offensive to the religious, the virtuous, and the wise;—because it makes no provision for the acceptance of their supposed good.—Blameless Saul could not bear to hear *that by the works of the law none could be justified*;—it lays the virtuous Pharisee on a level with the vilest sinner.—Righteous Saul could not believe that God had concluded all men under sin;—it represents the strict religious man as farther from God than an harlot, &c.—Self-esteeming Saul could not bear to hear that harlots and publicans should enter the kingdom of heaven sooner than himself.

The gospel is equally offensive now to people of the same character.

IId. The place where: when near Damascus. In the Jewish language *Damesce* (a bag of blood) thought to be the very spot on which Cain slew Abel.—But here was a Cain ready to slay many righteous Abels.—Wonder at Christ's forbearance in permitting this mad persecutor to proceed five days and a half without molestation!—Just ready to lay his fangs upon the poor disciples, and no doubt feasting upon their blood in his way.——Behold the entire sovereignty of grace!—Paul is taken in the very height of his madness and rage.—What had he done to entitle him to the favour of Jesus?—Or to qualify him for receiving of mercy?

mercy? Grace lays hold on him in the height of rage against Christ.—Grace brings down the stoutness of his heart in a moment: proud Saul is brought to the ground.—All this without *repentance, faith,* or *prayer;*—grace lays hold of him, and these come of course.

In this the gospel sets an open door before the very vilest sinner.——Every possible aggravation attended Saul's sin; learned, sensible, religious; skilled in the Jewish law, which admitted of no oppression.—He sinned knowingly, and greedily; it was to him as the breath of life.—He sinned maliciously, he was filled with rage.—He sinned impiously, making God an accessary to his barbarity, doing all things in his name.—Yet Saul was a chosen vessel—Paul was the greatest apostle; perhaps the greatest saint in glory.

Learn hence,—We ought not to despair of the conversion of any, however near to Damascus.—If ever man sinned as one abandoned of God, it was Saul of Tarsus;—If ever man seemed to have sinned beyond recovery, it was mad Saul;—If ever man looked like a devil incarnate, it was raging Saul.——Yet divine love never lost sight of him, divine mercy never gave him up, divine power soon subdues him.—The love of Christ is no sooner felt than it constrains.

IIId. The manner how. This chief commissioner was converted to and by Christ himself.

It is strange, but true, that those designed for greatest usefulness, are sometimes left to run the greatest lengths in sin ere converted.

(1.) It was about noon on the sixth day, Acts xxii. 6. that suddenly there shone from heaven a great light all around.—How great must the personal glories of Jesus be to cloud noon day sunshine.—This glory overcame even obstinate Saul; like lightning struck the mad persecutor to the ground.

(2.) Bereaved of power to act, and thus disarmed by Christ, he heard a voice, saying, *Saul, Saul, why persecutest thou me?*——He calls him by his name, *Saul, Saul,* to remind him of his namesake Saul doing the Devil's drudgery for him, in persecuting David, the father, the type and figure of Christ.—Saul, Saul! to inform him that he well knew him.

The callings of Christ are not to nations as some think, but to individuals, and by name, Isa. xliii. 1. *I have called thee by thy name,* &c.

(3.) Christ expostulates with him, *Why persecutest thou me?*—Why me, Saul? for what demerit of mine?—When sojourning among you, what injury did I to thy nation and people? I gave health to the sick, soundness to lepers, sight to the blind, hearing to the deaf, speech to the dumb, yea, life to the dead.-——I taught the way of truth, and showed the only method of acceptance with God.——I bore thee upon my heart, served with thy sins, loved thee to the death, and rejoiced in the prospect of thy salvation.—I took the charge of thy person, became bound for thy safety, stood in thy law place, and bore thy curse.——Look on my hands, my feet, my head, my side, and say if I have not suffered enough!——Because I am the friend of sinners, who came to seek and save those who were lost, setting a door of hope before the vilest offender:—because I spoiled principalities and powers, and made a shew of them openly, thus defeating the designs of hell,—do I merit persecution?

Why persecutest thou me in my members and followers?—I am the head of the church, and feel myself wounded in the wounds inflicted on my saints, in whom I live, Gal. ii. 20.——All injuries to them are injuries to me, Matth. xxv. 40. ——Isa. lxiii. 9. *In all their affliction he was afflicted.*——Zech. ii. 9. *For he that toucheth you, toucheth the apple of his eye.*

How careful should we be towards the saints?

(4.) This brings Saul to ask, *Who art thou Lord?*——Well might he ask this question, struck with such grandeur and glory, and being thus interrogated.—With all his great learning and knowledge he knew not Christ—he knew him not; yet would persecute him.—Zeal is often blind.

blind.—He was willing to know for himself who it was that conversed with him in such a strange manner.—No sooner does Saul pray, *Who art thou, Lord?* but,

(5.) The Lord answers, *I am Jesus*, &c.——Jesus, thy Saviour, thy best friend;—Jesus whom without cause thou persecutest.—*It is hard for thee to kick against the pricks:* A proverb borrowed from stubborn oxen and slaves who were pricked on in their works with goads—By the Greeks applied to those whose impotent rage hurts only themselves.—Christ's using it shews the impossibility of doing any thing against him really hurtful to his kingdom.—The certain danger to which the malevolent expose themselves. Learn hence,

That those who kick against the law, do it to their own hurt, Deut. xxxii. 15.——*Jeshurun waxed fat and kicked—I will heap mischiefs upon them, I will spend mine arrows upon them.*——Thus the Lord rebukes Eli, 1 Sam. ii. 29. *Wherefore kick ye at my sacrifice*, &c.—*Behold the days come that I will cut off thine arm, and the arm of thy father's house*, &c. ver. 31.

Kickers against the gospel are yet in greater danger; Heb. x. 29. *Of how much greater punishment suppose ye, shall he be thought worthy who hath trodden under foot the Son of God, and hath counted*

counted the blood of the covenant wherewith he was sanctified an unholy thing.

All backslidings are a kicking against divine authority, and shall wound the kicker himself; Jer. ii. 19. *Thine own wickedness shall correct thee, and thy backslidings shall reprove thee; know therefore, and see that it is an evil thing and a bitter, that thou hast forsaken the Lord thy God, and that my fear is not in thee, saith the Lord.*

(6.) Grace wins the heart and hand—*Lord what wilt thou have me to do?* Saul is now Paul—instead of persecuting farther, he is for doing: what a change!—He is all submission, ready to do any thing.—Grace reduceth a man to this state.—Yet still he is for doing, though fallen to the ground, and could do nothing.

Every sinner must be brought down as he was, by conviction of his sin and folly.—Every one will be for doing to please Christ; yet every one must be equally indebted to sovereignty.—Grace implanted moves immediately to action.

(7.) Our Lord's answer—*Arise, go into the city, and it shall be told thee what thou must do.*

Arise. He was cast down purposely to be raised up; wounded him, that he might heal him.

Go into the city. He was going there before at Satan's instigation; he now has Christ's command.—He was going a wolf, a Saul;—now a lamb, a Paul, a preacher.

How

How the Lord turns the heart and purposes of men!—He must go and be instructed by the very man he thought to have destroyed.

Jesus recommends the use of means, especially the ministry of the word, it being the power of God to salvation.——Peter must go to Cornelius—Paul to Ananias.

IVth. The witnesses of Saul's conversion—the men who journeyed with him; serjeants and peace officers; ver. 7. *And the men that were with him stood speechless, hearing a voice, but seeing no man.*—It was not the voice of him who spake to Paul, Acts xxii. 9.—So powerful was the thunder of the voice of Christ, that it threw them all to the ground.——There were two kinds of voices heard on this occasion—an outward and an inward voice.—They heard the outward voice with terror, but not the inward voice which converted Saul.——How sovereign is God! who can assign a reason why the ringleader is taken and his followers left!

This leads us to consider the **different effects of a gospel ministry.**

Upon one man it may operate **as thunder,** filling with amazement and terror, which never terminates in genuine conversion.—So Felix, Acts xxiv. 25. *And as he reasoned of righteousness, temperance, and judgment to come,* **Felix trembled, and** *answered,*

SERMON XVII.

answered, go thy way for this time; when I have a convenient season I will call for thee.

It may fall upon the ears of some like a confused sound of many waters, bringing neither fear nor joy, pleasure nor pain.—Perhaps, the voice, gesture, and manner of the preacher may affect the passions, yet leave the soul as it was.

There is the hearing of faith peculiar to the elect.—Faith's concern is with Christ, not the preacher; with the matter, not the manner.—Faith hears the voice of Christ inwardly in the soul, and effectually to every saving purpose.—This hearing at once fills the soul with awe and confidence; with filial fear and holy joy.—Ravishes the soul with wonder and admiration.

Vth. Some things accompanying and completing his conversion. Six in number.

His change of posture—his loss of sight—his being led by the hand—the continuance of this blindness—his abstinence from all meat and drink during that time—Ananias laying his hands upon him and baptizing him.

(1.) His change of posture: he arose from the earth, ver. 8.—The terrors of the Lord cast him down, and a saving touch raised him up.——Dan. x. 10. *And behold an hand touched me, and set me upon my knees, and on the palms of my hands.*—Ver. 16. *Behold one like the similitude of the sons of men touched my lips, and I opened my mouth and spake.*—Ver. 18. *Then there came again and touched me one like the appearance of a man, and he strengthened me.*——In Saul's case a miracle of mercy; he fell to the ground a sinful rebel, he rises an obedient saint, instead of the earth swallowing him up alive.——So grace raises up and fits for action those who are called by grace, especially to office work.

(2.) His loss of the sight of his eyes.—To put him in mind of his blind Pharisaic zeal.——The glorious vision of Christ totally bereaved him of natural sight: he saw so much of the glory of Christ that he could see no other object.

Note. All men by nature are blind to Christ, to themselves, and their true interest.

Nothing short of the glory of Christ discovered, and his voice heard, can make sensible of natural blindness.—The moment Christ discovers himself, the soul is blind to all other objects.—— The Sun of righteousness eclipseth all natural beauties.

(3.) His being led by the hand to the city.— He had Christ's command to go to the city—but how can a blind man find his way? natural means must be used.——Paul was the only person struck blind, yet the only person converted.—There were none but dogs near him, such as barked at and would have bitten the lambs of Christ.—— The late violent persecutor, and future great
Apostle,

SERMON XVII.

Apostle, must be led by the hand by a dog.——How glorious was the Redeemer's conquest!—He led captivity captive. Saul, Satan's captive, is now the Lord's captive.—Happy Saul! happy soul! who is struck blind by the glories of Christ!

(4.) The continuance of his blindness; *three days*, &c.—How transcendently great must have been the glory of that light!—What cannot the power of Jesus do, exerted in the light of his glory!—strike blind a mad persecutor, or fill a a dying Stephen with holy rapture.—How wonderful must that work be in the resurrection, when *we shall see him as he is!*—1 John iii. 2. *We shall be like him, for we shall see him as he is.*—This is the beatific vision, to see the King in his beauty, and to behold the land that is very far off.—The Egyptians were bound in darkness, whilst Israel were circumcised;—so here Christ ties Saul's hands, whilst he circumcises his heart, and fits him for his work.

Happy they whose hands of rebellion are tied, whilst their hearts undergo the same operation.

(5.) His abstinence from all meat and drink during that time.—From his astonishment, surprise, and grief, as Psal. ch. 4. *My heart is smitten and withered like grass, so that I forget to eat my bread.*—Every passion and power was here agitated to the utmost.—If now rapt into heaven, his long fasting is thus accounted for: the visions of God incarnate, and of the eternal world, were both meat and drink to him.—Moses fasted forty days when on the mount with God.—Or the Lord might cast him thus low, and keep him so for a length of time, in order to fit him for his future work which was great and hazardous.—Take it which way we will, this was God's intent.

VIth. Some things consequent upon his conversion.—The Lord's vision to Ananias.—Paul's frame and conduct.—The conduct of the church, and of the world, towards a preaching Paul.

(1.) The Lord's vision and commission to Ananias, in which four things are notable.

1st. His call and commission, verses 10,—12. *By name.*—The command is peremptory, *Arise and go*, &c.—His direction is plain; the street, the house, and the host's name is given him.—He is encouraged by the vision which Paul had, *of Ananias coming to him*, &c.

Learn,

Christ knows where we are—what we are—and what we are doing.

1. Where his people are—and loves the place the better for their sakes. Their walls are continually before him.

2. What they are: *chosen vessels*, ver. 15.—A vessel, to shew that man is a patient, not an
agent

agent in converfion.—A chofen veffel. In a great man's houfe, there are all kinds of veffels for various purpofes, and all his own.——Paul was a chofen veffel for honourable work, therefore required much fcouring to keep him bright, being to carry divine treafure to the Gentiles, kings, &c.——*We have this treafure in earthen veffels, that the excellency of the power may be of God,* 2 Cor. iv. 7.

3. What they are doing: *Behold he prayeth!*—Religious Saul had never prayed before—proud Saul was now brought to his knees—blamelefs Saul now cries for mercy—perfecuting Saul now prays to Jefus.

The foul no fooner lives than prays—no fooner prays than Jefus hears.—What encouragement to the vileft! he heard Paul.—What horror to the prayerlefs!—never wounded for fin, nor burdened with it.

(2.) Ananias expoftulates with his Mafter, ver. 13, 14. *Lord, I have heard of many of this man,* &c.—He had heard the extent of the evil Saul had done—it was not a vague report—he had heard by many:—he had even then a commiffion in his pocket to bind all who called on the name of Chrift.—The Lord's faithful fervants may be backward on the difcovery of apparent difficulties, as were Mofes and Jeremiah.——Here was a general willingnefs to obey, *behold I am here, Lord.*

SERMON XVII.

—But when he hears, the flesh shrinks back.—Christ's commands should have satisfied him.—Hearing that Paul prayed, shewed his conversion—yet he must inform Christ of Saul's character.

Learn hence, That it is our duty to inquire out praying people wherever they are.—If truly praying people, there is no harm to be apprehended at their hands.—That if we have but Christ's authority, we may venture any where, fearing no danger.

More particularly the fruits of his conversion as they appear in—the conduct of the church—his own conduct—that of the Jews.

(1.) The conduct of Ananias and of the church.

1. Ananias owns him as a brother. The enmity was taken away on Saul's part, and the fear on his.

2. He calls him to immediate duty, chap. xxii. 16. *And now why tarriest thou? arise, and be baptized, washing away,* &c.

3. They received him into their communion, 19. *Then was Saul certain days with the Disciples which were at Damascus.*

(2.) Saul's own conduct and spirit.

1. He had different views of himself; the chief of sinners now, instead of being a perfect man.

2. He arose and put on Christ by baptism and profession.—Having received the nature, he submits to the laws and ordinances of Christ.

3. He

3. He forsakes his former company, and associated with the Disciples.—Embraced for his companions the people whom he thought to have destroyed.

4. Straightway preached Christ in the synagogue, that he is the Son of God.

. (3.) As they appeared among the unbelieving Jews.

1. They were amazed, as well they might.

2. They were confounded, for Paul proved that this was the very Christ, ver. 22.

3. When they could bear it no longer, they took counsel to kill the turn-coat, ver. 23.

We have here seen,

1. The enmity of the human heart in its extent, rage and madness against Jesus.

2. The power of Christ in subduing that enmity and turning from darkness to light, &c.

3. The proper fruits of converting grace;—love and attachment to the name and people of Jesus;—a putting on the Lord Jesus by open profession;—a maintaining his cause and interest against all opposition.

THE END.

BOOKS

Published by the late Rev. John Macgowan, *and sold by* G. Keith, *Gracechurch-street;* J. Johnson, *St. Paul's Church-yard; and* J. Macgowan, *Paternoster-Row.*

I. DIALOGUES of DEVILS, in which the many Vices which abound in the civil and religious World, doctrinal and practical, are traced to their proper Sources. More especially, the Roman Catholic Errors are pointed out from the Antichristian Principles from which they spring.

The whole is conducted by way of allegorical Dialogues, between the following Dialogeans.

Fastosus, or Pride; *Infidelis,* or Unbelief; *Avaro,* or Covetousness; *Discordans,* or Contention; *Crudelis,* or Cruelty. In two Volumes 12mo. *Price 5s. sewed.*

II. FAMILIAR EPISTLES to the Rev. Dr. Priestley; in which it is shewn, (1.) That the charges brought by him against the Orthodox, are applicable to none, but people of the Doctor's own persuasion. (2.) That, notwithstanding his Endeavours to destroy the Doctrines of Christ's Divinity, and the vicarious punishment of sin, the Doctor has established both, even to a Demonstration. (3.) That what the Doctor calls rational religion, has, according to his own Account, been productive of the most unhappy and irrational Consequences. And, (4.) That the Doctor's Religious Pamphlets are a complete Refutation of themselves. *Price 1s. 6d.*

III. SOCINIANISM brought to the Test: or Christ proved to be, either the adorable God, or a notorious impostor; in a Series of Letters to the Rev. Dr. Priestley. In which it appears, that if Jesus Christ is not a divine Person, the Mahommedan is in all respects preferable to the Christian Religion, and the Koran a better book than the Bible. *Price 1s. 6d.*

Books published by the late Rev. J. Macgowan.

IV. A LOOKING-GLASS for the Professors of Religion, consisting of the following Tracts on practical Subjects. *Price 3s. bound.*

1. A Rod for the Sluggard, or the great Evil of Idleness represented.

2. The Changes of Ephraim, or the Backslider's Warning.

3. A Caution to Drunkards, or the Sin of Intemperance censured.

4. The Canker Worm, or the Gourd of Creature-comfort withered.

5. Joshua's Pious Resolution, or the Duties of Family Religion and Houshold Government enforced.

6. Perez-uzzah, or the Danger of Discord considered.

7. Some Thoughts on Occasional Prayer.

V. FOURTH EDITION OF DEATH, A VISION, or the Solemn Departure of Saints and Sinners, represented under the Similitude of a Dream. *Price 2s. 6d. bound.*

VI. THE SHAVER's SERMON on the OXFORD EXPULSION. *12th Edition. Price 6d.*

VII. A CURIOUS LETTER to the Rev. Dr. BLACKET, occasioned by his Sermon preached before the *Bishop of Exeter*, at the consecration of *St. Aubin's Chapel in Dock-Town. Price 6d.*

VIII. THE CLEANSING FOUNTAIN OPENED, a Sermon, occasioned by the Death of the late Mrs. Elizabeth Bennet. *Price 6d.*

IX. THE LIFE OF JOSEPH, THE SON OF ISRAEL. In eight Books. Chiefly designed to allure young Minds to a love of the *Sacred Scriptures. 2d Edition. Price 2s. 6d. sewed.*

" This History of the young Hebrew, so celebrated for his
" Chastity, his Wisdom, and the Vicissitudes of his Fortune,
" may be exhibited as a fit Companion for *Mr. Gesner's Death*
" *of Abel.*"

Monthly Review, Oct. 1771.

www.ingramcontent.com/pod-product-compliance
Lightning Source LLC
Chambersburg PA
CBHW081912170426
43200CB00014B/2712